The $100,000 Resume

The $100,000 Resume

CRAIG SCOTT RICE

McGraw-Hill

New York   San Francisco   Washington, D.C.   Auckland   Bogotá
Caracas   Lisbon   London   Madrid   Mexico City   Milan
Montreal   New Delhi   San Juan   Singapore
Sydney   Tokyo   Toronto

Library of Congress Cataloging-in-Publication Data

Rice, Craig Scott
   The $100,000 resume / Craig Scott Rice.
      p.   cm.
   Includes index.
   ISBN 0-07-052586-2 (alk.paper)
   1. Résumés (Employment) 2. Job hunting. I. Title.
  HF5383.R53 1998
   650—dc21   98-23198
                                             CIP

McGraw-Hill

A Division of The **McGraw·Hill** *Companies*

1 2 3 4 5 6 7 8 9 0 MAL/MAL 9 0 3 2 1 0 9 8

ISBN 0-07-052586-2

The sponsoring editor for this book was Betsy Brown, the editing supervisor was Fred Dahl, and the production supervisor was Sherri Souffrance. It was set in New Century Schoolbook by Inkwell Publishing Services.

Printed and bound by Malloy Lithographers, Inc.

Contents

Alphabetical List of Resumes

Acknowledgments

The following professional resume writing services provided examples of their fine work:

Artistix Communications (Ipswich, Massachusetts)
CareerPro (Los Angeles, California)
Creative Keystrokes Executive Resume Service (Alexandria, Virginia)
Executive Resume (Cedar Brook, New Jersey)
Say It with Panache (Van Nuys, California)
WSACORP (Shawnee, Kansas)

Introduction

So you want to earn $100,000. Well, consider this. Over a million people earn $100,000 or more a year, according to the U.S. Department of Commerce. It takes time, hard work, and an organized plan to win a job at that level. This book provides the system—and the sample resumes. *You* can provide the time and the hard work.

These positions turn over at about a 10% rate each year, according to government figures. That's 100,000 new $100,000 openings every year! Naturally, other people will apply for these jobs. They're your competitors. How can you beat them out? A great resume is a good place to start.

This book helps you develop a "master resume"—a powerful weapon for getting a $100,000 job. Winning resumes are designed to make two people look good: you and whoever passes the document along to the boss, who says, "Wow! Thanks! *This* is the kind of person we need!"

This book is designed to be read from beginning to end. You'll begin, in Chapter 1, with a look at yourself and your skills. In Chapter 2, you'll find information on hundreds of sources. These are people who may want your skills or refer you to others who do—people who should be targeted in your marketing campaign. In Chapter 3, you'll combine those skills and sources to develop a personalized marketing plan.

Chapter 4 offers dozens of guidelines for success. In Chapter 5, you'll read about how to put together a superior cover letter. Chapter 6 will show you how to assemble resume-supporting exhibits that will help your candidacy—supporting materials your competition usually won't bother to put together.

Chapter 7 will help you make the most of the advertised opportunities you read about in newspapers and magazines—and how to make sure your resume gets noticed. Chapter 8 will explain how to assemble a top-notch mailing campaign, with your resume as its centerpiece. You'll also learn strategies for starting an exchange of ideas that builds an alliance and a new friendship with the contact at the target company.

Chapter 9 will demonstrate how to shine at the interview. Chapter 10 offers a concise plan for effective follow-up. Chapter 11 offers you important advice on negotiating your way to $100,000.

Chapter 12 provides contact information for some of the best professional resume writing services specializing in $100,000+ resumes. Chapter 13 contains a wide variety of samples based on resumes that *have produced $100,000 jobs.* (Most of these were developed by some of the country's top professional resume writers for senior executives.) You'll examine specific guidelines for getting the most out of *your* resume, the heart of your marketing campaign. You'll probably want to come back to this part of the book again and again as you develop your own resume.

In the Appendix, you'll find a resume outline form, information on handling psychological tests, and more.

Ready for a surprise? If you're looking for a senior-level position—one that pays $100,000 or more—you already have "a new job": finding the position that's right for you! This task is almost your own small business. Your best bet is to get busy—very busy—with the right steps. That's what is outlined here.

Let's get started!

CRAIG SCOTT RICE

The $100,000 Resume

1

Study and List Your Skills

And this above all, to thine own self be true!
—SHAKESPEARE

If you don't blow your own horn, nobody else will!
—WILL ROGERS

Start smart, and you're halfway home.

Who are you, really? If you truly know yourself, you are way ahead of most people, because they rarely stop to ask the question. (But you can bet your prospective employer will ask!)

DISCOVER YOUR "HIDDEN TALENTS"

Often your talents are hidden because they let you do lots of valuable things—things you often forget about later on. An easy way to rediscover your hidden talents is to think about your life and your traits. As a "thought starter," make a short, half-page, five-minute list of your strengths and weaknesses. Focus mainly on your strengths. Think especially in terms of a job or profession and an employer.

You don't want to miss any important traits or skills. Once you've finished the list, go back and take a little more time. Think about any special skill or strength you picked up but may have neglected to enter. List it.

Now look at the "Major Traits" form. Fill this in, including the relevant items from your first short list. Blend the two lists. To the big list, now add any work-related compliments people have paid you, especially about matters that might be valuable to an employer. These are personality strengths, as opposed to "technical" skills, and they are often just as valuable.

Be honest with yourself. Do people consider you:

- Smart?
- Hard working?
- Skillful?
- Quick learner?
- Good person?
- Trustworthy?
- Kind?
- One who gets along well with others at all levels?
- Diplomatic?
- Calm?
- Analytical?
- Planner?
- Reliable/dependable?
- Willing?
- Above average?
- Enthusiastic?
- Self-starter?
- Doer who gets things done?
- Leader?
- Writer?
- Speaker?
- Creative with ideas?
- Team player?
- Other good things...?

If so, add those—especially in areas where you are unusually strong.

If you are good at music, art, writing, or leading, list these abilities on your "Major Traits" form. Lots of top jobs either need these skills or at least a little knowledge of them. Keep at it. You may find you have values that you forgot you had!

In the space, across the bottom of the form, enter a summary. In a sentence or two, cover your main three to six or so traits, characteristics, strengths, and abilities. These are important, because those are the **key** factors that can win the $100,000 offer!

MAJOR TRAITS AND STEPS IN MY LIFE

Grade School (action, team work, honors, posts)

_____
_____
_____
_____

High School

_____
_____
_____
_____

College

_____
_____
_____
_____

Other Training

_____
_____
_____
_____

Job 1 _____
_____
_____
_____

Job 2 _____
_____
_____
_____

Job 3 _____
_____
_____
_____

Other Jobs _____
_____
_____

Special Activities/Honors: _____
_____
_____

Now that you know who you are, or at least you have a better idea, ask yourself:

- Is it time for you to look for a job in a new industry? If you feel insecure about your prospects in your current field or if you aren't going up the ladder where you are, maybe it's time to change ladders.
- What are you worth on the market? The answer lies with your training, experience, demand and supply of your abilities, and sometimes just plain luck and location. A trained, starting secretary might be worth more than a physicist, if the secretary happens to be the only such person in an isolated, frozen northern lab full of physicists.

Table 1-1.

Average Wage Ranges (in thousands of dollars):

Training	No Degree	Bachelor's Degree	Master's Degree	Doctorate
Starting	$15–$20	$20–$30	$40–$60	$60–$80
Mid-career	$20–$40	$30–$60	$60–$80	$80–$100
Top	$50–$80	$100–$200	$100–$200	$200–$300

Source: U.S. Dept. of Labor.

Table 1-1 lists average salary ranges according to academic degree. Some people nearly always start lower and reach higher than these figures. The dollar figures include bonuses, stock options, and other benefits.

ARE YOU A "SKILLED" PERSON?

That's a key question, because the answer will relate closely to your chances to land a $100,000 job offer. Low skills sometimes do the trick, but not often. What can you do that the average employee can't? What are your most valuable skills?

Your answer depends on three things:

1. How you define the word "skilled."
2. Your level of training, experience, and ability.
3. Your own self-esteem.

Skill is usually defined as the ability to use a special kind of knowledge to get a job done. It usually means you have technical expertise or aptitude. In reality, there is no very good definition for the word in today's work place, even though employers are often crying for "skilled" people.

Training and experience are usually part of "skills." Someone with a lot of training and years on the job is usually more skilled than others, but not always. Ability is important and so is willingness. Employers of $100,000 people often specifically and frankly seek both high *attitude* and high *skills*.

Your **self-esteem** is surprisingly important. People who think they cannot do a job are always right: They can't do it. But people who think they *can* do it are often halfway home. One of the great values of college and graduate school is simply that they convince students that they *can* do what they have to do. They build self-confidence and self-esteem: "I finished the project because I didn't know I couldn't!"

DO YOU HAVE GOOD "SOFT SKILLS"?

Many talented people don't try very hard. Employers seek willingness. A positive attitude. These are called "soft skills" and are often demonstrated by what you have accomplished. It wasn't so much that you coached the drama club, but that you were willing and able to do it. That speaks volumes to an employer.

Employers often say, "I'll always take a willing, enthusiastic person with only moderate skills over a genius with no action. With the first person, the job gets done. With the second, it's like pulling teeth." Good "soft skills" can often take the place of mediocre or average technical skills.

ARE YOU A "SUBROSA SEEKER"?

Are you looking while you still have a job and don't want to get caught by your employer? If your firm is downsizing, your job search could hasten your dismissal.

Of all the negatives to a "quiet" search while still employed, the fear of being discovered is the greatest. With secrecy, you have little flexibility, especially with a major job lead source group: your networking contacts. Once you go to them, the word will possibly be out and your boss will soon know. Even answering ads is chancy. Sending resumes to recruiters or other companies, on the other hand, is pretty safe. These folks rarely talk to each other, especially about applicants.

However, a quiet search has its advantages. You burn no bridges; so you enjoy a salary until you leave. Most searches take about six months, and some take a year. If you are employed, your situation is not so urgent. You have reduced stress, worry, and anxiety. You can be a little more choosy, and you won't be pressured to accept "anything" just to get a paycheck. Also, as an employed person, you are more attractive and have a bit more clout with a potential employer than if you are on the streets. Quiet seekers are common. Thousands are looking. Some expect turnover and start looking the day they are hired!

So search "under the table" if the time seems right, but be discreet. If and when your situation is revealed, you will be free to contact anyone, including your major source: your networking contacts.

ARE YOU IN A SPECIAL GROUP?

Special groups include seniors, handicapped, women, non-English speakers, and minorities. Laws prohibit discrimination against these people, but discrimination is still there and still strong. Nevertheless, such groups are growing and are increasingly represented among the higher paid people every month. Some companies actually seek out some members of these special groups, in a genuine spirit of fairness and balance. And some *must* do so to comply with terms of government contracts. Hiring special people in top positions can actually bring in profits.

WHAT MIGHT YOUR PROSPECTIVE EMPLOYER BE SEEKING?

What do employers consider the "ideal" person? Think for a moment about their needs and wants. Try to put yourself in their shoes, if you can, and you will suddenly have more insight and more power. Pretend you are hiring someone like yourself. List the "specs" you would want filled. Now you know both sides of the needs and wants agenda. You're further ahead!

WHAT CAN AN EMPLOYER EXPECT FROM YOU?

Employers can expect to get the skills, ability, attitude, training, experience, and know-how that you covered on your big list. At the $100,000 level, they will expect an ability to hit the track running, to learn, size things up, and analyze the "big picture" within a few days. You should be able to help set new and better goals as well as design new and better steps for reaching those goals. Most of all, for $100,000 the employer expects results. These you cannot guarantee. No one can. The situation usually has too many variables, too many people involved, for "sure things." But you can guarantee one thing: a good try, and that almost always gets at least some results. The boss will notice.

BORAX IN DEATH VALLEY: WHAT DO YOU, PERSONALLY, EXPECT FROM AN EMPLOYER?

Answering this question is a part of knowing yourself. Taking a new job is a little like buying a house or a car. Some people are satisfied with anything. Some people want the moon. If you are reading this book, you probably want $100,000. But you probably don't really want just the money. Other things are important too. You probably wouldn't take even $200,000 to shovel borax all summer in Death Valley! (I wouldn't, either.) When thinking about your compensation, remember that your *benefits* or fringes can be highly important. Bonuses, stock options, insurance, and other perks can often far exceed the dollar pay, and so can "intangibles," such as location and working conditions.

Accepting a job is a little like getting married. As Mark Twain says, "You should keep your eyes wide open before marriage and half shut afterwards." Executive recruiters tell lots of stories about jobs that were filled quickly, without careful review, only to end in tragedy. After a while, employer and employee both thought they were shoveling borax in Death Valley.

Here's how you can both evaluate a company and better understand your own wants and needs. You are wise to list a few "must haves" (requirements or needs). Then list some "like to haves" (preferences or wants). List five or ten of each category on a sheet of paper, running down the left side. First enter the needs or musts. For example, your first "must" may be wage. Your second might be location. Then comes the type of work, moving expenses, and other things. Keep this list short.

Then below the "musts," list the preferences. Include things like:

- Fringes and benefits.
- Help in relocation.
- Spouse house hunting trip.
- Realtor contacts.
- Schools.
- Shopping.
- Churches.
- Cultural centers.
- Insurance.
- Day-care.
- Spouse employment help.
- Bonuses.

- Profit-sharing.
- Stock options.
- Recent growth.
- Exciting plans for the future.
- Vacations.

Once you have your list of requirements and preferences, go to the suggested blank "Company Evaluation Checklist" on page 8. Completing this checklist has several advantages. You may surprise yourself by finding that some important things are not really so important, while others have unexpectedly become essential. You now have a clear idea—before you start—of what you really want and need. You now have a criteria list you can use to judge a company, even if the company represents the only offer you get. You won't accept it and then say, "Oh, no, I forgot about …!"—and be back to shoveling borax again. If you get two or more offers, you can evaluate each and compare them against each other using the same yardstick. Otherwise, you may be influenced by one company's fine offer and excellent presentation, and forget to check, for instance, the job duties. Find out whether you have to shovel borax!

If one company meets all your needs and preferences and another firm meets none, your choice is pretty easy. Problems arise when two firms offer about the same benefits. Then you might give "weights" to some of your criteria. Some are far more important than others.

COMPANY EVALUATION CHECKLIST

Needs Required	Company A	Company B	Company C	Company D
Wage				
Location				
Type of work				
Company moving				
Others				

Preferences	Company A	Company B	Company C	Company D
House hunt				
Help buy house				
Realtor				
Good schools				
School near				
Day-care				

Preferences	Company A	Company B	Company C	Company D
Good shops				
Church near				
Cultures				
Spouse job				
Insurance				
Bonus				
Stock option				
Profit share				
Recent growth				
Growth plan				
Vacation				
Others				
Net				

SUMMARY

Ask yourself, "Who am I, really?" (in the eyes of a prospective employer). List your abilities, going through your major steps in life.

- What are you worth? Are you skilled? Part of the answer consists of degrees, as the salaries chart shows. Other parts are your job training and experience, your special field, and your soft skills (attitude, confidence, and people skills).
- Are you a quiet seeker? A subrosa search can be less stressful, less hurried than one while you are unemployed.
- Are you a member of a special group? Laws give you some protection, even advantages.
- What do you expect from a job? You certainly don't want high pay in Death Valley! Use the checklist to judge a company before you commit, on the basis of your "must haves" and preferences. This exercise helps you decide what is *really* important and what's not.

CASE STUDY

A young professional woman had acquired considerable education, but elected to take off ten years or so to raise her children. She then returned to the job market, but found that prospective employers expected still more specialized training, which she obtained. For years people had put her down as "just a housewife," and she thought of herself as a nonprofessional. Then she did a thorough personal evaluation, discovering that she had a lot of training, experience, abilities, and skills. These included formal preparation as well as soft abilities such as attitude, confidence, personality, and ability to work with, train, motivate, and manage people. She had forgotten or ignored these valuable abilities. She moved into the job market, knew what she wanted, evaluated several company opportunities, and soon landed an outstanding, professional position, leading to major big money assignments.

Rice's Comment: Making a true, brutally honest evaluation of yourself is not easy, but it has a great influence on how well you move up the dollar ladder. Successful $100,000 people usually know themselves very well. They know their strengths and weaknesses, and move into the market accordingly. You can do the same to get *your* $100,000.

2

Best Sources for $100,000 Jobs

Plan your work and work your plan.

—BLAINE

A rich man is just a poor man with money.

—W. C. FIELDS

The goal of this chapter is to help you find the best sources for your $100,000 job. Naturally, if you know the best places to apply, you raise your chances of getting the big bucks. It's time to look at who these people are, where they are, and how to reach them. Many of your competitors won't examine this issue thoroughly enough. Most will never even think of the many people you will be listing.

Remember: *You are always competing.* Many job seekers forget that. They think they are the only job hunters when they are among thousands. Yet most job seekers are not like you and have a different package of skills to sell. Others are a lot like you. As a result, most jobs have a dozen candidates—even at the $100,000 level. Your big challenge is to stand out from the others and make it easy for the employer to see you as superior. The guidelines in this book will make you stand out.

TWO BLIND PEOPLE

You and your would-be employer are a little like two blind people reaching out in the dark to each other. Employers are looking for people like you, but they don't know where you are. And you don't know where they are. One of the best ways you can find each other is to make noise, which is exactly what we will plan to do. Follow the directions in this chapter, and lots of sources will notice you favorably.

INCREASING THE ODDS

About 100 million people in the United States are working in 100 million jobs, and about 10% of them change jobs in a year. That's 10 million U.S. openings! If your city or state has about 2 million people, that's 1% of the United States. So 1% of those 10 million national openings are in your area. That's 100,000 openings within your distance during the year. Maybe only 1% are big jobs, but that's still 1,000, or about 100 a month. That's a lot of big job openings. Certainly you can get a shot at one out of 100! The odds are even more in your favor when you use the many advantages we offer.

PLAN TO "NETWORK" FIRST

Look through your personal phone directory and business cards. Over 50% of the people making $100,000 say they got their jobs through networking. This strategy can be your best job source. One reason is that, when decision makers pay six-figure money, they like the new employee to come recommended by someone they know, personally, not a perfect stranger off the street.

You have a great network, free for the asking. (Most people don't realize how many people they know.) Make a list of every "above average" person you know. Jot down at least 20 names. Are you a member of a club, one with perhaps 20 members? They all know you at least a little. That gives you 40 people, maybe a lot more. Don't forget people in your present or former company (unless you are looking quietly); you might add another 20.

That gives you a total of 60 personal contacts. Each of them knows 60, just as you do. That gives you a network of 3,600 good people, without even trying. (Some people know 100 people who each know 100, giving you a network of 10,000 people!) They are already there. You already made your effort, just by getting to know them in the first place. Don't contact any of these until you have your cover letter, resume, and exhibit, which we will plan in the coming pages.

WHO ARE YOUR BEST JOB SOURCES?

"What kind of person would hire me?" If you can't answer that question, look at the kinds of people who did hire you in the past and the kinds of people who even considered you or interviewed you. The answer to that question almost points you toward the "who." Make a list of those company types. You can find many such lists of each type in the library. Just tell the librarian you want a list of, say, 100 food companies or clothing stores or metal working firms. They are in a book entitled *Job Hunter's Guide, 1,000 Companies*. That should include several lists of your best company types.

Work Backwards!

Working backwards is a little like going to a dance or other social event to find a totally new friend. You'd start by asking, "What church, dance, school, or club might someone I'd like attend?" Then go there.

Similarly, in a job search, ask, "What are *employers'* sources? Where would *they* look?" Ask any company employment person. Their sources are no secret. Then you can be there, waiting for them! This could make your search easier. (Your competitors will rarely think to start backwards.)

Employer's Sources

Nearly all employers *start* with, and actively use, their files of mailed-in resumes. They also use *their* networks and personal associates, just as you do. More than that, they place local and national ads, and contact job placement agencies, headhunters, and recruiters. The big companies get thousands of resumes each year, and many put them on computer program. When an opening comes up, they simply punch in their specifications and up pops ten good candidates. So get in that computer! You might even qualify for two jobs!

Names or Titles?

Send to personal names, if you know them. Otherwise (mailing specialists say), use titles, not names. Those change too much. And send to top titles. (See Chapter 8, "Superior Mailing Action.")

When you send materials to the major officers within target companies, they just *might* look at your resume and jot a positive note on it, before passing it along. Even without a comment, the Human Resources person on the receiving end is never quite sure whether the material was noted. There is always a little more strength to your package if it is passed from the president's office, rather than going just directly from you to HR. Remember, wherever your package goes, that "Dear President" salutation is on your cover letter. The reader never knows for sure just how much interest the president might have in you.

Downsizing vs. Upsizing

Be especially aware of companies in your community (or further out) that are cutting back. Generally you want to stay away from such companies. They usually have more heavy hitters than they need, or some of their top people with "wage creep" have become far too expensive to keep. Expanding companies, however, offer good potential. Stay aware of them. Make a list of them, as you see them in your local newspaper, in magazines, or in *The Wall Street Journal*. (Free copies of the *Journal* are available to read at your library.)

YOUR BEST SOURCES

Since you now know where employers look, your own selection of good sources becomes easier. We already discussed your network. Much of this book is dedicated to building your powerful three-way "Package": resume, cover letter and exhibits. Then we will cover how to mail this package to your network, top employers, answer ads, and contact recruiters.

Should You Use Executive Recruiters?

Companies hire these people to find specified types of employees. If you send your resume to them, they will compare it with their job orders. If your qualifications match the requirements of one or more positions, you will probably be contacted.

There are thousands of such recruiters. The top fifty who specialize in $100,000 people are listed in the back of this book. Remember, however, that they work for and are paid by the employer, not you. So they respond only to their clients' wishes. They do not try to place you. But contacting them gives you very wide reach to 100,000 employers or more, and costs little. Also, you are taking the initiative. You are helping the blind man who is reaching out trying to find you.

> **CASE STUDY**
>
> A highly qualified candidate had sent his resume to several key officers at a major Midwestern company without response. Months later, a recruiter interviewed this same man and recommended him to the company. They made him an excellent offer and he accepted. Mailings had done nothing. The company officers apparently did not trust their own judgment. Their recruiter was assigned to do the staffing, and he did.

Consider Using a "Professional Executive Marketer"

These people are very different from recruiters. Executive marketers work for you, are paid by you, and actively try to place you.

The advantages are:

- They are responsive to you and can save you a lot of time and work.
- They do most of the steps covered in this book, including helping you prepare and send your resume.
- They know hundreds of prospects that you do not.
- They can be highly effective.
- They are in the yellow pages of any major city or listed with the chamber of commerce.

The negatives are:

- Their fees are high—usually several thousand dollars up front or a percentage of your first year's wage (or both).
- You still need to help them put together your cover letter, resume, and exhibits package, all of which are needed to sell you.
- *You* must still do the interviewing. Be very careful. Most of these firms are competent and diligent, but a few are just out to get your $5,000 or $10,000 fee, send resumes, run a few ads, and quit. Get recommendations from satisfied customers before you make any commitment or sign anything.

There is nothing wrong with using these marketing pros. They are especially worth considering if you have the money but not the time, or if you are simply not interested in or oriented toward marketing yourself. Job categories that may benefit from marketing pros include:

- Accountant.
- Engineer.
- Scientist.
- Lawyer.
- Banker.
- College dean.
- Government supervisor.

- Medic.
- Musician.
- Artist.

Telephone Sources

Dial 1-800-248-6800 for job openings available through *The Wall Street Journal*. Also, PRONET (a Web site) offers free employment information; just call 1-800-593-3088. Stay alert. New numbers are announced on TV news programs and in the newspapers almost every month. Visit or phone the business reference librarian at any large library for the latest information.

Cyberspace

The Internet is a fast growing resource, one you should not ignore. Many big companies expect their recruiters to scan the Internet. Most "job bank" services are free, with employers paying a fee if they hire. The largest is the American Job Bank, a service of the U.S. Department of Labor. You can access this site 365 days a year.

These Web sites require little technical skill. They often ask you to fill in a resume form. Most of these let you jump right into thousands of company lists. Others connect with ads in a dozen newspapers. Resumes for Web sites should mainly emphasize skills or achievements, not job titles. About half the jobs are for computer people, half for other professionals. Some people find a dozen openings in a few minutes. If you don't have a computer, check your local college or state employment office.

Out of hundreds of Web sites, the "Big Six" are:

- America's Job Bank: www.ajb.dni.us.
- Career Mosaic: www.careermosaic.com.
- Career Path: www.careerpath.com.
- E-Span: www.espan.com.
- Monster Board: www.monster.com.
- Online Career Center: www.occ.com.

For people over 50, AARP's WebPlace at www.aarp.org/bulletin/webjobs is worth reviewing. Your local library probably has books listing many other such sources.

Executive Want Ads

These appear daily in *The Wall Street Journal* and in the business section of Sunday newspapers in most large towns. (See Chapter 7.)

More Information

You'll find two valuable source lists at the end of this book. After your personal network, these can be very effective tools. They have done magic things for many job seekers and can for you, too, if you use them intelligently. Your competitors will almost never make proper use of these resources! See Appendix B, "100 Largest Employers of $100,000 People" and Appendix C, "50 Special Recruiters for Jobs Paying $100,000 and Up."

Always remember that "gold is where you find it." You can look in the likely places, but also check out what seems to be low-grade ore. You never know what you might find. Most major companies either own part or all of other companies that seem totally unrelated to the holding company. The Acme Stone Quarry may own the Modern Medical Hospital or the Red Apple chain of supermarkets.

Leave no stone unturned. Check out every new source that may come along (but don't spend your precious time without considering the pros and cons carefully).

SUMMARY

- Your goal of $100,000 is best reached by contacts and good sources. You are competing; so you must find more and better sources.
- Get seen! You and the prospective employer are like two blind people groping in the dark; put the odds in your favor. List many more sources than you think you'll need. Start with your personal network. Each of your contacts knows many people, generating a net of thousands.
- Start backwards. Ask, "Where would I find a good candidate if I needed one?" Then go there.
- Check out cyberspace resources, avoid downsizers.
- Check recruiters of professional executive markets.
- Use free phone numbers.
- Check the source lists in back of this book.

RICE'S COMMENT

All this may seem like a lot of work, and it is. High-level jobs are seldom won in a few casual steps. Is the new job worth it? That depends on how much a person wishes to see $100,000! Rest assured, however, that the search itself can be fun if you approach it with the right attitude.

3
Your Best Marketing Plan

Patience is essential to success.

—Disraeli

Success comes to he who hustles while he waits.

—Edison

The goal of this chapter is to enable you to build your own, superior personal "marketing plan." If you are *not* a marketing person, your competition probably won't have such a plan and *you* will! You're ahead of the game. If you *are* a marketing person, your competitors will probably make such a plan; so you should not let them get ahead of you. Yours must be better. This chapter gives you the steps and an easy, effective form for you to fill in to develop what I call an *S-O-S plan*.

This plan should be made early in the job hunt program. Do it after you list your skills and your prospects (Chapters 1 and 2), but before you create your "package" of cover letter, resume, and exhibit (discussed later in the book). That way, when you design your "package," it fits your plan nicely.

YOUR SITUATION–OBJECTIVES–STRATEGY (S-O-S) PLAN

The S-O-S plan is based on a method that works well for millions of large and small businesses, worldwide. You might as well use what they have already tested. After all, your job hunt is your own private "enterprise." Like a small business, you have challenges, opportunities, goals, and strategic steps—especially when you're hunting "big game."

The S-O-S plan works like this:

- The first *S* means *situation,* or an assessment of the facts facing you. This step includes a study of who you are and what skills you have to offer. Your situation also includes facts about your job sources and your opportunities.

You already now know all this, and you can use the facts in your marketing plan. So you are part done.

- The *O* stands for your *objectives*, your goals, or what you seek. The main goal is $100,000, of course. Other goals might be the kind of job and company, location, and other factors. For example, your objective might be either to enter a new industry or to move up in your present industry. Those are logical objectives. Once they are clear in your mind, such goals influence your strategic steps: resume, cover letter, and exhibits. Your Three-Pack will be sharply aimed at your specific objectives.

- The final *S* indicates your *strategy*. This is not your situation or your goals. It is the heart of your plan. It consists of the concrete steps you want to take for reaching your $100,000 goal. List the steps (using the form in this chapter), and you have a plan. Luckily for you, most candidates *start* here. They seldom have a clear understanding of themselves, their job sources, or their objectives. They are sailing in circles, without a situation compass or a map of goals. You have both! And that means your strategy will be working smarter, faster, and higher up on the dollar ladder.

Executing the S-O-S Plan

The steps are listed in the S-O-S form appearing later in this chapter. They appear in chronological order:

- Make a resume, cover letter, reference, and exhibits page as a "package."
- Send this package to your network, prospective employers, recruiters, and advertisers.
- Keep records and follow up.
- Close your deal.

You'll soon learn exactly how to do all this. Your plan just lists and schedules the steps so that you know what's coming.

Two Additional Strategies

Here are two added strategy options to consider, each of which can move you closer to your $100,000 goal:

Consider a "Multiple Campaign" Program. Suppose you qualify for two major fields, like marketing and management, production and training, or comptroller and auditor. List prospects for both. Develop resume and exhibits for both. Run both programs at once. Even jobs within a single category might permit multiple programs. For example, in marketing, you might have a separate campaign for sales manager and advertising manager or for market research manager and promotion manager. You become two people. Some applicants are four people! Employers rarely notice or care if you try this. They are just trying to fill a slot with the best person. This approach may double your chances to hit $100,000.

Fax or E-Mail Campaigns. When a street address is available, try following up with a cover letter and resume package to selected prospective employers via fax or e-mail. The advantage to fax and e-mail is speed, which is sometimes very important in a job hunt. These usually get immediate attention and create a positive impression.

Records

Your program can get lengthy and complex. Without records, you could easily mess up your $100,000 offer. Your log can be just a one-page chart, listing major mailings and responses. This helps you keep track of what you have done and what you plan. Also, set up a file called "Prospects Lists, Cover Letters, Resumes, Exhibits." Most important, create a separate file on *any* specific company that shows any interest; these are the "live" prospects and their files the most important records. Keep details on these companies, including a log of phone calls or letters. There is no need to record the turndowns. Toss them. They just clutter up your files. Many firms don't answer anyway, and that's the same as an answer. Some will answer many months later, usually to decline.

Advantages to Your S-O-S Plan

- You are well organized.
- You do first things first, by priority.
- Taking the task a step at a time, broken down to simple pieces, makes it all seem more doable, easy, and less overwhelming.
- When you have a good picture of your situation, you can pick a suitable group of prospective employers.
- By knowing your situation and your goal, you set up smarter, more effective strategies.
- Each step you take fits in a logical sequence.

HOW MUCH TIME DOES A JOB HUNT REQUIRE?

Some have been lucky and got the $100,000 job in a few weeks. Some have needed a year or more. Some people have had to build the program in two or three career moves, each a couple of years long. This meant climbing a career ladder in several deliberately planned steps. For the average seeker, figure about six months to a year. A great deal depends on your training, skill level, location, industry, and the economy of your region. If each of these is favorable, your search might be very short.

However long you search, remember that your big new job is *your* number one priority. Unfortunately, it is not number one for most of your prospective employers. In fact, it might be far down on the priority list. Employers can take weeks just to open, read, and judge your package. If they like what they see, they pass the material around. Often key people do a lot of traveling and may be out of town for a week or more. Meanwhile your package sits. Even prospects who are interested in you might not reply for weeks. That is why the whole process takes months. It's not that people don't like you; they just have other fish to fry. People who hire $100,000 employees are usually dealing with many projects, often involving millions of dollars. You just need patience. Keep busy and keep adding other prospects to your list.

YOUR BEST S-O-S MARKETING PLAN

(From this original, make a photocopy as your worksheet.)

MY SITUATION (You did this on the form you filled in for Chapter 1.)

My training is: _____

_____

_____

My experience is (functions, duties): _____

_____

_____

My best skills are: _____

_____

_____

I'm complimented for: _____

_____

_____

My major contribution would be: _____

_____

_____

❑ I am looking quietly.   ❑ I can announce freely.

I am flexible as to: ❑ Duties.   ❑ Location.   ❑ Full time/part time.   ❑ Work hours/nights, weekends, holidays.
❑ Compensation.   ❑ Employee or contractor.   ❑ Travel.   ❑ Benefits/insurance.

Remarks: _____

_____

_____

_____

Companies most likely to hire me are: _____

_____

_____

_____

Those companies are looking for "ideal" ❑ RE: _____

_____

_____

_____

20

MY OBJECTIVES

Wage (total income and benefits): _____

Duties: _____

New industry: ☐   Move up in present industry: ☐

Location preferred: _____

Other: _____

_____

_____

Remarks: _____

_____

_____

STRATEGY STEPS (Remarks [R] might include a planned date for doing this.)

1. Study myself (You did this.): _____

2. Set my goals (You did this.): _____

3. Make a superior resume (that's the next chapter). ☐ R: _____

4. Make a superior cover letter. ☐ R: _____

5. Make a superior reference sheet. ☐ R: _____

6. Make a superior exhibit sheet. ☐ R: _____

7. Make some backup, extra exhibits. ☐ R: _____

8. List my network names. ☐ R: _____

9. Contact my network with a package (cover, resume, exhibits). ☐ R: _____

10. List 100 best employers. ☐ R: _____

11. List 50 best recruiters. ☐ R: _____

12. Watch for published ads. ☐ R: _____

13. Mail letter-resume-exhibit package to these. ☐ R: _____

14. Keep simple files/records. ☐ R: _____

15. Add prospect names and mail more. ☐ R: _____

16. Interview employers. ☐ R: _____

17. Follow up on interviews. ☐ R: _____

18. Close the $100,000 deal. ☐ R: _____

SUMMARY

Be sure to *have* a market plan if you expect to reach $100,000. Make the plan soon as you list your own skills and prospective employers. The plan should have three parts:

- *Situation:* Skills, prospects, where you are now.
- *Objective:* Goals, money, where you want to be. You already have done much of this.
- *Strategy:* The steps to reach your goals.

Part of your strategy is your package of cover letter, resume, and exhibits. Add to that personal visits, mailings, answering ads, using recruiters, electronics, and Web site sources. Records are a part of strategy; they help you keep track of the "live ones" interested in you. Then come the interview and the magic follow-up.

Advantages to such a plan include:

- You are organized.
- You have priorities.
- You reduce stress.
- You create clear goals and logical steps to follow.

Allow six to twelve months, although possibly much less or several times that.

This chapter has a plan form covering your situation, goal, and 18 suggested strategy steps.

CASE STUDY

In hiring a professional woman to serve as human relations director for a major company, we complimented her on her well organized search. She was candid about her marketing plan. She even showed us how she had "borrowed" a marketing outline, organized her resources, and approached it thoroughly. We were glad she did, or we would never have found her.

Rice's Comment: We all use the S-O-S system in most of our daily work, even starting in school:

- *Situation*—I don't know this subject.
- *Goal*—to master it.
- *Strategy*—study like mad.
- *Situation*—I am in New York.
- *Goal*—get to a meeting in California.
- *Strategy*—hop a jet.

The same intuitive system, carried out carefully and thoroughly, will serve you just as well in landing that $100,000 job!

4

What Goes into a $100,000 Resume?

Maximize knowledge to minimize risk.

—JUSTICE BLACK

Learn from the mistakes of others. You won't live long enough to make them all yourself!

—MARK TWAIN

Each resume reminder that follows is worth cold, hard cash to you! Read them all, and learn how to outdo the competitors whose hot breath is on your neck—even if you can't feel it yet.

Does your resume have to follow *all* of the following principles? It wouldn't hurt, but many superior resumes have been assembled using only some of these points. In Chapter 13, you will see scores of samples from a wide variety of sources. For variety's sake, I've included lots of different approaches and philosophies for you to use as models. All the same, you increase the odds for success in your $100,000 job hunt if you familiarize yourself with all the principles in this chapter—and use them to your benefit when you assemble your resume.

See Appendix A for a resume template you can use to develop your own $100,000 resume. See Chapter 12 for ideas on where to find one-on-one resume help.

$100,000 RESUME REMINDERS

- *Resume readers may see hundreds of resumes every week.* They have the job of pulling just a few of the better ones. Don't expect readers to pore over every word. They won't! In many cases, resumes are scanned, not read.

- *Keep your resume objectives in mind.* One objective is to provide readers with a short, clear, attractive picture of your best qualities, as they apply to the job. (*Resume* is, after all, a French word meaning "summary.") Another goal is to outdo your competition, to look better than the others. You also want to give the reader a selling tool to show others—to make the reader look good as a supplier of high-quality people. Your real, bottom-line objective is to get an interview. Sometimes, resumes result in an automatic, pick-up-the-phone, "You're hired!" response. But this does not happen often, especially at the $100,000 level. These employers nearly always want to "see the body!" So your resume is a tool meant to help you get an interview.

- *Your strategy is to follow the key steps outlined in this chapter.* It is seldom some one thing that you say or do, but rather your total assembly, a hundred little "just right" touches that will make all the difference.

- *Accept it: Your resume will have deficiencies.* The chances are small that your background (training and experience) will match perfectly with all the job specs. It's a rare person indeed who provides an exact fit with every requirement of the job.

- *A well-assembled resume will not just overcome some background flaws, but can make you look even better than the candidate who's "got it all."* The reader, who has seen thousands of resumes, will recognize that yours, following these guidelines, is the work of a quality professional—worth $100,000. How you present what you do have to offer can make all the difference in the world. "Trifles make success, and success is no trifle!" said Michelangelo.

PAPER, LAYOUT, AND APPEARANCE

- *Remember your major layout goals.* You want your resume to be attractive, accessible, interesting, high-quality, useful, understandable. Your competition seldom sets those qualities as specific objectives, but you can. That alone helps you stand out from the crowd. Keep these goals in mind throughout the writing process, and your resume should nearly scream out, "Here is your ideal person!"

- *Resume paper quality is important.* The paper you select speaks for you. The paper should be medium weight, top-quality "resume" or "document" paper. Cheap paper looks cheap and feels cheap, and seems like everyone else's. Heavy paper gives a poor impression of overkill. Your best selection is probably 24 lb., 50% rag content or a similar stock. The paper you select should "feel" like quality. Pay a little extra for a good printer or paper source. Your resume is worth it. It may be passed through many hands (you hope!). Don't use any fancy weaves or rice paper, because these usually do not copy well or print well and can cause tiny breaks in the printed letter.

- *Make sure your paper takes ballpoint pen, pencil, and felt pen well.* Readers might wish to highlight something, put a star next to it, or write "Great!" next to some key point for the boss to see. Make that easy to do.

- *The paper color should be white, off-white, ivory, or eggshell.* It should say "quality" before anyone reads a word of it. Do not use other colors. You might come across as strange, and your resume won't photocopy as well.

- *The typeface you select is "your face."* Ordinary or super-plain type makes you look average, and you don't stand out. Don't get super fancy, either. That makes you look strange. Best to use something between the two extremes: strong, businesslike. Times New Roman, 12 point bold typeface is ideal. (It's available to nearly every word processing or typesetting system.)

- *Do not use dot-matrix type.* This went out years ago, and is hard to read.

- *Eliminate all layout, spelling, or typographical errors.* Proofread the resume yourself; then get a friend to look it over for you.

- *Paragraphs should be single-spaced, not double.* Double-spacing takes up too much room. Use short paragraphs. Double-space between paragraphs.

- *Try to leave about 25% of the page as white space.* You can do this by using a 1-inch margin all around. Expensive readership studies show that such spacing gets more attention and makes your resume airy, inviting, and easy to read. Leaving enough white space makes you look upscale. Resumes that are crammed and jammed border to border on the page look cheap and are hard to read. These resumes suggest that the applicant doesn't know how to condense key material.

- *"Document" lines are thin border lines about 3/8ths of an inch in from the edge, all around.* These are unusual and not essential but they add class. They remind the top executive of vital documents, and give you a little extra importance. Don't go any closer than 3/8ths of an inch, because many photocopy machines will not pick the lines up, and your reader may wish to copy your resume.

- *One page is a "magic" resume length.* It shows you can translate complex material into short, accessible documents. The one-page size also shows that you have consideration for your readers. They are well aware that your career has lots more than can possibly be covered in one page. Since some applicants feel very strongly that a multiple-page resume is worth considering at the $100,000 level, I have included a few multiple-page samples in Chapter 13. All the same, I feel you should know that many people who handle resumes (at all levels) tend to take a very dim view of the multiple-page format, no matter how many years of experience you have. Hollywood has an old saying: "If you can't tell the story in a sentence, then they won't be able to write a listing for it in *TV Guide!*"

- *Consider using the back of the resume,* if for special material that is not part of the resume, but should be considered as part of your candidacy.

- *Strive to set up a series of "stand-alone" sheets.* Resume readers don't seem to mind several total pages: a cover letter, a resume, and even several exhibits. But they should be one page each. Your reader can staple these together or use them selectively. You just gave them a better tool; you stand out. But what do you do when you find yourself holding a piece of paper that says PAGE TWO and you don't know where PAGE ONE is?

- *The folded resume is an unusual, eye-catching and impressive variation on the standard resume.* Here, an 11 × 17-inch sheet is printed and folded in half to form an 8.5 × 11-inch folder. This gives you four sides. The first side might be your cover letter. The inside two faces might be the resume spread over two sides. (Although they're not my first choice, a number of two-page resume examples appear in Chapter 13.) The last page might be miniature exhibits, covered a little later in this book. This approach has made some applicants stand out, since it is almost never done and has been effective in landing $100,000 jobs. It is also very handy for the sender, since it is compact, complete, needing no assembly.

  The disadvantage is that it limits your flexibility. You may not want to use some exhibits with certain employers.

- *The summary resume is an innovative approach that goes in the other direction.* This is an abbreviated, highly targeted resume that focuses only on a few elements from your background—those that match up exactly with the requirements of the job as you understand them. It's an excellent initial contact tool. You might wish to use this format early on in a relationship as a "low-risk" resume with nothing to rule you out—and everything in your favor. (Several examples of summary resumes appear in Chapter 13.)

- *Use a paper clip, not a staple, to hold sheets together.* If the reader wants them separated, that is easy to do. To some people, a prestapled set is limiting, awkward, and unwelcome.

- *Your envelope should be a standard #10 size ($9\frac{1}{2} \times 4\frac{1}{8}$ inches).* Use a first-class stamp. Give no indication of a bulk mailing. The envelope color should match your resume, usually off-white. Your resume and other material should be folded in thirds. When you seal the envelope, moisten the flap only about an inch or so up from the point of the flap. This makes your letter easier to open, and you give a good first impression. (Sealing it fully and adding tape to the seal makes the resume seem like a secret spy document and, more often than not, a real pain to open. Your materials get torn—not a good first impression.)

- *Your return address on the envelope should be printed.* People seeking $100,000 jobs usually have their own stationery. If you don't have some, get some. Typed or handwritten return addresses look amateurish at this level.

WHAT TO SAY

- *This is the heart of the resume.* Give it lots of thought and care. Great facts, poorly presented, can be fatal. The decision to interview or not to interview is based largely on the facts you select and how you present them. Take your time. Get it right. Do several drafts. Give yourself time to review each of them.

- *Your "tone of voice" is important.* It should be businesslike, calm, brief, factual, concise, friendly, and confident. Don't waste a lot of words. Avoid saying "I" any more than is absolutely necessary. When you give a fact such as "Ten years at ABC," the reader knows you are talking about yourself. Avoid self-centered or judgmental adjectives, "Ten tough years with the giant ABC Company."

- *Avoid emotionally loaded words.* Stay away from phrases like "suffered" through ten years at ABC Company or "admired" ABC Company. The purpose of the resume is to give an economical, clear, and attractive picture. Emotional words get in the way; they distract people from the facts that support your cause.

- *Use lots of action words:* Organized, analyzed, planned, established, executed, developed, designed, directed, founded, helped, joined, managed, produced, rebuilt, saved, solved, and tested. Use action words to focus on constructive, valuable things you did. A main question your reader nearly always has is, "What can this person do for us?" Use action words to answer this question. Employers know that what people did in the past is a good clue to their probable action in the future.

- *Pretend you are the reader.* Use words, facts, and phrases that would make *you* say, "This sounds like a good person to work for our company. We should get together for a meeting."

- *Make every word count.* The average resume reader will spend only about 100 seconds on your document, reading about 50 lines, or two seconds per line. Make each line as attractive, informative, and pleasant as you can. Make each one a gem. Write and rewrite, if you feel you are making the phrase better. Every little improvement makes a small difference. You are steadily moving ahead of others.

- *Drop anything boring or confusing.* If just one line is dull or complex, you will lose your readers. These people often have many distractions around them competing for their attention. Don't use fancy, complicated, or technical words or phrases, unless you are absolutely sure that everyone at that company knows what you mean.

- *Consider using "no person."* For example, say, "developed this, designed that, or accomplished something else." Make no reference to "Jones" or "he." The reader knows exactly who you are talking about. Start most phrases with a verb or action; then say what was accomplished. (Some people are more comfortable writing in the third person, however, and there's plenty of precedent for this.)

- *Consider switching to "first person" near the end or when it seems appropriate.* Real pros do this. For example, "I am in excellent health." The resume suddenly becomes more personal and ends with a friendly note.

- *Keep your phrases short.* Save words when you can. That lets you add more good things about yourself. Use neither jargon nor long or strange words. Use plain ordinary words. You keep their attention and they read about you with greater interest. The sentences in this paragraph are good examples. Notice how clear and easy they are to read.

- *Customize your "job objective."* Direct it at readers, so that they know your goal. This might be the headline and first thing you say, and often is just that. The best way to cover this is to stay short, clear, but wide enough to cover several possible jobs. As an example, for finance, you might say, "Job goal is CFO, Treasurer or similar." For production you might say, "Job goal is Production VP or similar." For marketing, "Job Goal is Marketing VP or similar." The same goes for general manager or chief of PR, air traffic, engineering, admin, research and so on.

- *Use an objective only where it fits.* If you are aiming for one very specific type job and either not qualified or not shooting for any other position at the moment, use an objective. It can help you and the reader. Many job hunters have "Objectives" on one resume, different words on others, and no goals on another. They keep a supply of each.

  Giving an objective has its advantages. It is a big help to readers. They know immediately how to classify you and the job you seek. This is especially useful if you are applying for the very job for which they have been running ads or recruiting. Now they can quickly accept your resume as a legitimate applicant. Their job is made easier, and you have jumped one hurdle and maybe crossed the threshold.

  There is a disadvantage to giving an objective. You have suddenly ruled yourself out of other jobs for which you might qualify. You have limited yourself. Anyone in the hiring mode may have several other open slots to fill.

- *Consider developing several separate resumes.* Most people who seek $100,000 jobs have enough experience to qualify for several different leadership positions. Some successful job seekers have a resume designed specifically for Job A, another for Job B, one for Job C, and so on. All the information in the resume for Job A is aimed only at that job. This sort of resume is more likely to stand out and win the position. It is ideal for selective situations.

- *If you have several resumes, customize your cover letter or, on special occasions, adjust your entire package of exhibits.* What applies well to one job, like sales management, may not fit well with others, such as advertising.

- *The general resume, written so as to apply to several jobs, is by far the easiest and most flexible approach.* It may not be as specific as the "A-B-C" approach, but employers often find highly attractive features. They are often interested in people who have good skills in two areas, as well as broad experience in others, making them more valuable to the company. (A person with 20 years in just one highly specialized job is perceived as being of limited use.)

- *Let the cover letter handle the objectives.* It probably mentions goals in almost any case, and so it makes the A-B-C specialized resume less necessary. The cover letter's first line should be something along the lines of, "If you need a production director or similar, perhaps I can be of service." You have given your objective.

- *Mention whether you know a foreign language.* Specify whether you are fluent in reading, writing, and speaking the language, or can only read or understand it. This is a major difference, but still valuable in any case. Use only one line. For example, "Fluently read, write and speak Spanish. Spanish family."

- *Leave no gaps in time.* Personnel people like to say, "If there are any gaps, applicants are hiding something. Maybe they were in prison." If you have a time gap, you can stretch the times before and after it a little. A few months seldom make a difference. If you were job hunting during that period, this is seldom important. (Of course, if you *were* in jail, you should handle that point very carefully, probably by raising the subject yourself during the interview and supplying a wealth of superior references.)

- *Cover the last four or five jobs or 20 years or so.* Much before that may not be important, unless it has a direct bearing on the job you seek.

- *If you have been unemployed during the last six months, don't say so.* Surely you have not been totally idle. List almost any reasonable activity, such as serving as a teacher, consultant, advisor to local firms, friends or relatives, or writer in a related field, or volunteer. Most readers will understand. They've been there themselves or talked to many who have, and they are unlikely to press you on this. Also some of the great and near great people have been "on the beach" at least once. But they still had needed and widely used skills.

- *Give job titles that mean something.* Your actual title may be nondescriptive and even confusing ("Review Specialist"). Modify and clarify it so that it applies to the job objective ("Review Specialist / Quality Control Center"). How you write about your past jobs can be very important. The easiest and best way is to give your job title and company, size (if important), and one or two major things you did for the company. For example:

1/90-6/95   **Treasurer, Abbott Labs.,** $900 mill sales. Set up new cost and mgmt. account system, and wrote annual reports. Firm doubled income in five years.

- *Use a terse, compact style that says a lot in few words.* Don't say, "Served as treasurer." They know you served. Abbreviate management. They know what "mgmt." means. Perhaps say "account" rather than "accounting." All those little things may not seem important, but you just saved enough space to say that the firm doubled its income—an impressive statement. Not everyone can say that. You are not saying you did it by yourself, but you obviously played a role in a successful operation. Employers like to know you come from success, not bankruptcy. (If the firm did go bankrupt, leave that out. That's called "selective editing"!)

- *Put two letter spaces after each sentence.* This opens your paragraph, gives it air, and makes it easier to read, which is one of your goals.

- *If you can, cover each job in about two lines.* That can usually tell as much of the story as they want at the moment. You may have accomplished five other big items, but to list them all here might be overkill. Just pick the two or three main items. (If you had only one or two jobs in recent years, naturally you should use three or more lines each.)

- *Show evidence of using your skills.* Knowledge isn't doing. An old story goes like this: A girl and her cat are sitting on their front steps, when a little boy comes along. He says, "Hi, does your cat know any tricks." "Yes," the girl says, "She knows hundreds!" "Oh, great," says the boy, "Let's see one of the tricks." "No luck," answers the girl. "I said she *knows* a hundred tricks, I didn't say she would *do* any."

- *Leave out short, early entry jobs, like delivery boy or store clerk, unless they have a purpose or make some key point.* They may have nothing to do with being a treasurer.

- *Don't dwell on any short-term "steppingstone" jobs like "drove delivery truck" or "flipped burgers while in college."* These usually have no bearing on the treasurer's job or the industry in which you are interested. They show you are industrious, but your last five jobs show that and may be more closely related to your objective. If you must mention them for chronology's sake, consolidate them into very brief summaries or telescope the jobs into a single group.

- *Leave out "reason for leaving."* People looking for $100,000 candidates will not expect to find such information in a resume. And successful $100,000 resume writers almost never offer it. Why? Both parties know that there are often many, complex reasons for leaving. At least three are: those given by the employee, those given by the employer, and the real reason, which no one may know for certain. Parting, like divorce, is such a mixture of facts and emotions that it can seldom be described accurately. If employers really want to know why you left, they can usually tell from the facts or asking during a reference check, though even then the accuracy is often one-sided and doubtful. Sometimes the reason is obvious (such as a downsizing, department elimination, buyout, closing, or bankruptcy). In most cases, the subject is ignored, and other facts help to provide the background. Don't waste the space.

Later on, you might be asked "Why did you leave?" The best answer is to say, "Circumstances were such that I saw little chance of moving up, and I left to take a better job." That makes neither you nor your employer look bad, and gives a perfectly acceptable reason. If asked for details, just elaborate on those ideas.

Leave out any mention of trouble. Don't say, "The company was experiencing financial difficulty," "The boss became mentally ill," or "I was fired for stealing money and punching out the boss." Never badmouth a company because readers will think you may do the same to them. In fact, you might mildly compliment them: "They hired lots of good people [including you!]."

- *Leave out your past compensation.* If you held highly responsible positions, the readers know the probable income range. Furthermore, since pay plus bonus, fringes and other benefits are hard to measure and change yearly, they are not easily stated accurately. Also, people tend to exaggerate their compensation; so any statement is promptly subject to question.

- *Seek a $100,000 position only if your previous pay was close to that level, such as $70,000 or $80,000.* You might also go for that level of compensation if you were doing or can do equivalent work to that $100,000 level, and you can support this conclusively. Bear in mind that very few people ever get a new job paying twice what they were earning, although it can and does happen from time to time. For example, the ship captain's salary for a given company may routinely start at $100,000. If the first or second mate wage was well below this, perhaps $50K, but he had to take over because the captain died on a long, dangerous cruise and did a superlative job, he might be promoted to captain at $100,000.

- *Leave out weaknesses.* In the interests of honesty or avoiding a later surprise, some people feel compelled to mention, on the resume, that they are not expert in some field or skill such as math, language, or law. Unless this is directly related to the job you seek, forget it. Calling attention to your weaknesses adds nothing. The matter may never be relevant or even mentioned. No one is expected to be expert or skilled at everything.

- *Avoid exaggeration, especially if the exaggeration is obvious or just plain hard to believe.* If the firm got a $10 million contract, don't say, "I won a $10 million contract," unless you really did it all on your own. Even then, it will be more believable if you say you "played the major role" or "helped the company land it." Resumes tend to overstate, and a little modesty is not only more believable but refreshing. It adds to your stature.

- *Your availability, your specific salary, or other requirements don't belong in your resume.* Salary is usually flexible and negotiable, within limits. Availability is assumed, and personal "demands" are harmful. So these elements might not even be in a letter. It's better to wait for the later discussion phase, when you are close to finalizing.

- *If a former boss likes you, you might give the supervisor's name with the job activity.* This saves checking a reference, but more important, says in effect, "I did such a fine job, my boss will give me a good word." This makes you look very honest, open, aboveboard, and confident.

- *Consider using an "honors" section.* Again, you need not list dates or places. Just enter elements like: "Won award for high grades or service to the school or civic group," or "Written up in the newspaper." If you've got room, you can include almost anything that might show you excel and were recognized, especially if the recognition is only remotely related to the job you seek.

- *Consider using an "other" section.* This gives you maximum flexibility to put in items that don't fit well elsewhere, such as "night desk clerk to put self through college." Anything that shows you are a dedicated hard worker can be a plus.

- *Consider using any small, clever picture you might have.* If you won a rare, major award, you might have a fingernail size picture of this award in the margin next to the statement. You might even consider including a picture of yourself!

- *Your education is important.* List only colleges and degrees, with honors if they apply. You can do this in one or two lines. For example, "B.A., and M.S. on scholarship to Duke Univ. Honors." You might want to list a course or two directly related to your field, such as, "Six courses in accounting."

On its own, a degree seldom lands the job, unless you have a Ph.D. or Master's in the given field. But the lack of a degree can hurt you, and your competition will play degrees up strong. Still, you probably shouldn't lead your resume with your degree information. Employers at the $100,000 level are seldom looking for a degree as a prime specification. (Exceptions are colleges, hospitals, or high-tech groups.) First, you should prove that you can do the job well, by showing career accomplishments. Then close off with the degrees, almost as an afterthought. People who think the degree will get them the job (outside of advanced technical jobs) are not being realistic. They are putting far more importance on it than do most employers. Someone said, "Some people take years to overcome their education!" (or at least to put it in perspective).

- *Omit minor education activities.* Only if you have nothing else, list the quoits team.

  Instead, focus on top academic honors, such as "3.8 GPA," "Elected to the National Honor Society," or "Phi Beta Kappa membership."

- *Consider what your reader might have done.* If the decision maker is in medicine or management, mention associated activities that might mean something in that field, such as president of the finance club or head of the cardiovascular volunteer group.

- *Mention whether you ever taught college, high school, or grade school.* Even if you taught as a substitute, with boy or girl scouts, with a civic group, or at church, summer camp, or anywhere, mention this experience as part of your education. Holders of $100,000 jobs are usually leaders and often expected to teach others. Experience of that type can put you ahead of others.

- *State whether you ever did any public speaking anywhere.* Mention this unless it was with a program that now has a negative image. (Even then you can be vague: "Did considerable public speaking with various groups.") Candidates for $100,000 jobs often must do public speaking, if only to small groups.

- *List anything you published—briefly.* For example, "Wrote three published magazine articles on accounting." $100,000 people are often expected to put things in writing, although not necessarily as an accomplished author.

- *Mention whether you have ever held a leadership position.* $100,000 people are usually expected to lead a group, large or small. Leadership might be in sports, military, academics, civic or social groups, or even volunteer groups.

- *List membership in a trade or professional association.* Examples are the American Management Association or American Bar Association. List these if there is space.

- *Highlight any volunteer efforts.* For example, "Volunteered during serious local (fire/ flood/ quake/ blizzard/ epidemic/ riot/ drought/ explosion/ other)." Or describe your role in a fundraiser or work you did in scouting, hospital, elder care, disabled people, church, or service club. This type of activity shows you are public spirited, dedicated, willing to serve and to work hard. Companies now expect their execs to do more community service than they did in the past.

- *Many people list a Skills section.* A person seeking a $100,000 position probably has lots of training and experience, and could well have dozens of skills. These are usually best stated in the cover letter and should be obvious from the jobs held. Repeating them here might be unnecessary, but special situations or a particular opening might call for a short list.

- *Enter whether you are licensed for any relevant profession.* Examples are law, medicine, piloting, undertaking, engineering, accounting, architecture, museum management, finance.

- *Mentioning your spouse can be a plus.* Call this paragraph "Personal." If you have a spouse who has done anything noteworthy in your field or any related field, say so. For example, "Spouse of 10 years has won honors as a tax accountant (or CPA, etc.)." This shows you are proud of that person and demonstrates that you have a long-term solid relationship and a stable personal life.

- *Mentioning children can also be a plus.* If you have children, a few words show they come from a good family, such as "Our three children all graduated high school with honors." This shows that your family are solid believers in accomplishment, loyalty, team spirit, the long term—not likely to be a personal problem to you. A family can be an advantage, since many resume readers tend to be seniors with older, traditional values and strong family beliefs. Making brief references to family also shows you are dependable, the number one trait sought by upper-level leaders, according to recent studies.

- *Say nothing if you are single, divorced, not married, have no family, or are gay/lesbian.* Skip the family subject. Instead, say something about your health. If your health is fine, simply say, "Health, Excellent." You need say no more at this time, but it could be an important plus for you. (You can say this even if you are under a doctor's care for a disorder, such as high blood pressure or diabetes, or are taking prescription drugs, as long as you have the matter under control.) A large percentage of mature adults (your competition) have health problems. If you have none, this is a good place to stand above others in a very important matter. Employers are understandably reluctant to hire a person who is now or soon will be seriously ill. Illness can be very expensive. Bringing up the subject is a sort of reminder that this should be checked out with other applicants.

  If your health is not fine, just skip it at this point, although the subject is likely to come up. In any case, you may be asked to submit to a physical examination by a company-paid physician, with findings provided to the employer.

  Make only supportable statements. Most people exaggerate and some blatantly lie in resumes; readers learn to take the statements with a grain of salt. The better it sounds, the more doubt they have. You may be asked to substantiate any point. Be ready to do so.

- *Mention exhibits.* (See Chapter 6 on exhibits.) If you have room at the bottom, add "References available." You might bring in exhibits by saying, "References and exhibits available." If you don't have room, you can mention that point in your short cover letter.

- *References can be important, but they usually do not belong in the resume.* Their names simply take up space and will serve no real purpose, unless they are famous or well known to the reader. (If so, mention them!) Otherwise, you might make the "references available" statement in your short cover letter. And be sure to have your list ready.

UNUSUAL RESUME IDEAS

Creative ideas that worked include:

- Sending your resume in an empty, but corked, good label wine bottle with a note saying, "I heard by the grapevine you wanted to uncork some good people."

- Include an old shoe with your resume and a note: "I finally got my foot in the door and hope I'm the sole candidate!"

- Attach your resume to a flat inner tube: "Hope you get pumped up by this!"
- Pass along a tee-shirt with your resume printed on it, or a video tape of you outlining your resume's highlights.

More sedate suggestions include:

- Recording your resume, in your voice, on a tape cassette, "For listening in your car."
- Placing your resume in a gift-wrapped box, "In case you want a gifted person."
- Sending your resume with a packet of flower seeds, "In case you want someone to grow with, who really blooms!"
- Sending a short chain of three links, each labeled, "Willing," "Talented," and "Available."
- Including your resume with an industry-related book.

Use these "creative" approaches only for certain employers, not just anyone. They are ideal for answering advertisements that usually draw hundreds of applicants. They are also ideal for students leaving college and seeking entry jobs, competing with thousands of other candidates. Creative contact methods are also good for sending to people in the advertising, publishing, communications and entertainment business. (These tactics may put off more conservative employers.) These ideas are also good when you have one or several specific job slots in mind and you have tried more conventional methods without result. For a more detailed overview, see Brandon Toropov's *303 Off-the-Wall Ways to Get a Job* (Career Press), from which these ideas have been extracted.

REMEMBER YOUR TARGET AND JOB LEVEL

If you are looking for a $100,000 job, your resume reader is likely to be earning much more, perhaps twice that. Such a person is probably older and conservative. Further, if you are looking for $100,000, you are usually talking about a very responsible position where you manage millions of dollars in cash or other assets, and possibly people's lives. That doesn't mean you can't have a sense of humor, but such a trait is rarely essential, unless you are in the entertainment business.

SUMMARY

Remember these resume writing tips: one page if you can, quality paper, good type, letterhead, spacing—25% white space. Direct tone, action words, brief, clear, reader aimed. Leave out the negatives; focus on the positives. A blank form you can use to draft a resume is in Appendix A, in back of book.

RICE'S COMMENT

Most resumes look pretty good. Only a few are exceptional. Follow these guidelines and yours will look like a million bucks or at least $100,000.

5

Your Cover Letter for the $100,000 Job

Perception is reality.
 —TOLSTOY

Work smarter, not harder.
 —DRUCKER

Your cover letter could be your ticket to $100,000. Why? It is your first "Hello," your "Good morning," your beginning, your opportunity to jump ahead. The cover letter is where 90% of applicants make fatal mistakes. For example, they almost always start with the wrong sentence. They talk about themselves and a problem, rather than talking about the reader and a solution.

The bad beginning doesn't eliminate them, but it sure misses a great chance to jump ahead of others. Remember, the reader sees thousands of cover letters, and they must separate them into "winners and losers."

MARVELOUS MINOR MIRACLE

Here is an example of a cover letter that focuses on solutions to reader problems. It worked! This actual superior cover letter helped get $100,000 offers! (It has been slightly altered for confidentiality.)

Typeset letterhead name, address
City, State, Zip
Phone , E-mail, and FAX numbers   Date

Dear Jim,

If you can use a qualified, seasoned STAFFING OFFICER, TRAINER, MARKETER or MGMT AUDITOR, perhaps I may be of service to you.

Have served as:

— Chief consultant, top award-winning trainer, over 15 years. Small business.
— Management and marketing planner, large and small companies.
— Author of three articles on: Staffing, Marketing, Management
— Key exec for two Fortune 500 companies. (Vice Pres. of one.)
— New business specialist. (Big ticket items, multi-mill and more.)

Can serve you well and enjoy most marketing, start-ups, new projects, staffing, coaching, training, motivation, building morale, and teamwork. As employee or private contractor.

Have reputation for reliable, much above average quality performance, getting on well with people at all levels. Flexible on hours, weekend, location, travel, and income. Recent wage package was near six figures. Many references available or at any of my past employers.

I look forward to hearing from you. Perhaps we could have a coffee nearby?

Cordially [handwritten]

Name [handwritten]

Enclosed:
Resume
Exhibit page

[Handwritten note] P.S. I would be honored to serve the ABC Company. Your organization has a fine reputation.

$100,000 COVER LETTER FORM

	[Typeset name, address,
_____	phone, fax, e-mail]

_____

_____

[full date]

Dear _____:
(Spell name or title correctly, handwritten)

If you can use a:

_____

_____

_____

(List 3–4 key skills or job titles, preceded by a couple of favorable adjectives, like "seasoned.")

I have served as: (Did what? Licenses. Honors. Results. List 4-8 items in four lines.)

_____

_____

_____

_____

Would serve you well and enjoy (doing) _____

_____.

Have a strong reputation for (reliability, work well with others, high-quality work. Flexible on hours, location, travel, income, recent wage area.)

_____

_____

_____

I look forward to (Hearing? Coffee?) _____

[Close, by hand] _____

[Signature] _____

Enclosed
Resume
Exhibit Page(s)

P.S. (This brief, handwritten compliment is very important, because it is one of the most frequently read parts of the whole letter!) _____

_____

_____

SUMMARY

Your cover letter can be your ticket to $100,000. Decision makers read cover letters, especially if the letter is closely tuned to the job involved. Use the model and form in this chapter to build your own $100,000 letter. Stay away from openings like "I am looking." Instead, begin with something like, "If you need ...."

CASE STUDY

This cover letter format was used by several people who landed major jobs. One of the best examples was a person who had sought a position as vice president of a major New York bank. Armed with a great resume, she prepared a strong cover letter based on the model you just saw, along with a one-page exhibit as a package. She sent the package to the bank president. It got her an interview, but then a turndown. She was depressed, but she kept on with her search. Then two weeks later, she got a call saying that the chairman of the board had seen her package and wanted to talk to her. They had a visit and she was offered the job. She took it and later became president of a branch bank.

Rice's Comment: Your cover letter is one of the most effective tools you have. Almost everyone reads this document. It is surely worth preparing with care. If so, you will move a long way toward that $100,000 job.

6

Exhibits That Won $100,000 Jobs

Hold their attention and interest in you.
—LEO BURNETT

What is past is prologue.

—SHAKESPEARE

In this chapter, you will see how to make a prize exhibit or two. With such tools, one New York candidate, who was running even with another, suddenly became the $100,000 selection. Good exhibits often make the vital difference. They aren't essential, because many candidates don't have them and still land jobs. But for a little effort, they can be the memorable cherry on the sundae, when others have no such topper.

WHAT'S AN EXHIBIT?

An *exhibit* is almost any item, but is usually a sheet of paper that documents the claim, "I can do this, possibly for you, which is another good reason you should hire me." An exhibit is one of your credits. It can be a special honor, a recognition, or a big project. We will look at a whole string of ideas, and it won't take a lot of work. Some things are obvious, like a special performance award, such as "Supervisor of the Year for 1998." If nothing pops to mind, read through your resume and try to think of anything related to your accomplishments. Look through your files. It's often a simple thing, some achievement that you might not have considered very important but that shows you can make superior contributions. Give yourself double credit if you can find anything that is visual: a picture, photo, or diagram.

WHAT'S A SUPERIOR EXHIBIT?

Don't go job hunting emptyhanded. Your exhibit can be almost anything that is to your credit. Naturally, make it the best you can find. After all, some of your better competitors *will* have something to show.

A superior exhibit is a single page that tells a story of accomplishment in, or related to, your field. Ideally it has several small items, like newspaper clips or pictures. The best exhibits use visuals and are easy to understand. An example is an award scroll or picture of a silver cup for designing a high-selling circuit breaker. Usually, you wouldn't include a blueprint for the same item. That's too esoteric, too specialized, unless your target employer is in electronics, in which case it's OK.

You should have three kinds of exhibits:

- Your *reference list*.
- An all-purpose *exhibit sheet*.
- A few *specials* to use as opportunities occur.

The Reference List

Employers rarely hire total strangers; they want someone to stand up and vouch for you. So some kind of list is essential for a $100,000 job. Often this list helps make the final decision. Most candidates have a short list of four or five well primed references. That's fine. But you can do better. Don't list five—list fifteen or twenty people! Show their names, titles, companies, and phone numbers. Street addresses are not needed. They are almost never checked by mail. Phone contact is far more common.

References should be people who will say a good word for you. Such a large list by itself says, "An army of people think well of me. I do well everywhere." It also says you are not afraid to be checked. With this many names, you have a giant advantage over most other candidates, who have just a few. A half dozen people could easily be coached, but not twenty.

Group and label your references by company or profession. Phone them and get their permission ahead of time, of course. Then send a resume to refresh their memory. Hold this reference list out from your resume mailing, but give it later at the right time, usually at the close of an interview, with the thank you letter as a follow-up tool, or whenever it's requested.

The All-Purpose Exhibit

The all-purpose exhibit can be used in many places and times. In one of the best our recruiting team ever saw, the candidate had written six magazine articles in her field. She "shrank" the title page of each of these down to about half size, cut them up to about the size of playing cards, and then pasted them on a sheet in an overlapping fan arrangement. She added a typed box listing the subjects, magazines, and dates, and then made many photocopies. She sent out this all-purpose exhibit with her cover letter and resume (to form her "package"), and also gave it out during her interview. She said she had more compliments on this than any other job device she had ever prepared. And she landed a $100,000 job!

Variations of this by other people show items that the person helped develop, such as exciting or highly successful new products or interesting graphics from reports or service announcements. This can give you a superior exhibit that no one else can offer.

"I just don't have anything like that," many people say. Nevertheless, you probably *DO* have something in your background that you may have forgotten. People seeking $100,000 are usually in the $50,000 to $80,000 range and tend to do things that get some publicity, publication, honors, recognition, awards, or prominent notice for themselves, their department, or their company—and then they filed it away. Take a look through your files for:

- Newspaper articles on you and your company.
- Annual report pages you helped prepare.
- Organizational charts you helped create.
- Product pictures, packages, services, or ideas you helped produce or market.
- Print or TV ads with pictures you can shrink, paste, and caption.
- Maps or flight plans you helped produce, with explaining captions.
- Pictures of a department team, people who got results and whom you helped hire, organize, or motivate.
- Graphs of sales, revenues, or other data.
- Financial charts, bar charts or pie diagrams, money-in/money-out results.
- Checklists you've developed.
- Public activities of the company, in a pie diagram, by sector.
- Communications by type of media, such as a pie diagram.

You might also adopt:

- Pictures or write-ups about yourself.
- Images of worksites or land surveyed.
- Artwork done.
- New systems.
- Space photos.
- Autos driven and sold.
- Civic ceremonies.
- Sports occasions.
- Lab setups.
- Buildings, roads, or bridges designed, or structures built.

You get the idea. You want your reader to say, "*This* person might do this for us."

Your Special Exhibits

Special exhibits might simply be more narrowly focused all-purpose exhibits. Some successful $100,000 candidates had five or ten such items they may never use, but they are in their brief case file, "just in case" a special opportunity came up during their interview. This type of preparation is highly impressive and puts you way above others. These extras are also ideal to send in follow-up, thank you letters, when you don't want to repeat your original exhibit, or to give to someone who has already seen your first exhibit.

Consider setting up a miniature flip chart set in your brief case. These might be simple, colorful charts, or just pages with a few key words about a plan in your field like accounting, economics, statistics, law, supervision, marketing, or transportation. They should be on standard pages or heavy paper, explaining a plan, outline, proposal, project, or other subject in maybe ten points. Such an exhibit is ideal for a five-minute close to an interview. Almost no one else has such a thing. These will greatly impress your interviewer and usually take less than an hour to prepare.

CASE STUDY: THE FLIP CHART ON THE WATER GLASS

A company president asked a candidate to lunch. He knew they would have almost no space for papers, but he had an important "captive" audience for a short time. So he put a simple plan on a small flip chart. This was several 3×5 cards. Each card was glued to sheets of a matching, pocket-sized spiral pad, bound at the top. When the president said, "Tell me about yourself." The candidate said, "Well, I just happen to have a small suggested marketing plan on this little flip chart." It was designed to lean up against a water glass or coffee cup, with the pages turning over to lay across the top. The president was much impressed; no one else had ever done that. A major job offer followed. This was a truly superior exhibit that was actually easy to prepare.

CASE STUDY: COLOR SLIDES

One successful candidate had a short set of color slides on marketing. He had helped develop a lengthy set for his employer. Since the material was not confidential, the candidate simply had a much shorter, 20-piece set made up in duplicate. He used these as a five-minute end of his first interview. The president of a billion-dollar company said to him, "No one has ever given us such an interesting job interview! I think we have a deal."

CASE STUDY: A BOOK DEAL

One woman used a copy of her book, which dealt with the profession in question, as a special exhibit at the end of an interview. The corporate officers were very impressed. No one could say she wasn't qualified! She got the job.

Other special exhibits might be an actual small piece of equipment, a packaged product (as a gift), or a model of a large item. Whatever it is will put you far ahead of others. You give your interviewer a superior tool for selling you.

SUMMARY

An exhibit is "the cherry on the sundae," the topper, the clincher that puts you a step ahead of others. It is anything "extra" that shows that you are better or exceptional, or that you can do more than others. Make sure you've got this edge over your competition!

The exhibit should tell a story, especially in a picture.

Develop three types of exhibits: a long reference list; an all-purpose exhibit that might be a collection, summary, or montage of a few exhibits on one page; and special exhibits for special occasions, like small flip charts, overheads, or color slides.

If you take this approach, you *will* be noticed.

Rice's Comment: Sometimes the exhibits alone have been far more impressive than even a good resume. Employers see thousands of resumes, but few well prepared exhibits. As part of an outstanding package, your exhibits will help to point you toward $100,000!

7

Strong Answers to Ads

Don't rape. Seduce.

—RICK BUDD

In the land of the blind, the one-eyed man is king!

—JAMES FOSTER

Occasionally, $100,000 jobs are advertised. Most such jobs, however, are filled in other, far different ways. When these jobs *do* show up in the newspaper, they are usually in "display" ads, little boxes a few inches square. Sometimes the ads mention the salary in the headline or in the text, but usually you must guess. The aim of this chapter is to give you a superior system for answering ads, so that you get invited for an interview.

THE JOB SUGGESTS THE WAGE

The ad normally talks about two things: (1) the job duties and (2) the kind of person sought to perform those duties.

When employers advertise a job opening with highly responsible duties and need a person of major skills and experience, they are not thinking about minimum wage. That sort of job is usually near or over $100,000. Examples of such jobs are a senior actuary, pilot, engineer, vice president, general manager, major department or division manager, senior scientist, college dean, medic, administrator, minister, journalist, managing editor, or broker.

Another clue is major financial authority. If the ad says this job has the authority and responsibility to supervise a large number of people or a high volume of product, major equipment or investments, then it is probably at or above $100,000.

To find these ads, scan publications like *The Wall Street Journal, Time, Forbes, The New York Times,* or the Sunday edition of most major city business sections. The *WSJ* is especially good for $100,000 jobs. The large, high-paying display ads in all these papers usually attract many applicants. Most are totally unqualified. You can stand out from the crowd.

HOW TO STAND OUT

There are five major ways to step ahead of the competition:

- First, send a superior package.
- Second, make sure your cover letter fits the ad like a glove.
- Third, create a somewhat unusual, off-beat resume.
- Fourth, send the package to several top officers at the address in the ad.
- Fifth, answer lots and lots of ads.

The Superior Package

This is the subject of the book. Making a strong answer to ads is just one example of the flexibility and power you get once you have a really strong package.

Customize Your Cover Letter

Play the ad back to the reader, sentence by sentence—which almost no one does. This pleases the reader, because it shows that you read the ad carefully, and it gives your reader ammunition to take your materials to a higher person. Show that you have what they are requesting—and more!

Create an Unusual Resume, Just for Them

In Chapter 4, you read about some ideas for creative approaches to employers utilizing customized, off-beat resumes. These are unique and will certainly get you noticed. But remember, you must still show the interest, desire, and ability to take action, along with solid reasons why you can help the target organization. A gimmick is nice, but it has to be accompanied by a reason to set up an interview.

Send to Several Top People

The ad may give the company name. If so, send to the president, CEO, executive VP, appropriate department head, and director of human resources, as well as the name given in the ad. Someone else may notice you in connection with other openings the company did not advertise. Even if the ad does not give the company, consider sending your package to several titles at the address given.

Answer a Lot of Ads

Reading the classifieds shouldn't be your only contact method, but devoting some time to promising ads makes sense. Some candidates answer ten or twenty every weekend, for weeks. That gets your package out to many companies who are looking for people. That beats letting your materials sit in a desk drawer! Accept interviews even from unlikely companies. This keeps you in practice, and who knows where a contact may lead?

SUMMARY

The biggest and best jobs in the $100,000 area are seldom advertised. Plenty of qualified people are often already in the company, on file, or available through a $100,000 recruiter—but not always! Some such slots *do* get advertised.

The ad might not give the salary, but the job type suggests the wage.

The best sources for such ads are *The Wall Street Journal,* published weekdays, *The New York Times* Sunday executive ad section, and the Sunday editions of most major city papers.

The few ads bring in hundreds of underqualified and unqualified dreamers who take too much work to screen. So you must stand out. Apply with a stand-out package of cover letter, resume, and exhibits. Customize your package, if you have time and if the ad gives you enough information. Send to several people at that company, if the name is given, or to the address, if that is all you have.

Answer lots of ads. These are real slots, and should probably be pursued before you launch a cold mailing to a company that may have no openings whatever. Don't expect much, but be ready for a phone call.

CASE STUDY

A young professional in California answered a lot of ads using a good package and had many interviews. One was for an assistant financial training director. He was not a trainer, nor was he a finance major. So had no chance, right? Well, he prepared a customized resume that emphasized his willingness to learn the finance field, the high points of his moderate experience, and his fondness for teaching. He got an interview, was thoroughly prepared with materials, exhibits, and lists, and displayed a very upbeat enthusiastic attitude. The company made him an offer. He thought it over, felt the money too low, so took a pass. They called him again, had lunch, raised the offer, which was still below $100,000, but had real possibilities. He took the job, spent a year at it, and moved to another slot in Boston, far above $100,000.

Ask Yourself

1. How will you prepare your package? _____

2. How can you "customize" it? _____

3. What ad sources will you use? _____

4. How many ads can you answer each week? (Remember, you should leave time for other job search methods too!) _____

5. Will you accept most interview invitations? _____

Rice's Comment: Answering ads, like any other step, can lead to mixed results—from lots of responses to nothing but wastes of time. But they are a source that wise seekers of $100,000 will use.

8

Superior Mailing Action

Ideas rule the world.

—EMERSON

Modern management's major mistake is miserable communication.

—DRUCKER

A good mailing program means sending your package of your high-quality cover letter, resume, and exhibit sheet to your many high-potential job sources.

TEN STRONG ADVANTAGES TO MAILING

1. You are in control and being proactive by reaching out to people, not waiting for them to contact you. As the song goes, "If you wait for the boss to raise your pay, you're going to be waiting 'til judgment day."
2. You can contact good prospects at your own pace.
3. Your program is superior to your competitor's.
4. You are putting your materials to use, not letting them sit in a desk drawer.
5. By staying active and busy, you are using your time and effort productively and keeping your spirits up.
6. Mailing costs little in comparison to the goal you are seeking.
7. The program is efficient, in that you can reach far more prospects per day and per dollar than by most any other method, and companies are familiar with the system and set up to work with it.
8. Mailing is selective. You reach just the people and places you wish.
9. You make hundreds of contacts fast. You could not possibly make these contacts in person. Some might lead to nothing at the moment, but could produce major offers months from now. (This often happens.)

10. For years, good mailings have been the greatest tool for getting the $100,000 job. They still get good results. Recently, however, because so many middle management professionals are using mail, other programs (like using your resume package with networking contacts and recruiters) are becoming just as important, or even more so.

DISADVANTAGES TO MAILING

1. Mailing does cost money. The typical cost for postage and printing for sending one resume package is about $1.

2. Mail takes work to gather prospect names, write a cover letter and resume, gather an exhibit or two, print and collate all these, and set them up for mailing.

3. Mail takes *time*. A mailing of 50 takes most people about a day. The mail takes a couple of days to reach the prospect. Then you have to allow at least two weeks or months for a reply, since recipients have many other projects and you are not a high priority.

4. You have to have your phone covered in person or with an answering machine.

5. There is no guarantee. After all that work, over half never answer. Out of the total, you might hear nothing.

WHO SHOULD GET YOUR MAILING?

The various sources covered in Chapter 2 can be summarized as:

1. Your network of references, friends, associates, club members.
2. Replies to appropriate "Exec Wanted" newspaper ads.
3. Executive recruiters.
4. Large companies that hire $100,000 people.
5. Best companies to work for.
6. Other new targets of opportunity that come along.

Mailing Starts with Your Network

Don't be shy about using your personal network. Embarrassment is a major obstacle for many job hunters (particularly men). Many people are reluctant to ask for help. Don't be. Many of your competitors will certainly use their contacts, and you should too!

Gather your courage, pocket your pride, and make the calls. The average job hunter knows 60 businesspeople.

You have a lot of good reasons to use your network. After all, what are friends for, except to help each other? And many of them may have once asked for help themselves. You won't be the first to ask them for help, and someday they may need your help. They know it; so they build a few brownie points with you, at no real effort. Also, they take pride in the fact that you asked them; it makes them feel important—sort of sets them up. They like showing a company that they know a good person who is available. And certainly you would help them, if they asked, wouldn't you? Maybe you already have helped people in the past. Perhaps they all won't assist, but if only half the 60 help you, that's still 30 professional allies. And that's a lot of horsepower—for free.

You Do a "Triple Whammy" When You Contact Your Network

By going to your network, you:

1. Enlist a good reference, and that alone can be impressive or helpful.
2. Are almost asking them for a job. (Perhaps they *do* have openings, or know of some.)
3. Enlist them as a placement or recruiter person to be your salesperson and to solicit among their hundreds of friends.

Women sometimes call this "The Old-Boys Club," which is partially true—but smart women use the same procedure!

Phone or visit those original 60 contacts, even if they are not in the business world. They know people who are. The calling is work, and it costs a few bucks, but it is worth it. Your contacts will give you encouragement. Simply tell each of them that you are looking and ask if you may list him or her as a reference. Few will ever refuse. Then give or send them your package: "This is to refresh your memory, in case you are called as my reference." Your contacts will appreciate that. You just gave them a great tool and an incentive, something few job hunters ever bother to do. Have lunch with them, where practical. They will often say, "Hey, you should go see Jan or the XYZ Company because they are looking for your type." Your search may be over!

Network your civic club people in the same way—especially chambers of commerce and service clubs, like the Lions and Kiwanis. You may want to join a new club, at least for a few months; most are usually always seeking new members. Many top execs are required to join local service clubs, and you might eat lunch next to someone you could hardly meet any other way.

Turn Important Contacts into Better Salespersons

Give some of your contacts a few resume packages, one for their own information and the others labeled "For a friend." Offer more if they want them. Smart operators end up with a whole staff of top-level, free salespeople, passing out their resumes to people they never heard of. Just one energetic person can be highly helpful. Sometimes two recommend you to the same employer, which adds major impact to your name.

Now Go to Your Big Lists

Your networking may not bring results for a few weeks, if ever. Don't just sit, wait, and worry. Take action! Mail to your longer lists of recruiters, customers, nearby companies, former company suppliers, large national companies, and best companies. Then mail to the want ads, perhaps on a continuing basis of a dozen, once a week.

Send Large Mailings to Titles

Address your package to "President," "Executive VP," "CEO," or "VP (of department where you fit)." These people seldom read resumes, but they do pass them on to their human resource director. As we've seen, these persons aren't always sure whether the boss read the resume or not, but they know where it came from and treat it with care.

WHAT RESPONSE CAN YOU EXPECT?

Unless you have a skill in big demand—a "hot" property—the average professional can figure that 5% of companies mailed will show some "interest," usually as a request for an interview. These 5% might lead to one "offer" per 100 letters, at best. It's probably safer to figure one offer in 200 to 300 letters.

HOW MANY PACKAGES SHOULD YOU MAIL OUT?

The estimated return of 5% will help you decide how many packages to mail out. People don't realize that most companies have no present openings for a given, standard type of professional. Maybe one in 20 has an opening for you, even if you have a strong skill. Don't feel as though you are not wanted. Employers may greatly admire your credits, but simply have no vacant slot. And these statistics vary widely with the industry, the location, the skill, and the strength of the economy. So 100 packages might generate ten job offers, or only one, or none. If you want five offers, you should probably plan on sending at least 500 packages.

Note: Many of your competitors prepare their material, mail to a dozen companies, and then feel demoralized because they don't get a single offer. They overrate the market demand for their skills—and their own importance.

WHEN TO MAIL?

You should mail after you have your sources listed and the package ready. Most wise hunters send in batches of about 100, roughly a week apart. Your network people are likely to be the most productive; so they should be covered first, by mail or in person. That might be enough right there, leading to several offers. More likely in today's uncertain economy, you need to go to your next group, which may be answering ads. Then come mailings to the recruiters, large companies, best companies, and any other companies that seem appropriate.

Done right, a simple system saves you a lot of time and work. Start with your source list. Now you know your count, at least for the first mailing. It's best to mail in batches. You can make changes from one group to another, or hold off mailing to a group while you fix a problem.

Use printed envelopes. These are costly, but, at your level, you definitely don't want to use hand-addressed return envelopes! Most pros simply use peel-off typed labels run through their computer printer. If you run batches of 100, have 100 package items printed or photocopied (cover letter, resume, and exhibit). Many pros handwrite the date, salutation, signature, and PS on the cover letter. This looks more personal. You should address, fold, stuff, and seal just the inch or two near the tip of the flap. Use first-class stamps, and then mail the batch. The average work time to do all this: about 2 days per 100 letters.

DEVELOP A SIMPLE MAILING PLAN

A simple mailing plan gets you much better results than improvising, and saves you a lot of work. The plan puts all your tools and steps together and in order, so that you don't waste time. And it does this all on one page. On page 51, you'll see a sample form to use or change as you wish. The spaces are for "date done."

MY MAIL PROGRAM PLAN

Mailing Number	Mailing #1	Mailing #2	Mailing #3
Mailing to (prospects)	_____	_____	_____
Approximate number of prospects	100	100	50
Cover letter (date written)	_____	_____	_____
Resume (date written, one time)	_____	_____	_____
Exhibits (date ready, one time)	_____	_____	_____
Cover letter printed	_____	_____	_____
Resume printed	_____	_____	_____
Exhibits printed	_____	_____	_____
Cover salutation/signature*	_____	_____	_____
Envelopes printed	_____	_____	_____
Envelopes addressed**	_____	_____	_____
Package: collate, fold, staple	_____	_____	_____
Stuff, stamp, seal, mail	_____	_____	_____
Special item/remarks	_____	_____	_____
(things to do)	_____	_____	_____
	_____	_____	_____

*Your cover letter, resume, and exhibits might be identical for some of these prospects. Wise applicants use a blue felt pen to write a salutation, like "Dear Manager," date and sign your cover letter ("Sincerely/Jane Smith"). This gives a personal touch to your package, suggesting you did not send out many, although most employers pay little attention to this.

**Mail-to addresses might also be done by hand in blue felt pen. (Blue shows it was not printed.) This gets a little more attention and doesn't take much more time than typing.

About 65% of the people you contact will never answer in any way. About 30% will send a "So sorry" form letter, because they think it is good business. (After all, you might end up working for one of their customers, and they want you to think kindly of them.) The remaining 5% are the ones who write or call and say, "Let's talk." Those are the "live ones." Treat them very carefully. They are golden.

A SLIGHT RESPONSE? GO TO WORK FAST

If you get even a minor response, such as checking on a point in your resume, do some major homework, promptly. Someone is looking at you. You may have a live one! Track down as much information about the company as you can. (Check the local library.) Expand the prospect's interest. Get the company's annual report, if possible. Consider sending the firm some extra, highly targeted material and then following up by phone.

A PROMISING RESPONSE? GET ON THE HORN!

Prospective employers often send letters saying something like, "We enjoyed reading your material. If you should happen to be in town, please give me a call." What they are probably saying is that they can't pay to fly you out. They suspect, however, that you will be in their town (especially a big city, like New York or Chicago), perhaps at someone else's expense, and would honestly like to talk. Write and thank them for their interest, telling them you sure will be in touch, if at all possible. If your plans include travel to the city in question, call well beforehand and set up a meeting.

Some will simply say, "Please call me." Do it promptly while the person remembers sending the note.

When in doubt, make the call!

"WHEN CAN YOU COME IN?"

Some of the people you mail to will phone you to set up a visit. These are by far the best prospects! Your package has generated real interest.

Keep a note pad near the phone. List on it the key facts to ask about:

- Individual's name (spelled correctly).
- Company name.
- Phone number and extension.
- Date.
- Time.
- Place of meeting, if they set one.

When on the phone, write accurately, and repeat the phone number, meeting date, time, and place. In their excitement, many people forget these important facts. If in doubt about any of them and you have the phone number, call back "to confirm." Ask for a copy of the latest annual report, if available. Your contact will be pleased you want to read about the organization.

If they are located out of town and ask you to travel, find out whether they will provide the ticket and expenses. Most will. If not, you might elect to pay for this. (I once forgot to ask about that with a firm in Miami—and got stuck with a $300 tab. The company declined to pay, since I had not asked about it initially.)

On Telephone Etiquette

Keep a pleasant, businesslike tone of voice. Answer any questions in a short, friendly way. Include any pleasant comments that fit in well. If you have a good opinion of the firm, say something like, "You people have a fine reputation." Close with a recap of the information, and thank your contact for his or her time.

Reconfirm and Start a Dialogue

If you meet Ms. A on the phone, promptly send her a thank you and confirming note. This shows you are interested and do your homework. If she sends requested material, send another thank you note. You now stand out above other candidates. She will like that and remember you.

Here's a simple log sheet that helps you keep your facts straight. Make a log for *every* live, interested prospective employer, so that you don't forget something important!

LOG FOR COMPANY: "A" _____

Date	Person Contacted	Action	Next Step	Other
_____	_____	_____	_____	_____
_____	_____	_____	_____	_____
_____	_____	_____	_____	_____
_____	_____	_____	_____	_____
_____	_____	_____	_____	_____
_____	_____	_____	_____	_____
_____	_____	_____	_____	_____
_____	_____	_____	_____	_____
_____	_____	_____	_____	_____
_____	_____	_____	_____	_____
_____	_____	_____	_____	_____
_____	_____	_____	_____	_____
_____	_____	_____	_____	_____

Keep Careful Records of the Live Ones

Maintain a separate file for each live prospect, since you might get only a few. There is little point to keeping records on the "no answers" or form letter answers. (Some, however, send a "so sorry" form, yet actually phone you at a later date.) The only important ones are those few who show an interest in you. Those files should contain your log sheet plus any letters they send. These are prospective income sources.

SUMMARY

Your mailing goal is to make lots of contacts and get as many offers as you can with the lowest cost in time, money, and effort. A good mailing plan does this. The advantages are mainly that *you* are in control, making hundreds of contacts, fast, at relatively low cost. The disadvantages are that mailings take some time, work, and money—and might not get you much in return.

As soon as you have your prospects listed and your package ready, send it to hundreds of your potential job sources. Focus first on your network. Don't be shy or it will cost you. Be sure to network your friends and social contacts. Make them all salespeople. This gives you many advantages.

Use a set of mailing mechanics and the steps as outlined. Use the plans chart. Answer all inquiries promptly. Answer the phone with special care. Try to build a dialogue. Keep careful but simple records of all good responses, using a log. Then follow through on your opportunities.

> **CASE STUDY**
>
> A young professional member of my own family recently followed the system in this chapter very carefully. She ended up with more big job offers than she needed, took one, was soon promoted, and is very happy on her path to $100,000!

9
Win with the Ideal Interview

I asked the time and he built me a watch factory!

—Wm. Blake

Enthusiasm is contagious.

—Ory

You put in a lot of time, work, and money to get to the interview. You contacted all potential employers and passed your package on to them. Now someone has invited you to visit the company—a golden opportunity. Out of hundreds, you're suddenly on "The Short List," among the chosen few.

The interview is the fork in the road. It is vital. If you do well, you might be in. Do poorly, and you'll surely be out. Employment at this level is very *personal*, and preparation is the key. Few, however, bother to prepare. You will be ready and relaxed. You will stand out from the others.

START BUILDING THE IMAGE

Your goal is simple: You want to build an excellent image, to have the interviewer feel that he or she likes you and wants *you* as an employee. Give this person reason to say something like, "We should talk further" or, even better, "I have some people I would like you to meet." The first interviewer is rarely the person who can say, "Yes, you're hired." But that first person can either end it, or introduce, and later recommend you, to the person who can say yes.

Before the Interview

Study the company well before you get there. Easy sources of information to use before the interview are:

- The company's annual report, if it has one.
- Library information, including *Moody's Manual, Million Dollar Directory, Barron's,* or *The Wall Street Journal.*
- Your investment broker. (Brokers have access to research groups and can also suggest nearby people to visit.)

You should also "ask around" about the company. Go to friends, club members, retailers who may sell the company's product. Your goal is to know the facts—the pros and cons—and to be able to talk to the company employees as if you are already employed on the team. You will stand out.

Prepare a list of 10 to 20 questions about the company. Phrase the questions so that they are friendly, reasonable, appropriate, and nonthreatening.

The questions should deal with the company's opportunities, challenges, goals, and plans. These are very important. To lighten things up, ask about your contact, where she comes from and her views on the business. Do *not* ask about wages, benefits, vacations, or promotions. It's too early to talk about such issues in the interview.

You might want to jot the essentials of these questions on a small card, in case you are asked out for lunch without your briefcase. Now, you'll never need to grasp wildly for subjects or ask bad questions.

Call and recheck your interview time. Do this a few days before your interview. This does no harm and shows that you are interested, thorough, and professional. It reminds them about the appointment and gives them the opportunity to reschedule if changes have occurred. They will appreciate the reminder. Few other candidates will do this. You will stand out.

You should also send a short confirmation note, recapping the time and place of the meeting. Also, thank your contact for setting up the meeting. Again, you will stand out.

Dress for success. Be guided by how your prospective employers might dress. Don't try to one-up them (for instance, with a boutonniere). Even if it is casual Friday, don't be casual! Show up in a simple conservative suit. If they say, "It's casual day around here," drop the jacket and tie, roll up the sleeves of your shirt, and you're casual. You're one of the gang. Don't arrive that way!

Some points for women: Your appearance should not ignore your femininity, but it should be professional. Avoid using strong perfume or wearing low-cut blouses, dangling earrings, or jangling bracelets. Remember: People dress professionally because they want to demonstrate respect and responsibility. During your interview, ignore obviously accidental gender slights, if any should occur.

Before your interview, whether male or female, look in the mirror and ask yourself, "Would you trust this woman (or man) to manage a million dollars—this morning?" That's the work $100,000 people do!

Bring plenty of backup material. Use this if it's needed or if an opportunity comes up. Examples are extra resumes (interviewers sometimes misplace theirs), an extra cover letter; or exhibits you couldn't send, like a news clipping, a flip chart, slides, an article about you or a book you wrote, or a product you helped introduce.

Arrive early. Visit with the receptionist, if you can. Most are a wealth of information, and some say more than they should. Be incredibly polite. Show respect to anyone and everyone you meet; that intern might be the president's daughter. Tell the receptionist you're early and ask her how long she has worked there. Ask if he or she knows the person you are to visit and if she has any advice for you. Sometimes they say surprising things like, "Yes, be sure to ask her about the big new project in Chicago!" If any company literature is on display, scan the first few pages while you're waiting.

When you're ushered into the office:

- Smile.
- Use the contact's name ("Hi, Mr. Smith").
- Thank the person for seeing you.
- Start upbeat.
- Stay that way.

During the Interview

Maintain a pleasant attitude, staying alert and interested. Interviewers are usually thinking, "Will Ms. Big like this person?" Sometimes they want to go through your resume with you, asking for details on key points. This is an excellent opportunity. Give facts, in short, reasonable, pleasant sentences. If they request more data, be ready to give it. Don't argue or debate. Appear to be relaxed, even if you are not.

Realize that, while you are a little uneasy since this is an unusual activity for you, the same is true for most interviewers (except for personnel people). People at upper levels have lots of professional skills, but interviewing is seldom a regular task for them. Don't be overly casual, "talk down" to them, or treat them as children. Just relax and try to put them at ease. Make a small joke or two at your own expense.

Use first names, if you're invited to do so, but always use a tone of respect. Shake hands with the interviewer. Accept coffee or tea if it's offered. (It's an important symbol of friendship.) Thank her. If convenient, sit with the sun in your face, so that you are in the spotlight, not your contact. Let the interviewer set the pace. Watch her body language and yours. The usual opening is, "John, I'm glad you could come in." Your response: "Thank you for asking me. You have a great company." "Thank you."

When asked about your experience or education, give brief, pleasant answers. You may be able to go through your entire resume. This is a great opportunity to match yourself to their company. Build on those points.

Watch for good signs. You'll be doing well if your contact shows a special interest in your resume (remember, she may see hundreds)—talks about the company, walks you through the building, tells you what you would be doing, responds to your questions, or introduces you to others. She doesn't do this with every candidate. Close as pleasantly as you can. Thank her sincerely for the visit, telling her you really enjoyed learning about the great company. *Mean it.*

When the interviewer starts to talk, pull out a pad and pen. Ask, "Is it OK if I take some notes?" That nearly always impresses them. Listen carefully for key points. They are a big help for you later. Note problems, goals, and plans or programs, especially test results or plans for new products. Chat briefly

---

CASE STUDY

On one occasion, a surprised executive asked to see the list of questions! Then he spent the whole lunch hour going over the answers. The job was nearly won right there! The list had proved to be a great personal selling tool.

about these and carefully write their answers down. These notes are very useful after the interview.

The interviewer might ask, "Do you have any questions?" You're covered because you have your 10 to 20 prepared questions. "Yes, I do have a few," you might say, taking out your list. You will impress the interviewer. Only about 10% of interviewees ask questions, and fewer still bring a list.

Pose your questions, and then ask your interviewer to elaborate on the responses (always a safe bet!).

The Social Lunch or Evening Dinner

A sit-down meal offers a great opportunity. Employers give such invitations only to "finalists." You have them in a relaxed situation, where they are likely to give special attention to anything you say. At such a time, your contacts are likely to be much more forthcoming. Be sure to have your question list and a pocket pad to jot down information. Be very careful about liquor. Drink if they do, but nurse one glass of wine all evening, if you can—or stick to club soda. You want to stay as sharp as possible. Be cordial, pleasant, friendly, and always professional. They are measuring your behavior.

They might put tough questions to you. The easy way to answer them is to have practiced answers that are basically what they want to hear. Answer slowly, not as if by memory. To stall for time to think, you can always slowly repeat the question to yourself.

Examples:

- "What were the three most important projects you've completed?" (Have a list with you that outlines all the essentials.)
- "Why on earth do you want to leave [or did you leave] your present company?" ("Well ... I had hoped to ... go where I can make a better contribution.")
- "Why us?" ("You have a really good reputation, and perhaps you can make better use of my skills.")
- "What is your greatest job weakness?" ("Well, — I sometimes try a little too hard to reach company goals — or I often feel I should be doing better.")

Don't overreact to strange questions! They could be trying to see if you can stay cool under pressure. They may not believe all you say, but that isn't the point. You get an "A" in diplomacy and look good compared to others, who sometimes get angry when tough questions arise. Actually, you have a great advantage here, since they don't realize that you know what they are doing. You can play the game. Breathe deeply, speak slowly, and don't pretend to know what you don't.

Some employers deliberately try to get you angry, as a test of your self-control. Practice responding to surprising questions.

- "What makes you mad?"
- "Do you believe in God?"
- "Have you ever been fired? Why?"
- "Why did you leave your last three jobs?"
- "Who are you, really?"
- "What would we need to guard against if you worked for us?"
- "Do you take home office supplies?"

- "Do you curse/use obscenities on the job?"
- "Have you ever had a fight on the job? Explain."
- "Ever been arrested?"
- "Have you ever had too much to drink?"
- "Ever drink at lunch? On the job?"
- "Are you Republican or a Democrat?"
- "What fact would people be shocked or angry to know about you?"

You get the idea. The point is not to get the "right" answer, but to stay cool and polite.

Multiple Interviewers

In a multiple interview, two or three people interview you at once. They might fire aggressive questions at you, sometimes rapidly, without waiting for the answers. They are ganging up on you. They don't care much about the answers. They are really trying to find out how you handle an assault. Remember: They don't usually bother to do this unless you are a finalist and a big salary is involved. They may know that the job will put you in similar situations on major contracts. So stay cool, calm, and pleasant. Show no anger. Try to give brief and careful answers to each question. You can actually turn the game to your advantage if you smile and say, "Hey, folks, please slow down just a little. You are asking good questions and you deserve good answers." But rule number one is to *keep your composure!*

CASE STUDY

Four company presidents got an applicant into a deluxe Atlantic City hotel room one hot summer evening, served drinks, and then started the multiple-interviewer harassing technique. Within minutes, the applicant said to himself, "Oh, I get it! They're just trying to get me mad. It won't work. I'll use General Eisenhower's slogan, 'I only get mad on purpose, when I want to, not when others want me to.'" He answered the questions calmly, to the best of his ability, and with good spirits. Then they suddenly stopped, and said they would meet him for breakfast. In the morning they were the picture of cordiality. Halfway through breakfast they said, "Oh, by the way, we would like you to be president of our large Canadian division."

Before You Go

Before leaving the interview, ask, "If I have other information, may I send it along?" Most interviewers will say, "Sure." This is vital. The door is wide open to you to follow up effectively.

SUMMARY

Your interview is a magic moment and a fantastic opportunity. Your goal is to make prospective employers want you on the team. Learn all you can about the company. Recheck the time, date, and place, and reconfirm them by note. Dress for success. Arrive early. Visit with the receptionist. Probe for clues. Have extra resumes and exhibits. Show a very respectful, pleasant, yet relaxed attitude. Ask for permission to take notes. Have question lists. Be ready for tough questions and a social lunch or dinner. Be prepared for stressful questions.

CASE STUDY

One candidate, on his way to an interview, parked his car right next to a well dressed, senior lady who also had just arrived. Her arms were full of packages. She dropped one. He picked it up and offered to carry another. She gratefully accepted and thanked him, saying that the parking lot was extra full because of an important meeting and she was bringing materials for this meeting. The two got to talking about the meeting and the new building as they walked past the long line of cars. They helped each other through the big, heavy main doors, and talked some more as they waited for the slow elevator and then during the long ride to the top floor. They made a few jokes about "overloaded" executives and finally got to the office. She thanked him again and then disappeared. When he was brought into the interview, guess who was scheduled to visit with him? The two already felt relaxed, almost like old friends. She joked that they "had already been working together." The visit went well and he was eventually hired.

Rice's Note: The following ten steps were taken by top-quality upper executives whom *we* interviewed, enjoyed meeting, and ended up offering major jobs. Some applicants arrived late, were poorly dressed, bored, unpleasant, and asked only about when their vacations would start. Then they had the brass to phone a few weeks later, wondering when they were going to be hired!

TEN STEPS TO A $100,000 INTERVIEW

1. Did you remind yourself, "This is it"? _____
_____

2. Did you reconfirm time, date, and place, if reasonable? _____
_____

3. Can you *study* the company a bit? _____
_____

4. Will you be well dressed? _____
_____

5. Will you arrive early and visit with the receptionist? _____
_____

6. Will your attitude be pleasant, alert, interested? _____
_____

7. Will you answer questions carefully without losing your composure? ___
_____

8. Are you ready to ask friendly, reasonable questions? _____
_____

9. Will you watch for good signs? _____
_____

10. Will you close pleasantly? _____
_____

10
Follow-Up Clinches It!

The real problem is apathy, but then who cares?

—Stover

Delays arranged while you wait.

—Twain

You close. You shake hands. Now what? Most candidates do nothing! Winners, on the other hand, act almost as if they are already hired, but working for free. Here's how you can do the same—and land that $100,000 offer you deserve.

AFTER THE INTERVIEW

Review Your Notes

Take a good long look at all their comments. Note especially where their needs and your skills match up well. Make special note of new projects and ideas you discussed.

Look for any comments the interviewer made about the company's *situation* (its problems, competition, opportunities), as well as its *goals* and *strategy* (the plans, programs, or intentions for the near future). You took special care to collect that data, and now it is about to pay off big.

Gather more facts about the company. Find out more about their business and their industry. Check the library again; do some more digging.

Send a Strong Thank You Note

Send a thank you to every person you met. Check your notes for names. If you are not sure of spellings, call the company. Tell the receptionist you plan to send thank you notes and want to be sure you are spelling the names right.

The note should not be just a "quickie" but a thoughtful, personalized note of thanks. Compliment the company and make a point or two about how you match their needs and fit into their projects. In the body of the note, speak positively of several people if you can. This will greatly please the reader *and* encourage them to pass your note around, doubling its impact.

YOUR SECRET PLAN

Now you are ready to prepare your secret plan. This step is an inside, professional secret, and you also might wish to keep it to yourself. This is the first time the following strategy has appeared in print.

Remember those 10 to 20 questions you had on your list during the interview? You're going to turn the answers into an S-O-S plan: situation, objectives, strategy. Since you base the plan on the contact's *own* words, it makes you sound brilliant. People talk about these things so much among themselves, they rarely remember that they gave you all that data. Even if they vaguely recall doing so, they will be amazed that you both listened and remembered. What follows may apply to the company, a branch, a department, or just one important project.

Situation

If interviewers tell you their problems, you're in great luck! Those facts will fit fine into the first part of your plan: situation. Add any facts you have learned about the industry (size, trends, major players). Then add facts about the company, possibly five or ten points from annual reports. Talk about industry size, trends, major players, company or project problems, opportunities, threats, competition, trends. You want enough facts for about a page or two, double-spaced.

Objectives

Goals might be harder to get, because your contacts don't always mention them, but their comments might give you clues. If not, you can state "assumed goal of 10% growth" or some such improvement. There's nothing wrong with admitting ignorance in this area, nor with aiming at growth.

Strategy

Here is where you really shine. Here is where you play back any plans, steps, ideas, even hints about what the company might be doing in the future. Check your notes carefully. Add anything that might be deduced from what they said or from their problems, such as, "We want to improve our dealer interest through personal visits, direct mail, advertising, special events like breakfasts, or special dealer offers."

Then add your own ideas of strategy steps that might fit. Examples are:

- Improve training, where possible.
- Build improved enthusiasm and teamwork.
- Search for ways of improving customer service.
- Consider any upgrading of machinery, computers, or other equipment.
- Review possibilities of incentive or motivation programs.

Also think in terms of improvements in product, packaging, pricing, promotions, advertising, personal visits, distribution, dealer, public or industrial relations.

Use a little imagination or adopt ideas from other people. Each step might be stated as a separate sentence and item.

Note: You are *not recommending* these steps, only proposing them. You can't go very wrong with that, and you get credit for even thinking of these steps!

NOW YOU HAVE A PLAN!

Prospective employers might not accept anything you suggested, and you never really recommend anything specific. But you *did* have a plan. Drucker says, "A man with a plan is quite hard to ignore. Women, too." Planning shows forward and constructive thinking. Employers like that. And almost no one else will do it.

When your plan is ready, get someone with business knowledge to review it and make suggestions. Edit the plan appropriately and add a simple, light-colored cover sheet, maybe slate blue, green, or yellow. Find a picture from the company's annual report or maybe its logo. Paste this onto a sheet of white paper with the title, "Suggested Plan for the XYZ Company [or department] by John Jones." Include the date and place. Then photocopy the text onto your colored sheet.

Write an introductory letter, with words to this effect:

When parting from our recent visit, I asked permission to send on any further material. This is submitted purely as an example of what kind of service I might provide. The material is based only on incomplete data, possibilities, or labeled assumptions. I don't claim that what follows is completely accurate yet.

But, actually, it *is* fairly correct, because it is based on things *they* told you—their own plan!

THE CLINCHER

Perhaps they read your plan and you are invited for a second interview. "Let's meet for lunch on Friday and talk some more." This is a great sign! You're clearly a finalist and nearly home. Don't blow it now! Be ready to go through the whole process again, perhaps with different people. Candidates for major jobs often make the mistake of getting too confident and assuming they are hired, when they are still being tested. Don't get too casual or too familiar. Keep selling. Treat everyone with respect. Take notes. You are very close now. The job is yours to lose.

DON'T BE DISCOURAGED BY A DECLINE

Declines are almost routine. Your resume is often sent to the human resource director, who can't match you to any known low-level slot openings and so sends you a polite decline. Meanwhile, copies of your package might be still circulating. You might interview with several companies, but you don't have a job offer.

All is not lost. If the interviews went well, you probably came pretty close. You made a positive impression and perhaps a few friends. Even when they decline you, write and thank them for their time and their great interview. Make them think, "Here's a really unusual person. We can't help liking him. He wants to work for us. We should keep him in mind. He didn't fit job A, but Sam's retiring next year, and maybe ... ." In several actual cases, interviewers have called back months after such a letter with other offers—sometimes even better ones.

So keep in touch, no matter what. Write a note a few months later saying you are still looking; ask for referrals. These contacts are valuable. Don't let them die. They could bring live leads.

SUMMARY

Smart follow-up can make all the difference. You have your foot in the door. Use it. Review your notes for facts and ideas. Send each interviewer an interesting thank you note. Study. Get more facts about the company and industry. Prepare your Secret Plan. Build this on the target company's situation, objectives, and possible strategies. Include a colored cover, an introduction, and special letter emphasizing that what you've generated is just a sample. Keep contacts alive, even if the interview doesn't turn into a job offer.

CASE STUDY

A candidate listened carefully to remarks made by the people he met. He got permission to take notes, and did so thoroughly and accurately. He then went home, wrote thank you letters, and passed along a careful plan. No one else had done that; the interviewers were highly impressed. He was invited for a second interview and was offered a major $100,000 position, which he took.

Rice's Comment: Candidates make a major mistake by not generating a superior follow-up campaign. The winners use this opportunity to win those $100,000 jobs.

11
Salary Talk to Yes

Enthusiasm is the world's greatest asset!
—CHESTER

My goal? To build a great cathedral!
—MICHELANGELO

An offer, if it comes, often happens on your second interview—or maybe much sooner than you had expected. Be ready and wise in handling the offer. To negotiate your best deal, create a plan in three parts: *your* situation, *your* dollar objective, and *your* dollar strategy. When you read this chapter, you'll see that you should do a little homework and personal thinking.

Note: *Be prepared for a setback*. Being prepared for a step backward is especially important if your company has cut back staff. Among people who are downsized, only about 60% relocate at their same or better wage. The other 40% take a cut.

YOUR SITUATION

By now you have taken all the right steps. You applied to the right prospective employers, sent them a good resume and cover letter, had an excellent interview, and followed up perfectly. The employer is about to make an offer. By now, you know about the type of job under discussion. You should also know what the job pays or at least the range of salary appropriate to this industry.

The brutal reality is that employers usually have a strict budget window that they must follow, perhaps $80,000 to $100,000. Why is the window so rigid? Having been on both sides of the desk, I've discovered at least three reasons:

1. That was the range initially put in the budget for this job.

2. Other employees' budget patterns are at that general level. If the employer gives you more than the approved figure, it causes internal problems. Your pay would exceed that of others, perhaps others who have greater training, experience, and seniority. Disparities like that can lead to low morale, complaints, anger, and resignations. Those are heavy expenses.

3. If the employer gets you to accept just $80,000, then the company has room to give you a few $10,000 raises without busting the budget or getting special approval.

Most people take any offer, without discussion, because they are happy to have a job offer. The money might not be as much as hoped, but it's still pretty good.

Certainly, you should make at least a small effort for a higher salary. There is almost always some room for discussion, unless you have been told that the figure offered is totally "firm and nonnegotiable." Even then, you certainly should at least inquire about fringe benefits that often exceed salary. If you want to try for more than the offer, though, I will explain some guidelines that have worked well for both parties in recent years.

YOUR OBJECTIVE

For example, your goal might be to get $100,000 or more either in salary or in total income (cash salary and benefits). Besides salary and benefits, you should also measure company reputation, management quality, company future, and your immediate prospects for moving up, and other such intangibles. Potential can be worth a lot, perhaps far more than salary.

The employer's goal might be to find the least you will accept. Perhaps they want to get you at the lower $80,000 figure, although they won't tell you that. They might begin with an even lower offer, perhaps $70,000. Either you will accept the offer, as some applicants do, or the company can move up to $80,000 and let you feel you won a concession.

STRATEGY

In normal price bargaining (say, for an antique automobile), the offer is $70,000, and the seller responds by asking for $120,000. Now there is $50,000 between the $70,000 offer and the asking prices. Buyer and seller haggle and eventually split the difference, ending up at $95,000. But wage bargaining is often quite different. Unlike buying real estate or a car, it's a lot more personal.

You might have three simple strategy plans.

- *Plan A:* You try to get as close as you can to your $100,000 goal by using bargaining strategy.

- *Plan B:* You have a single fallback position, and will go down as far as the *least* you will find acceptable, although you won't state that early on. (The employer also has an upper-range figure in mind, the *most* they will pay. Hopefully these overlap a lot, so that you both can be happy.)

- *Plan C:* They offer below your "least acceptable" figure. Now you can either say, "Forget it" and go elsewhere, or take the job for the stopgap income and keep looking.

Your best bargaining strategy guidelines, says a ten-year Harvard negotiating study are: Know your goal and fallback positions. Your plan is to probe gently to find their best offer. Realize that most disagreements rapidly become emotional and that can become almost "no-win." Do all you can to avoid that and you have a better chance to win. Be factual. Show that you understand their words by repeating them. Stay friendly, pleasant, even complimentary. Watch your tone of voice; it speaks volumes. Speak slowly and calmly, without excitement. Show respect. Let them know you understand their needs; even play back their position. But also state your position as clearly and pleasantly as you can. Change the issue so that it is not "You vs. Them," but deal with it as "the problem to be solved so that we both gain." Let the other side save face. If you get stuck, suggest other compensation options, like fringes.

Your first reaction to their offer might be a truly sincere, "Great! But ...". Say out loud: You really appreciate their offer. You are honored to be with such a fine company and fine people. Say out loud: You would work very hard to bring all your abilities, full time and full force to the job. However, you feel that you offer them some extras that other candidates don't usually bring. Have a list. After you've outlined what you have to offer, you might point out that they are getting Cadillac quality, but their current offer seems a little more in line with a Chevy or a Pontiac.

To make your case, you should probably use visuals, perhaps a couple of flip cards to show the group. While showing off your bulleted list, say: "I bring you extra education, extra professional training, extra experience, experience specially suited to your operations, extra strong references, extra plans and proposals, and an extra positive attitude, so that I can hit the track running, to produce extra fast results. All that should probably be worth a special salary."

They will know what you mean. They know that you want the job and like the company and fit beautifully but that you have a problem with the money. You've made your point in a civil way—gently, pleasantly, without insult.

Their response will likely be a defense of the initial offer, unless they are so impressed with you and want you so much that they make a higher offer on the spot. But they will probably try to sell the best offer first. They might never expect you to accept it, but they want you to feel, if and when they go up a notch or two, as though they made a great concession to a great deal. They might say something like, "Yes, but this is a Cadillac opportunity." Or, "OK, you're right, but we bring you in at a Pontiac wage and you'll soon be moving up to a Caddy."

Normally, you go around this track a couple of times, perhaps with no movement by either of you. Maybe they go up a notch or two. In any event, you'll probably want to take the opportunity now to shift gears.

Ask, "What can you tell me about fringes? Do you offer a bonus, stock, profit share, insurance, or other benefits?" This opens a whole new subject, one they know a lot about and be eager to discuss. They may try to show that the fringes more than make up for the salary amount you feel is lacking. They often present an impressive list. Some items might surprise you.

Take careful notes. Ask about moving expenses, day-care, or help with your spouse's job search. If you don't understand something, especially on financial issues, *ask* for more information on that point. Get all the relevant details on insurance, profit sharing, bonus, stock and stock options. If these fringes are very attractive, you might settle for somewhat less up-front salary than you had planned. Or you might choose to go back to the salary issue.

Here is where you might try some creative variations on salary, if your financial situation permits. Some examples:

- "Would you consider my requested wage if I agreed to no further requests or expectations of an increase for a given number of years?"
- "Would you agree to start me at half the amount requested for a six-month probation and, if I pass, increase me to the full amount?"
- "Would you agree if I were to work *for free* for three months and, if I prove satisfactory during that time, you provide the full wage?"
- "If none of these items appeal to you, can you suggest some other similar variation?"

If they cannot, you have pretty well run the course. Either settle for what you can get, or say, "Well, I'll think it over." That's when you have found (and they are likely to make) their highest offer. If they can go to $100,000, they will then. If they don't, you have a choice to make.

Beware of Dirty Tricks!

These are not common, but keep your eyes open. If you suspect lies from people on the negotiating team, deal mainly with the people you feel you can trust. If they try to refer to some phony authority, try to find the real one. If they make casual offers of benefits, ask if they will put them in writing. If they try to use high-pressure tactics or other head games, back away and wait awhile. If they try a personal attack, don't be offended, but realize it's just a device. If they say "take it or leave it," make a counteroffer: "Would you consider this ?..." At almost all costs, avoid a breakdown or termination. They have other options: your competition. Keep your decisions in the "talking and exploring" phases.

Major Mistakes

High wage seekers often commit basic negotiating errors. Some are far too aggressive and demanding. They take a tough, belligerent tone of voice. They get angry, offensive, and insulting, showing no room or flexibility to bargain, then walk out in a huff. These people blow some very good opportunities.

Don't burn bridges or walk out in anger. You have a valuable discussion going. Stay friendly. Ask for a little time to think things over. They might come back to you, as they often do with higher-paid people, with an even better offer. Or you might change your mind.

In time, people often find a new career they liked even better and see even better income. Remember "stopgap" employment with this company. You might even consider being a consultant in your profession, as a private contractor. Downsizing has an advantage in that it puts lots of top people on the street and so makes companies short-handed. They might still want and need these services, but they don't want a full-time $100,000 person. Some will hire a part-timer at $40,000 or 50,000, and you might be able to work on this basis for two clients!

SUMMARY

Know your situation and the realities of the the company's budget range. Your Plan A is to bargain for more, especially if the employer is obviously chasing you. Plan B might be to have a fallback figure, the least you will take. Plan C might be your plan if they don't even offer your least acceptable number. You might either part company or take what you can get and keep looking. The employer's goal is agreement within their range. Stay calm, pleasant, and respectful while you probe to find their best offer. Point out your "pluses," check the fringes, and salary variations.

CASE STUDY

An employed candidate sent her package to a major Chicago advertising agency, and they called her in for an interview. It went well; they made her an offer. She thanked them but said she was going to keep on looking. A week later they called her to have lunch with the president. She did and showed him a special set of exhibits. He introduced her to several key people and told her they would call her within three days, which they did. They made her an offer that was far above her present income. She hesitated on the phone and then said she really wanted some additional thousands. The key person said, "OK, you have a deal! How soon can you come on board?" She was playing from strength. She had a job. She was in no hurry. She realized they wanted her, because they asked her for a second interview for lunch.

Rice's Comment: Negotiating is "iffy." Most people don't like it. Some situations almost cry out for a little bargaining, as in the case of this advertising professional. Some situations make it clear that a salary figure is *not* negotiable and would be a mistake to try to haggle. When it is worth trying, however, the bargaining guidelines in this chapter have worked very well in landing that $100,000 job.

12

Superior Resume Resources

The following resume writing services are among the very best in the country. If you're looking for one-on-one help in developing your own $100,000 resume, and you want to build on the ideas and strategies contained in this book, I strongly suggest that you contact one of the following organizations:

Artistix Communications
41 South Main Street
Ipswich, MA 01938
508/356-4014
508/356-7613 (fax)
e-mail: jvv@shore.net

Artistix Communications provides a range of job search assistance work. Strategies include writing and formatting resumes and cover letters, career counseling, job search planning, interview techniques, and salary negotiation. For people interested in self-employment, Artistix also writes business plans. Joanne Vaccaro-Vallis is a professional consultant for Artistix, certified to administer the Myers-Briggs Indicator and a member of the Professional Association of Resume Writers. With over 15 years as an entrepreneur, Joanne is sensitive to the needs of her clients, and guarantees satisfaction and results.

CareerPro
3600 Wilshire Boulevard, Suite 1604
Los Angeles, CA 90010
213/736-5224

Brad Bucklin of CareerPro offers a wide variety of resume writing and personal marketing consultation services. CareerPro boasts a long and distinguished record of success for its clients.

Creative Keystrokes Executive Resume Service

800/817-2779 (Outside U.S.: 703/768-7210)
800/817-3428 (fax) (Outside U.S.: 703/768-7227)
e-mail: ljsmith@creativekeystrokes.com
internet: http://www.creativekeystrokes.com

With over 20 years' success guiding executives and professionals in diverse industries worldwide through the career transition process, Creative Keystrokes president Laurie J. Smith regularly draws referrals from executive recruiters, outplacement agencies, counseling services, and military officer associations. Selected from a national candidate pool to serve two terms on the Professional Association of Resume Writers (PARW) Certification Board, she contributed substantially to the development and implementation of industry standards. She founded Creative Keystrokes to serve as the executive's comprehensive career management resource, providing highly individualized service, customized search strategies, and high-impact, targeted marketing materials with the "sizzle that gets results." Tele-service worldwide from Alexandria, Virginia, USA.

Executive Resume

P.O. Box 79
Cedar Brook, NJ 08018
1-800-563-6359

Executive Resume, founded in 1991, provides a broad spectrum of personal career-marketing services for professionals and executives seeking to advance or change their careers. Services range from the preparation of powerful resumes and employment letters designed to optimize each client's marketability, to the custom design and management of an entire job-hunting campaign. Executive resume's services may be utilized regardless of geographic location.

Say It with Panache

14413 Burbank Boulevard
Van Nuys, CA 91401
818/780-8215
818/780-8215 (fax)

Esther Maron, president of Say It With Panache, offers 30 years' background in Human Resources; she has taught a popular two-day workshop at colleges and has conducted her resume business in the same location for the past 13 years. She works with both national and international clients.

WSACORP

11933 Johnson Drive
Shawnee, KS 66216
800-973-2677
913-631-9898 (fax)

WSA services more $100K+ clients than any other resume company in the United States. Since 1976, WSA has been helping executives, managers, and professionals with their career advancement. WSA's business is one of creating opportunity by introducing the right talent at the right time to the right companies. This is accomplished through the design of high-impact resumes and their targeted distribution in the marketplace.

13

$100,000 Resumes

Here are plenty of samples based on resumes that got the job done!

ADMINISTRATIVE OFFICER

CAROL ANNE WESLEY

216 West Juniper Avenue ■ Clarksburg, OH 23622
709-559-3725 (W) ■ 709-865-2298 (H)

Experienced general administrative officer with nearly 13 years experience in financial institutions. Extremely knowledgeable in Human Resources, Systems and Procedures, Public Relations, and cost/benefit analysis.

Primary responsibilities include the management of Human Resources, Purchasing, Security, Maintenance, Travel, and Public Relations. Receive the highest ratings for the ability to assess problem situations and promptly implement corrective actions.

PROFESSIONAL EXPERIENCE

NATIONAL BANK OF OHIO   1991 - Present
Assistant Vice President, Administration
Direct all general administrative and operational support activities. Manage 134 professionals and hourly employees.

- *Developed and implemented alternate methods for processing residential and commercial loans, increasing efficiency and reducing administrative costs by $140,000 within the first year.*

- *Reorganized every administrative support department, decreased staffing, implemented centralized controls, and improved access to database information through automation.*

- *Negotiated electric utility rates with Ohio Electric and achieved an annual savings of nearly $85,000.*

- *Negotiated settlement of two union contracts and the decertification of a third union which led to annual savings in excess of $475,000 in the first year.*

- *Worked with a major consulting firm and successfully implemented a financial forecasting system for operations, leading to savings of more than $1,000,000 per year.*

- *Administered the installation of real-time computerized control and ordering system.*

WESTERN FEDERAL SAVINGS BANK   1984-1991
Director, Human Resources and Administration

- *Centralized Human Resources, Purchasing, and other support services; created management systems for coordinating all branches resulting in annual savings of more than $1.2 million.*

- *Ensured organizational compliance with legal guidelines by revising or installing 9 major personnel policies, and by updating employment applications and employee handbook.*

- *Installed policies and programs which reduced professional and hourly employee turnover by near 300%.*

- *Directed the conversion of a totally manual administrative system to a completely computerized and automated system. Savings were estimated to exceed $300,000 in the first year.*

- *Selected as a business community liaison to spend one day a week working with a major non-profit organization in order to improve and update their operating and administrative systems.*

- *Created training and development programs that were recognized by the Chief Executive Officer as a major factor in improving morale and productivity.*

EDUCATION

Master of Business Administration - Management - University of Wisconsin
Bachelor of Business Administration - Management Studies - California State University

ADVERTISING EXECUTIVE

PAUL MILLER

6278 Pontiac Street, Greenwich CT 06831
555/555-8762 (days) 555/555-0915 (evenings)

OBJECTIVE: To become Advertising Creative Director for Windward Associates.

SUMMARY

Award-winning advertising professional with 6 years of achievement as an Advertising Director for a national printing chain with 32,000 employees and 970 operations. Campaigns launched coincided with dramatic (174% over three years) growth of regional revenue totals.

ACCOMPLISHMENTS

Responsible for creating all advertising for Adams-Fowling's Northeast region (Maine, Massachusetts, Vermont, New Hampshire, Connecticut, Rhode Island, New Jersey, New York, Pennsylvania, Maryland, Delaware, and Washington, DC) during remarkable growth phase.

- Helped to bring about fastest growth in volume and profits of any region in company history.
- Cited for "superior promotional and marketing achievement" at 1996 Corporate Convention, Adams-Fowling Print Huts.
- Nearly doubled sales in a 36-month period through aggressive marketing and advertising campaigns that used print, broadcast, and Internet media intelligently and effectively.

MEDIA MENTIONS

"A sharply outlined and expertly targeted campaign ..." *Marketing World* (December, 1996)

"Utterly unique." *Ad World Achievements* World Wide Web site, October, 1997

"Stunning." *Adams-Fowling This Week* (company newsletter), June, 1997

EMPLOYMENT

Adams Fowling Print Huts, Greenwich CT 1994–Present. Advertising Director.

Metworth, Forsyth, and Green, Hartford CT, 1992–1994. Advertising Associate.

EDUCATION

B.S. in Marketing, Barrington University, Barrington MO, 1992

ADVERTISING EXECUTIVE (SUMMARY FORMAT)

EXECUTIVE RESUME SUMMARY FOR
Brenda Lawson, President, ABC Corporation

If your search for a "senior advertising executive with a demonstrated record of top-level achievement" is still in process, you may be interested in someone who offers ...

- 18 years of experience as senior executive for $8 million to $200 million organizations.

- A record of demonstrated achievement in sales, marketing, client services and operations management—with particular skills in fast-paced, team-oriented environments.

- Generation up to $16 million in business revenue annually, development of 435 agencies in 37 states, and direction of 22 employees—while sustaining 29% pretax margins.

Contact

JACK SMITH * 542 Oak Street * San Francisco CA 94930 * 555/555-5555

APPLICATIONS CONSULTANT

JANE SMITH

51 Mountain Road, Boston, MA 03455   617-277-3333

APPLICATIONS CONSULTANT/IMPLEMENTATION/PRODUCT DEVELOPMENT

Extensive qualifications in all facets of project lifecycle development, from initial design through documentation, implementation, user training and enhancement. Accomplished project manager and trainer skilled at designing and implementing materials used to present complex, technical information to a cross functional range of decision makers, end users and in-house trainers.

PROFESSIONAL EXPERIENCE

1989–present   TECHMED, BOSTON, MA

Fast track promotions through a series of increasingly responsible positions.

Required ability to synthesize and understand complex medical and technical information to create training materials and to teach software modalities to troubleshoot applications and interface with client and product development in the creation of solutions.

NEXT GENERATION CONSULTANT - PRODUCT DEVELOPMENT
- Research medical and technical information: ensure that new products interface with existing applications
- Design training materials: formulate goals, content, and implementation
- Demonstrate prototypes to current and potential decision makers in healthcare organizations; train marketing and sales forces on product benefits

Achievement: Selected members of an elite group working with the founder of TECHMED to develop "Next Generation" software

SUPERVISION HIS APPLICATIONS, IMPLEMENTATIONS
- Managed 10 Applications Consultants; hired and trained as needed
- Coordinated travel schedules and site visits; made assignments according to staff abilities and client needs to ensure proper client support
- Interfaced with technical staff and product development in testing and troubleshooting; ensured that functional changes interfaced with product enhancements
- Documented new product design, developed visual aids and supplemental educational materials

Achievement: Selected to facilitate seamless transition at alpha and beta sites and to train other staff on enhancements

SENIOR APPLICATIONS CONSULTANT, HIS
- Trained new hires, evaluated performance, determined readiness to conduct training at clients' sites
- Provided training for more complex clients
- Updated materials for new software and systems

APPLICATIONS CONSULTANT, HIS
- Traveled nationally and internationally to train end users on software functionality
- Trained groups of 4–8 within 6 months period at TECHMED and in client environment; provided support, then assigned maintenance to other staff
- Investigated and solved applications problems; interfaced with information systems directors in providing progress reports and achieving application goals
- Developed, authored and modified training materials

EDUCATION

1986 Connecticut University, Hartford, CT

Bachelor of Arts

Major: Speech Communication. *Minor:* English - Cum Laude.

CERTIFICATIONS

CPR, Aerobic and Fitness Association of America

BROADCASTING EXECUTIVE

JOHN BRILL

543 Third Street
San Francisco, CA 94930
555/555-5555

Qualifications

* Sixteen years experience as a Vice President with WXY Broadcasting Company, Inc.
* Comprehensive knowledge in radio station operations from sales and marketing to programming and staff management.
* Extensive financial management background.
* Excellent personnel management, motivation and communication skills.
* Have consistently increased market shares and profit margins.
* Considerable experience in acquisitions and divestitures.
* Decisive; able to work effectively on deadline and in stressful situations.
* Active with community organizations and projects.

Experience

1988 to Present   KBB FM and WWKK   San Francisco, CA
WXY Broadcasting Co., Inc.
Vice President/General Manager

Began as the Vice President/General Manager of KBB with a market revenue share of 4.3% and a 28.0% profit margin. The market share rose to 5.3 in 1993 and currently stands at 6.4 through April 1994. KBB's profit margin increased to 43% in 1993 and is over 50% through four months of 1994. Conversion ratios are currently at 2.30. After taking over as Vice President/General Manager of KBB in mid-1982, profit margins have grown from 30% in 1992 to 42% in 1993. The Conversion ratio is 1.50.

1985 to 1988   WWWW-FM   Ukiah, CA
WXY Broadcasting Co., Inc.
Vice President/General Manager

Increased the profit margins in the declining Easy Listening market from 14% in 1985 to 17% in 1987.

1982 to 1985   WXY Broadcasting Co., Inc.   Albany, NY
Radio Station Division
Vice President/Controller

Responsible for overseeing the financial operations and analysis of 7 AM and 6 FM stations as well as the soft rock division. Also directly responsible for the acquisition and divestiture of properties.

1978 to 1982   Sethway Productions (TV production and syndication)   San Francisco, CA
WXY Broadcasting Co., Inc.
Vice President/Controller

Responsible for financial operations and analysis of this television production and syndication company with such programs as The Jerry Davis Show, Night Magazine and *Here and Now* Magazine.

1977 to 1978   Sethway Productions   New York, NY
WXY Broadcasting Co., Inc.
Controller

1975 to 1977   WVK-FM   Chicago, IL
WXY Broadcasting Co., Inc.
Controller

Education   Michigan University   Detroit, MI
B.S. Degree Public Administration

Organizations   Samaritan Club of San Francisco
Abused Children's Outreach of San Francisco - Board of Directors
San Francisco Broadcasters Association - Board of Directors

References   Available Upon Request

CEO/INTERNATIONAL

JOHN SMITH

555 Brentleigh Avenue • Salem, MA 01970
(555) 555-5300

SENIOR EXECUTIVE
General Management • Customer Service • Multi-Site Operations • Business Development

High caliber, customer service/business strategist with over 13 years' success managing multiple-site operations, reengineering operations for maximum customer satisfaction and efficiency, and launching service-oriented start-ups throughout U.S. and Canada. Multi-faceted general managerial skills in strategic planning, operations, customer service, finance, marketing, and government/community liaison. Award-winning customer service expert exceptionally successful developing and managing multisite, customer-focused industry leaders from concept to robust viability by applying abilities to:

- Pioneer innovative programs such as co-branded credit cards and express, 24-hour, and automated counter service which deliver quantum leap improvements in customer service
- Propel operations to recognition as customer service leaders in their industry (e.g., Banner, 1.5 yrs.)
- Standardize and manage up to 30 geographically dispersed sites in diverse international locations
- Conceive and implement state-of-the-art training programs which produce customer-focused, entrepreneurial spirited teams of 500+
- Reengineer operations for better service, quality, productivity, and image; lower manpower and operational costs; and phenomenal increases in revenues and bottom-line profitability
- Develop and implement highly effective quality response/customer satisfaction survey programs

U.S. citizen with multilingual English/Afrikaans/French fluency.

PROFESSIONAL EXPERIENCE

BANNER SOUTH AFRICA, Cape Town, South Africa   1994–1996
    U.S. $50 million rental service company.
PRESIDENT & CEO

Took Banner franchise from concept to successful operation, attracting private investor groups led by the Winston Group for this start-up "green field" joint venture. Negotiated master franchise agreement, by-laws, shareholder agreements, and business plan, as well as handled all government relations. Directed 500+ employees at 30-site operation. Oversaw all product development activities. Built business from ground floor to position as industry leader in service, product, pricing, and quality, with over $50 million in annualized revenues, through various initiatives emphasizing excellence in customer service:

- Introduced customer-focused programs and innovations including fleet diversity, unlimited mileage, fully automated counter service, 60-second express service, first-ever co-brand credit card, 24-hour road service and reservations center.
- Created innovative quality response card program with customer return program.
- Implemented fully equipped training center providing classroom training, psychological role play, and 100% computer-based counter training.
- Assertively represented industry to improve service and reduce costs as well as negotiate access to strategic airport location.

Earned nomination after only one year and reached finals in prestigious "Marketing Best" Award competition, recognizing creativity and high quality in service industry marketing programs.

EASTHOLM INDUSTRIAL LTD, Cape Town, South Africa   1993–1994
  U.S. $100 million commercial and industrial investment holding company with controlling interests in
  U.S. Rainbow Manufacturing, Vera textiles company, Overprint soft plastics manufacturing, and Pizzano.
CHIEF FINANCIAL OFFICER

Directed financial operations including financial/investment planning, cash management, capitalization, M&A transactions, investment bank negotiations, proposed acquisition economic viability studies, and re-engineering recommendations for manufacturing and production. Key catalyst in guiding company through explosive growth and major reengineering efforts:

- Delivered significant improvement in service as key contributor to outsourcing initiative which slashed Rainbow production time 80% from 40 to 8 days.
- Managed M&A transactions with Vera ($30MM linen manufacturer) and Rainbow, a joint venture which included 145 retail outlets and a 60,000 sf manufacturing plant.
- Re-engineered Vera's manufacturing processes and restructured capital equipment investments to produce marked reductions in manpower costs and improvements in quality and productivity.

ZENITH MANAGEMENT CONSULTING, New York, NY   1992–1993
INDEPENDENT CONSULTANT

Offered management consulting services focusing on customer service and operations logistics to U.S. and Middle Eastern companies. Provided strategic direction to Middle Eastern companies and individuals on corporate and financial strategies and opportunities; engaged to analyze and develop service programs, operational reviews, productivity and efficiency studies, and economic viability analyses.

- Assisted Auto Flair with asset purchase and merger with tour-oriented rent-a-car company resulting in 100% increases in revenues and market share.
- Guided restructuring and operations administration of Auto Flair New York region.
- Assisted Banner master franchise in South Africa with comprehensive operations reengineering initiative including cost reduction and manpower reduction/upgrade programs, franchise sales, and restructured financing resulting in 44% reduction in expenses and 33% revenue increase.

VORTEX, INC., dba Auto Flair, Mobile, Alabama   1989–1991
PRESIDENT & GENERAL MANAGER

Founded and built 7-location, 60-employee franchise from concept including due diligence, asset purchase negotiations, and implementation. Directed operations, sales and marketing with direct capital and cash management responsibility. Initiated solid customer service programs and creative pricing, implemented new fleet, and launched innovative niche marketing program.

- Increased revenues 120% in two years and market share 4% (150% increment).
- Captured local market, allowing full utilization of fleet during off-peak periods.
- Won nomination in first year and reached finals for *Mobile Daily Item*'s "High Growth Firm" award.

THE BANNER CORPORATION, Los Angeles & San Francisco, CA   1982–1989
GENERAL MANAGER (City Manager) California

Fast track promotional track from hire as Station Manager. Held full P&L responsibility for multi-location region spanning operations logistics, customer service, HR, marketing/sales, union relations, and quality control. Aggressive customer service improvement and marketing efforts generated significant increases in market share and revenues.

- Earned Banner annual award for excellence in service.

EDUCATION

Texas National University: MBA, 1986 • B.A. Business Administration, 1983

CEO/MANUFACTURING

BOB SMITH
123 Main Street
San Francisco, CA 94930
(555) 555-5555

Senior-level Executive with diverse experience in management and rapid growth who took a company from a $2 million loss to a $1.5 million profit with sales increasing from $10 million to $30 million.

Hands on operations, marketing, product development and direct sales experience for diverse product lines.

- 400% profit increase and 21% sales increase achieved in less than 24 months.
- Doubled sales to $10 million, tripled profits to $2 million in 3 years.

Board Member: Northern California Real Estate and Trust Company; Good Sam Club of San Francisco.
First adjunct professor of venture planning and 1994 guest lecturer for Max Hunt Center at University of the West.

Excellent health, physically active. Will travel. Love California where 3 generations have resided.

.MBA, Phillip Business School, 1978. B.S., Pharmacy, Pratt University, 1976

PROFESSIONAL EXPERIENCE

THE BELLWAY COMPANY, San Francisco, CA 1994–1994
$20 million company manufacturing artificial materials and environments for zoos, aquariums, museums and entertainment industries.
Executive Vice President
- Established domestic sales group and secured international license candidate (Malaysia).

RE-METER, INC., Detroit, MI 1993–1994
$13 million company manufacturing high tech electronic equipment.
President
- Doubled sales and profits. Established 70-person national and international sales organization.
- Owner decided to remain as CEO.

JHI, INC. Chicago, IL 1991–1992
$100 million manufacturer of truck mounted refueler systems serving multiple industries.
President and Chief Executive Officer
- Successfully consolidated divisions increasing profits 20%, and brought company to sale.

OFFICEWARE, INC. Chicago, IL 1988–1991
$28 million closely held contract furniture manufacturer.
President and Chief Operation Officer
- Increased sales 25% and doubled profits in 3 years.

BB MEASURES, INC. Chicago, IL 1985–1988
$10 million high precision test equipment manufacturer for highly accurate navigational and industrial measurement applications.
President and Chief Executive Officer
- Strategically guided company through rapid growth transition from regional job shop to international manufacturer.
- Turned around company and brought in sale offer of $7 million.

EASTCHEM CORP., INC. Chicago, IL 1981–1985
$30 million public company subsidiary specializing in agricultural, pharmaceutical, health and industrial chemicals.
President
Director of Marketing
- Pulled company from Chapter 11 bankruptcy to complete international sale of business 3 years later.

BARBOL, INC. Chicago, IL 1977–1981
Subsidiary of Porter Industries.
Marketing Manager • Senior Product Manager • Product Manager
- Successfully developed $3 million veterinary medical products business.

CEO/REORGANIZING FOCUS (SUMMARY FORMAT)

Your advertisement in the January 23 *Anytown Bulletin* suggests that you're looking for a "senior executive with a demonstrated record of effective relationships with franchisees." Accordingly, I'm passing along this...

THUMBNAIL SKETCH OF VERA BOONE

- 7 years experience as interim CEO and Senior Vice President for Causeway Business Forms Corporation.

- Proficient at streamlining and structuring corporate functions to boost revenues, profits and franchise owner satisfaction.

- Oversaw 609 domestic and international franchise operations with $178 million annual revenue.

- Led 40% of all corporate staff.

- MBA from Zimmerman University and a B.S. in Accounting from Johnstown College.

VERA BOONE * 123 Main Street * Salem MA 01970 * 555/555-5555

CEO/TRAVEL AND TRANSPORTATION

JOHN SMITH   815 Rider Street • Houston, TX 75000
                                                                     (555) 555-5555

Senior Executive: Marketing, Product Development, & General Management
Specializing in Leading Edge Technology for the Travel and Transportation Industry

Over 18 years' success developing and implementing domestic/international marketing campaigns throughout the U.S. and worldwide, and setting strategic direction to aggressively position companies for market share growth and profitability in intensely competitive global marketplace.

High profile industry expert/consultant, trade event speaker, and contributor to industry journals. World traveler with keen intercultural sensitivity and business sense who introduced technology to third world countries and delivered 110% single year sales increase to leading software company.

DEMONSTRATED ABILITIES TO:

- Develop leading edge products and re-engineered processes which serve as models and catalysts for change industry wide.
- Reorganize functions and establish systems to provide efficiency at lower cost, increase visibility, and drive customer satisfaction.
- Transition companies threatened by obsolescence to dominate with cutting edge technology.
- Develop strategic partnerships/joint ventures and creative revenue generation programs.
- Build dynamic, high performing teams and simplify systems to minimize training needs.
- Identify opportunities and weigh cost/benefits of outsourcing versus in-house handling.

PROFESSIONAL EXPERIENCE

TRAVELWARE, INC., Houston, Texas   **1993–Present**

Leading international travel industry developer and marketer of complex information applications for travel management companies, corporations, and airline reservation companies.

President & CEO: Recruited to reorganize and lead travel industry third party information system development company with near-obsolete product line to position of prominence as industry high technology leader.

Restructured firm into functional departments, outsourced where appropriate, and built strong team of development, support, and sales professionals:

- Reduced service calls 31% and produced dramatic reduction in end-user quality problems.
- Cut customer support costs approximately two thirds with client-transparent subcontracted International Phone Data Center customer support facility.
- Consolidated two development offices, reducing costs 22%.
- Significantly improved service by ensuring preparation of detailed specifications prior to product development.

Introduced new, leading edge products both in technology and functionality:

- Increased market share while transitioning company from DOS technology to object-oriented development tool and introducing new Windows line of applications.
- Developed client server and Intranet/Internet managed travel point of sale system to place control in client's hands, increase customer satisfaction, and save agency time.
- Introduced simplified agency system which increased efficiency 27%, eliminated need for training, and generated $40K in pre-release stage.

Launched aggressive new product, marketing, and joint venture initiatives:

- Developed strategy to retain 60% market share in face of competition with new technology.

- Negotiated/managed highly profitable joint venture relationships with U.S.T. Air, Apollo Air, and Manchester UK travel distribution networks.
- Repositioned company and opened markets in Europe, generating 100% annual growth for past three years.

JONES, INC., Dallas, Texas   1991–1993

Management consulting firm providing executive level advisory services to domestic and international corporations, airline reservation systems, technology and communications firms.

Senior Partner: Singly and in partnership with other consultants, undertook projects spanning business planning, marketing/sales programs, strategic information technology planning, market research, and senior executive coaching for client base including: Damper, Smith Noonan, Hotels, Inc., American Speed, Matrix Two, Goal Travel, Travel Matters, ASIT and Historic Communications, The Travel Bureau, MaxiDox, and others.

- Developed long-term strategic information management plan for major multinational company.
- Developed 5-year information management and new systems plan for Goal Travel.
- Developed sales and marketing plan that helped Yryoaro open U.S. market and achieve over $4MM in sales.
- Created marketing strategy to gain MaxiDox $5.5MM in business with fly-up-and-away travel plans for Yankee Airways, Apollo Air.

DECORUM INTERNATIONAL, Atlanta, Georgia   1988–1990

International reservation company.

Vice President & General Manager, North America: Managed start-up joint venture between nine European national airlines and Yankee Airlines with full responsibility for vendor marketing, public relations, multinational subscriber marketing, corporate communications, and vendor contracts for North America and South Pacific.

- Negotiated distribution contracts valued in excess of $130MM per year with nearly all major North American airlines, hotels, and car rental agencies.
- Key participant in strategic planning effort leading to merger with Yankee, and acted as intermediary between European based management and Yankee.

EARLY CAREER TRACK

President/General Manager - Networth International, Inc., Oregon: Grew company from $600MM to $1.3 billion in annual sales.

Vice President Licensee Marketing and Industry Affairs—BETA Inc., Miami, Florida: Researched and evaluated new members for investment in global business consortium; developed joint marketing programs; handled vendor negotiations; directed data management and consolidation.

General Manager—LAMM Enterprises: Managed South American establishment dealing in business management, transportation services, investment banking, and property management.

International Airways, Korea: Supervised joint venture to open Sales Offices, install the VariData reservation system, and handle government liaison.

Instructor - University of Alabama: Developed/delivered Marketing-Business Management lectures.

EDUCATION

MBA coursework, University of Maryland, 1980–81, 80% complete

Post-Graduate Diploma—Management Studies, Black University, New York, NY, 1979

CHIEF FINANCIAL OFFICER

BERT MASON • 8766 Deeley Drive • Boston, MA 01923 • (555) 555-5555

Senior Executive experienced in financial leadership, business development, and strategic planning in diverse industries who was key player in taking sales from $9.7 million ($4.5 million assets) to $35 million ($24 million assets) in 9 years.

- $600 K+ annual savings in employee medical and company property/casualty coverage through innovative methods.
- Turned acquisition from negative cash flow to $3 million positive cash flow in 2 years.
- Reduced average "Days Sales Outstanding" from 60 to 40 days.

Track record in merger, acquisitions, divestitures, SEC reporting and IPOs.

- Negotiated $12.5 million acquisition and arranged financing; became debt-free through cash flow within 18 months.
- Realized significant profit by marketing and negotiating sale of condo project earmarked for divestiture.
- Sold distribution and manufacturing companies totaling $2.3 million sales.
- Designed innovative strategies to invest money and minimize taxes for corporate/personal investments.

Experienced in administration of employee benefit programs and consolidation of administrative functions.

- Trustee for profit sharing plan that grew from $1.2 million to $8.1 million net assets in 9 years.
- Developed and implemented 401(k) plan that tied in with existing profit sharing plan.
- Facilitated sophisticated, computerized inventory control system for NYSE manufacturing company.

Results-oriented leader adept at increasing revenue, identifying problems, defining solutions and implementing new processes and procedures. Skilled in negotiations, communications and employee motivation.

B.S., Accounting, Top 5% of graduating class, Accounting Excellence Award, Alabama State University, 1973.

C.P.A., Alabama and Florida.

--- **PROFESSIONAL HISTORY** ---

LORRIO, INC., Chicago, IL - Vice President and Treasurer / Chief Financial Officer   **1987–August 1996**
$38 million manufacturer of plastic profile extrusions.
Directed all P&L and financial functions, staff of 20. Board Member and Trustee/Administrator of $1 million pension plan and $8 million profit sharing/401(k) plan.

UNITED MORTGAGE, Chicago, IL - Vice President / Controller   **1985–1987**
Largest originator of residential mortgages in state of Illinois with $1 billion in loans originated.
Directed 20 professionals in $2 billion portfolio management, implemented general ledger system and upgraded financial procedures.

J.J. CAMPBELL, Baton Rouge, LA - Vice President / Secretary / Treasurer   **1984–1985**
$20 million asset portfolio in the areas of commercial construction, real estate development/holdings and oil/gas properties.
Managed both personal and corporate financial functions and tax planning for E.H. Hurst.

RIGWORKS, New Orleans, LA - Assistant Corporate Controller   **1982–1984**
Leader in the land based, mobile rig, petroleum well servicing industry.
Managed all accounting, financial, tax planning/reporting and daily cash management activities for company with $150 million revenues, $350 million assets.

HOSPITAL SYSTEMS, INC., New Orleans, LA - Vice President / Chief Financial Officer   **1980–1982**
$13 million provider of primary emergency care, physician placement service and minor emergency clinics.
Directed financial/tax functions for medical entities and owner's personal portfolio.

Prior experience includes 6 years with JAMES & BOREN and 2 years with $130 million manufacturer.

CHIEF FINANCIAL OFFICER

Jane Smith
7872 Blue Hill Avenue
Rahway, NJ 07670

Objective: To become Chief Financial Officer for Vendway Industries. Superior skill base includes:

* Asset analysis
* Liability and stockholders equity analysis
* Revenue and expense management
* Tax accounting
* Investment management
* Development and analysis of financial statements

Career Summary:	Skilled in financial management and systems analysis with particular skills in accounting, auditing, tax preparation, costs and pricing procedures, inventory control and collections. 9 years of experience as a Chief Financial Officer, Certified Public Accountant, and Customer Support Manager for consulting firms and a $13 million audio equipment company.
Key Accomplishments:	Redesigned critical accounting systems for maximum efficiency at each new post. Designed highly customized financial reporting formats that made systemwide overhaul of marketing efforts possible. Expert in Excel and Lotus 1-2-3 operations (conducted advanced training seminars in each), and in many other programs, such as database management and Internet access software. Certified Public Accountant in New Jersey.
Employment History:	Achievement-oriented, highly efficient financial professional with a record of quantifiable success at ...

Weaver Audio Equipment Systems (Rahway, NJ), 1993–Present: As Chief Financial Officer, responsible for financial operations with 80 employees, implementing a reporting system for 6 subsidiaries and reducing auditing costs by $45,000 through automated reporting systems. Manage portfolio of $22 million.

Walker Business Services (Boston, MA), 1990–1993: As Customer Support Manager, worked with computer consultant to develop systems that allowed customer service reps automatic access to payment and order histories of callers.

Nash Associates (Boston, MA), 1988–1990: As Accounting Specialist, quickly placed in charge of development of new organizational payroll system only three months after hire. System is still in place and operating smoothly.

Education:	B.S. in Computer Science, Wellstone University, Waverly MA, 1987.

CHIEF FINANCIAL OFFICER (SUMMARY FORMAT)

CONCISE PROFESSIONAL SUMMARY: JANE SMITH
777 Lucky Drive, Dallas, TX 75265 * (555-555-7465)

From your July 13 ad in the *Dallas Morning News:*

"Fischer Corporation seeks a seasoned financial professional..."

• 8 years of experience as a Chief Operating Officer and Chief Financial Officer of Sunway Systems, a $92 million corporation. Certified Public Accountant.

" ... accustomed to working in a high-growth environment ... "

   • Responsible for sound financial management of a $92 million organization with revenue growth of 520% over three years.

" ... and comfortable negotiating large-scale contracts."

   • Excellent track record in negotiations, business acquisitions and multi-unit operations.

"Successful applicant will possess significant depth of experience in both financial systems and hands-on management."

• Adept at establishing sound financial infrastructures and developing superior management teams. Named Executive of the Year in 1996.

CHIEF OPERATING OFFICER

Ben Smith
984 Vessey St., San Francisco, CA 92101
555/555-1356

Profile

Chief Operating Officer for **Emark Hospitality Systems** (San Francisco, CA), a dynamic, highly profitable emerging company in the restaurant services and data management products industry. Skilled at:

Boosting revenue

Developing exciting new products for key customer bases

Managing and motivating employees at all levels

Coordinating design and marketing teams

Resolving daunting corporate operating problems

Creating and critiquing catalog and ad copy

Establishing revenue-enhancing pricing structures

Strategizing highly successful trade show campaigns

Imparting an entrepreneurial approach to daily business problems

Successful new product and service rollouts initiated include:

+ FoodBooks (Restaurant/Hospitality Accounting and Purchasing Software Package) — representing $1.5 million in annual revenue
+ TablePro (Restaurant Traffic Management Terminals)— representing $2.1 million in annual revenue
+ StaffSharp (Employee Staffing Service)— representing $1.6 million in annual revenue

Since I arrived at Emark three years ago, sales have increased from $220,000 to 6.2 million annually.

Other Employment Experience

Genesis Foodservice (Fullerton, CA)—General Manager (1989–1995)
Senior manager of the West Coast office of this $18 million hospitality firm.
TonyCo (San Rafael, CA)—Regional Manager (1988–1989)
Blue Boy Pizza Kitchens (San Rafael, CA) — District Manager (1984–1988)

Education

Bachelor's degree in Mathematics, minor in Theater Arts, Baldwin University, Kentfield, CA, 1983.

COMMODITY TRADING SPECIALIST (SUMMARY FORMAT)

RESUME BRIEFING FOR:

Alan Smith, President, Eaton and Eaton

Eaton and Eaton's Requirements	Vera Lesser's Background:
"Senior executive with deep experience in corporate strategy and investment."	✓ Senior executive with deep experience in corporate strategy and investment.
"At least 10 years of experience in commodity trading."	✓ 19 years of experience in commodity trading (stock indices, currencies, etc.) for seven major commodity funds, including my current employer, Pan-American Fund.
"Strong technical analysis and administration skills a must."	✓ Expert at strategy development, money management, execution of orders, and general administration, with heavy accent on fundamental and technical analysis.
"Demonstrated record of successful portfolio management at high levels is also essential."	✓ Manage portfolios from $1 million to $150 million.

VERA LESSER • 123 Main Street • Salem, MA 01970 • 555/555-5555

CONSTRUCTION SUPERINTENDENT

JOHN SMITH
4215 Shattuck Avenue
Hartford, CT 06831
555/555-5555

Overview

* Over 16 years of experience in the construction industry with over 10 years as Foreman/Superintendent for multi-million dollar projects.
* Established a positive relationship with inspectors in the City of Hartford.
* Excellent interpersonal communication skills; relate well with people at all levels and from diverse backgrounds.
* Strong, troubleshooting abilities; identify problems and quickly implement effective solutions.
* Knowledgeable in all construction and safety procedures dictated by OSHA; maintain a clean, accident free record.
* Experienced in hiring and supervising up to 500 union sub-contractor personnel.
* Computer literate on: Expedition, Microsoft Word, WordPerfect software.

Employment

1997   **Ortega**   **Hartford, CT**
Superintendent
Project: Questor Industries

Supervised the construction of a $28 million 68,000 sq. ft. office space and 10,000 sq. ft. class 1,000 clean room facility. Completed the project in budget and within time allotment.

1992 to 1997   **Ramp Construction Company**   **Hartford, CT**
Superintendent
Project: ViaWay Industries

Responsible for supervising the seismic upgrade of this vintage 1923 U.R.M. building as a low income residential hotel with 53 units. Completed the project within time allotment.

Project: Smith Homes, Inc.

Supervised the construction of a 107 unit low income residential hotel in South Central Los Angeles. Construction was completed on time and with fee intact.

Project: Marywell Units

Supervised a $1.3 million 40,000 square foot tenant improvement project including a self-contained telecommunication center and uninterrupted power source. Completed project ahead of schedule and doubled company's fee.

Project: Case Center

Supervised the construction of a $6.3 million, seven-story low income residential housing project. Utilized poured in place concrete for a subterranean parking structure with four floors of wood framing. Completed within time allotment.

1990 to 1992	**Johnson Construction**	Hartford, CT

Superintendent
Project: Dewey Plaza

Oversaw the construction of a $30 million, eight-story tenant improvement project with a marble entry, a complex drywall reveal system, and computer room. Completed project on promised date, a first in Dewey's history.

Project: Ranch Office Park

Responsible for tenant improvement of this multi-tenant complex.

1988 to 1990	**Mack Construction**	Hartford, CT

Assistant Superintendent
Project: Smith Museum

Supervised the remodel and structural upgrade of Smith Building. Performed extensive structural re-work of steel frame and concrete for the new museum.

1986 to 1988	**Owen Construction**	Hartford, CT

Assistant Superintendent
Project: ABC Airlines Connector Building

Coordinated the construction of a connector building at Hartford International Airport. Assisted in maintaining airport operations during construction. Oversaw quality control of all subcontractors.

1980 to 1986	**Carpenter/Foreman**	Hartford, CT

Project: Jones Tower Plaza

Assisted in the construction of this $30 million project consisting of four pre-case towers and a poured in place concrete commercial building.

Education

Las Vegas Trade Technical College	**Las Vegas, NV**

Blueprint Reading

CT Welding School	**Westwood, CT**

Light Gauge and Structural Certified

Valley Occupational Center	**Griswold, CT**

A.A. Degree/Carpenter Apprenticeship School

Certifications

Concrete Pump Safety, Excavation Competency, CPR & First Aid

Honors & Awards

Earned the Ramp Construction Safety Award and the Premium Responsibility Award, 1993–1996.

CONSUMER PRODUCTS CEO

Michael Smith / 47 Bellevue Place, Calabassas, CA 91399 / 555-555-8356

"Whatever a man does he must do first in his mind."
—Thomas Edison

OVERVIEW

Seasoned professional who has served as Owner, President, CEO, and Business Manager at dynamic organizations. Skilled in all areas of business operations and financial management. Exceptional strength in accounting, sales forecasting, budgeting, staff management, and public relations. Demonstrate a "passion for effective cost control" (CapLine annual report, 1/97).

EMPLOYMENT HISTORY

Chief Executive Officer: Fillmore Company, San Francisco, CA (1993–1997)
President: CapLine Corporation, Key West, FL (1987–1993)
Vice President of Operations: Everstone Products, Detroit, MI (1985–1987)
Owner: DayWear Corporation, Oakland, CA (1985)
Business Manager: Fastway Drug Stores, Hartford, CT (1983–1985)

RELEVANT SKILLS AND EXPERIENCE

Resource Management and Cost Control

- Increased profits from startup to $2 million (DayWear Corporation)
- Oversaw mineral development projects of up to $4 million (Fillmore Company)
- Posted average 20% return on company investments (CapLine)
- Maintained lowest production costs, by percentage, of any period in company history (CapLine)
- Initiated aggressive inventory management program that ensured adequate retail stocking at 117 retail outlets (Fastway Drug Company)

Corporate Administration

- Chaired committee for standardizing financial reporting systems, resulting in reduced overlap between departments (Fillmore)
- Led team that acquired Engelhart Co., a transaction described by the *Wall Street Journal* as "as shrewdly executed as it was carefully considered." (11/4/96)
- Responsible for launching new company distribution branch

Strategic Planning

- Developed 3-year plan that turned around moribund operation
- Isolated key new markets for successful startup company
- Identified key corporate goals for execution at all levels

EDUCATION

B.S., Business Administration, Reading College, Reading, PA (1981)

CONSUMER PRODUCTS/
COMMUNICATIONS PRODUCTS CEO

JOHN H. SMITH

316 Walnut Drive • Media, PA 19063
610-756-2300 (W) • E-mail: jhsmith@greatnet.com

Exceptionally broad-based senior-level executive experienced in domestic and international sales, marketing and financial management, strategic planning, start-ups, mergers and acquisitions, general management and new business development.

Demonstrated success at developing and implementing sales and marketing plans, improving productivity, negotiating contracts, and identifying market strategies for new product introduction in a wide variety of industries.

Rebuilt entire core business reversing 4 years of losses and achieving sales of $124M with $9.5M in profit within 2 years.

Grew consumer products division from $3.2M in sales to $9.6M in the first year and $28.2M in the second year.

Achieved #2 market share and increased sales by $29M within 18 months of obtaining exclusive distribution rights for new telecommunications product.

Improved on-time delivery from 43% to 91% through production planning and computerized forecasting

M.B.A. • Finance • Colorado School of Commerce   ✦   **B.A.** • Political Science • Rhode Island University

---

PROFESSIONAL EXPERIENCE

NATIONAL PRODUCTS, INC., Philadelphia, PA   **1993-PRESENT**
PRESIDENT AND CHIEF EXECUTIVE OFFICER
Develop and execute annual and long-range strategic marketing and business plans, as well as all financial and general management activities for a packaged consumer products company.

- *Developed a strategic plan and negotiated the acquisition of a growing competitor, adding more than $120M in revenues over a 32 month period.*

- *Added 3 additional products and eliminated 2 marginal products increasing revenues by 43% in 8 months.*

- *Reduced operating expenses by $2.3M through the reorganization of the sales force and eliminating unproductive positions within the administrative support functions.*

- *Eliminated 1M+ back ordered components, generating more than $4M in needed cash flow. Achieved an 87% reduction in the product defect rate.*

- *Eliminated virtually all high interest, short-term debt within 14 months of assuming control. Negotiated favorable credit lines totaling $35M with 2 banks and a major brokerage firm.*

SKY-TECH COMMUNICATIONS CORP.,   **1983-1993**
PRESIDENT AND CHIEF OPERATING OFFICER - (1988-1993)
Recruited to turn around troubled telecommunication products company. Reversed both market share and operating losses, within 20 months of assuming control, while going from 2 products to 7. Featured in the National Business Review.

- *Sold off more than $11M in commercial real estate, eliminating two defaulted mortgages.*
- *Negotiated a $14.2M acquisition, becoming debt-free through cash flow within 29 months of closing.*
- *Turned around an ailing division and increased sales by 68%. Improved margin to 29%, nearly 6% above the industry average.*

EXECUTIVE VICE PRESIDENT - (1983-1988)
Opened new markets, introduced new products, updated production facilities, redefined marketing and sales strategies, and directed the start-up of a new production facility.

- *Reversed market share decline and increased unit sales by more than 18% in 1 year.*

CONSUMER PRODUCTS/OPERATIONS EXECUTIVE

JANE SMITH
345 "E" Street, San Francisco, CA 94930
555/555-5555 (Daytime Message Number)
555/555-6666 (Evenings)

SUMMARY

19 years of experience as Vice President, Director and Manager of Operations for $3 million to $200 million organizations. Skilled at planning and analyzing, purchasing, MIS, cost accounting and managing all aspects of the manufacturing process.

ADMINISTRATION

A tested senior executive with a record of significant managerial and administrative accomplishment.
- Directed up to 225 manufacturing personnel.
- Expanded company's annual growth by 41% and boosted sales from $4 million to $35 million with a net profit of 360%.
- My company was nominated as *Trends* magazine's best business for 1993.

PLANNING

Skilled in all facets of divisional and corporate planning.
- Reviewed, revised, and implemented budgets and targets at all levels.
- Assisted in the development of accurate cash flow projections.
- Developed business plans for review by major financial institutions.

PRODUCT DEVELOPMENT

Assumed leading design role in over 40 new consumer product launches.
- Oversaw introduction of FreeHands computer dictation equipment. (Estimated first-year revenues of $4 million.)
- Developed specifications with key vendors for successful launch of CardWay three-dimensional baseball card holder. (Estimated first-year revenues of $6.7 million.)
- On selection team that established specifications and negotiated contracts ($100,000 to $3.5 million) with independent contractors and suppliers on over 25 projects.

OPERATIONS

Significantly increased operational efficiency in a wide variety of settings.
- Increased quarterly output in Cupertino, CA facility by 24% through reconfiguration of assembly line operations.
- After reviewing manufacturing processes increased personal efficiency of line workers in Trenton, NJ facility by an average of 19% during one-day training seminar.
- Oversaw redesign of Verona, NJ facility that reduced manpower requirements from 75 to 11.

EDUCATION

M.B.A. and a B.S. in Business Administration (from Bensonhurst University, El Paso, TX, 1977 and 1979, respectively.)

EMPLOYMENT

VP/Operations, The Jones Organization, New York, NY 1991–Present
Director, Home Breakthroughs, New York, NY, 1989–1991
Manager of Operations, Berescroft Products, Boston, MA 1984–1989
Design Engineer, Berescroft Products, Boston, MA, 1979–1984

CONTROLLER (SUMMARY FORMAT)

YOU WANT:

At least ten years of "significant bottom-line experience" from your new Controller.

I OFFER:

11 years of experience in corporate finance as Controller and Secretary for organizations ranging in size from $6 million to $220 million organizations. Helped to boost sales volume by $15 million and cut production costs by 21%.

In addition, I am:

- Skilled at financial analysis, forecasting, and implementing internal control systems
- Adept at developing short/long range plans and efficient use of resources.
- Highly proficient on IBM mainframe and PC computer systems.

RECOMMENDATION:

We should talk!

Martin Smith • 456 First Avenue • New York, NY 10017 • 555/555-5556

CONTROLLER/CFO

JANE DANIELS

555 Main Street
Reston,j105
 VA 22090
555-555-9813

Summary of Qualifications

Eight years of top level experience as a Controller and Chief Financial Officer for a multimillion-dollar organization. Superior communications, planning, and analytical skills. Expert at procurement and investment activities, with particular proficiency in forecasting, budgeting, credit matters, and collections.

Professional Experience

Controller and Chief Financial Officer, KC Auto Repair Systems, Boise, Idaho, 1990–Present

FINANCIAL ACHIEVEMENTS

* *Significantly reduced bad debt organization-wide; campaign resulted in 0.7% annual rate, lowest in organization's history*
* *Controlled accounts for 27 facilities in the Pacific Northwest*
* *Prepared budgets of up to $3.2 million*

MANAGEMENT ACHIEVEMENTS

* *Supervised staff of up to 50 employees*
* *Conducted, with senior managers, annual personnel reviews of all employees in headquarters location*
* *Developed "superior" training programs for team members that were praised by Chief Executive Officer in annual performance evaluations*

DATA MANAGEMENT ACHIEVEMENTS

* *Developed system supporting daily (rather than weekly) updates from field offices*
* *Authored customized computer system training manual distributed throughout organizations*
* *Worked with consultants and vendors to select highly efficient new computer system that resulted in an average of 13% greater productivity from finance team members within corporate headquarters*
* *Seamlessly integrated headquarters system with systems of field offices*

Herzberg Restaurants, Oakland, California, 1989–1990 Senior Accounting Supervisor

Crenway Group, San Francisco, California, 1988 Accounting Clerk

Technical Skills

Proficient in: Mainframe environments, IBM, and Macintosh systems. Expert at major spreadsheet, data management, and Internet navigation software.

Education

B.S., Accounting, Capitola University, 1988

DISTRIBUTION SPECIALIST (SUMMARY FORMAT)

TO: James Allen, ABC Industries

FR: Mary Jones

You seek an "experienced distribution professional with significant ability to work seamlessly with our marketing department."

I offer:

> 14 years of experience in regional and district Distribution Management for a major consumer products firm with operations throughout the eastern United States.

I am:

> Adept at directing sales, marketing and distribution activities for my employer's nearly $950 million annual operations, streamlining operations and inventory control with computers, and managing field operations and customer service functions.
>
> My current duties require: scheduling yearly deliveries of 22,000 autos, managing up to 22 employees, and accurately forecasting production needs.
>
> I have a B.S. in Business Management from the University of Santa Cruz.

**MARY JONES * 343 Capitola Avenue * Santa Cruz, CA 94555
555/555-5555 (home number)**

FINANCE/OPERATIONS EXECUTIVE (SUMMARY FORMAT)

CONCISE PROFESSIONAL SUMMARY
JACK WILSON

ABC is looking for "an experienced senior-level financial professional."

- *Jack Wilson has 16 years experience as Controller, Chief Financial Officer and Director of Finance for a $42 million company with up to 316 employees.*

ABC is a "fast-paced wholesale distribution organization."

- *Jack Wilson is skilled at tracking up to 18,000 inventory items, establishing highly effective interactive accounting practices, maintaining tight cash/credit management and overseeing warehouse operations.*

ABC is looking for a "self-starting team player comfortable working at all levels of the organization."

- *Jack Wilson successfully opened and managed a $9 million distribution center and expertly managed up to 155 employees.*

For a more detailed picture than this brief summary resume can provide, contact ...

•JACK WILSON
3567 Second Avenue
San Rafael, CA 94930
555/555-1556 (days)
555/555-2857 (evenings)

FINANCE/OPERATIONS EXECUTIVE

✦ JANE JONES ✦
123 MAIN STREET
SALEM, MA 01970
555/555-5555 (daytime)
555/555-6666 (evenings)

Labor omnia vincit. ("Work conquers all.")—Virgil

SUMMARY:

12 years of experience as a Finance and Operations Executive for $5 million to $225 million and FORTUNE 250 companies.

EMPLOYMENT HISTORY:

DANWORTH TECHNOLOGIES   Boston, MA
Vice President, Operations (1989–Present)

* Automated accounting functions, resulting in increased operational efficiency and $2.4 million in annual savings.

* Spearheaded consolidation team; combined three overlapping work groups and reduced labor costs by 16% while increasing productivity 11%.

* Managed staff of 94 employees; six of my team members were named "Key Contributors" at companywide awards ceremony, 1996.

PSL ASSOCIATES   Danbury, CT
Finance Manager (1987–1989)

* Raised $1.5 million in venture capital for this startup operation.

* Negotiated overseas plant agreements.

* Developed substantial knowledge of Budapest, Hungary business scene.

CENTRAL TECHNOLOGIES   New York, NY
New Markets Specialist (1985–1987)

* Launched two successful international businesses for this national engineering firm.

* Developed report on Asian economic opportunities that served as basis for $2.6 million investment.

* Hired and motivated key team members.

* Trained overseas office staff in operational procedures.

* Boosted sales revenue from $0 to $30 million in two years.

EDUCATION:

B.S. in Business Administration (Pinney University, 1982) and an M.A. in International Management (Vance University, 1984). Fluent in Hungarian and Japanese.

FINANCIAL EXECUTIVE

Frank M. Barcoh
(213) 561-5354

27763 Remcona Drive
Palos Verdes Estates, CA 90049

OBJECTIVE

Business / Financial Consultant

SUMMARY OF KNOWLEDGE AND EXPERTISE

FINANCIAL ANALYSIS
BUSINESS ACQUISITIONS / DEVELOPMENT
AUDITING - INTERNAL
ORGANIZATIONAL STRUCTURE
ACCOUNTANT / AUDITOR
CASH FLOW / COST CONTROL
LABOR RELATIONS
CREATE / IMPLEMENT POLICIES / PROCEDURES

SECURITIES INVESTMENT
FINANCE
COMPUTER SYSTEMS DESIGN
SKILLED NEGOTIATOR
RISK / FACILITIES MANAGEMENT
OPERATING PROCEDURES
ACCOUNTS ADMINISTRATION
DETAIL / RESULTS ORIENTED

ACHIEVEMENTS

- **Increased** annual net profit by 250%.
- **Increased** valuation of company by 400%.
- **Designed** management systems and internal controls.
- **Successfully negotiated** 25 yr. lease saving $5 million on 350,000 sq. ft.

- **Managed** growth from $40 to $100 million in services.
- **Designed** innovative computer system.
- **Reduced** error rate from over 15% to less on 2%.

PROFESSIONAL HISTORY

3/86 - Present **FINANCIAL / BUSINESS CONSULTANT**
Barcoh & Associates, Los Angeles, California
- Clients include companies in video production, document storage, public storage, software sales, property management / development.
- Provide expertise in setting up busines operations, computerized and accounting systems, creation of marketing and business strategies.
- Set-up administrative, accounting systems and business start-up advertising.

8/81 - 3/86 **SENIOR VICE PRESIDENT / GENERAL MANAGER**
Merlo Business Archives, Los Angeles, California
- Overall responsibility for the successful and profitable operation of business.
- Performed profit and loss responsibilities, accounting operations, risk management.
- Supervision of 80 employees.
- $4 1/2 million dollar firm. Multiple facilities - 600,000 sq. ft.

Previous: **CHIEF FINANCIAL OFFICER**
First Security Group, Los Angeles, California ($1 billion annuity / financial firm)

EDUCATIONAL HISTORY

University of California, Los Angeles

M.S. Business Administration / Accounting

B.S. Business Administration / Accounting

FUNDRAISER

CAROL ANNE WESLEY
216 West Juniper Avenue
Clarksburg, OH 23622
709-559-3725 (Bus.) ♦ 709-865-2298 (Res.)

Professional fund raiser experienced at developing marketing communication strategies designed to create a stronger image and greater positive awareness. Played key role in increasing revenues for two renowned humanitarian organizations.

Strengths include revitalizing the Donor Relations Department, maintaining favorable relationships with top executives, entertainers, and members of Congress, and developing new marketing plans for managing productive fund raising efforts.

An aggressive problem-solver and decision-maker with the ability to set realistic priorities and initiate viable courses of action designed to attain objectives. Outstanding communications, interpersonal and organizational skills.

Continually cited for ability to reach the individual small donor by recruiting influential volunteers and preparing motivational marketing materials during nationwide fund drives.

PERSONAL STRENGTHS AND ABILITIES

Knowledgeable in both donor relations, administration and operations. Possess excellent communication and interpersonal skills, as well as superior sensitivity to donor concerns and needs. Major strengths include:

- An outgoing and convincing manner
- Excellent listener with an ability to understand
- Goal-directed and a self-starter
- Creating effective written materials for diverse groups

- A high energy level and very professional
- Relate well to a wide variety of people
- Knowledge of tax laws and estate planning
- Dealing with pressure and meeting tight deadlines

CAREER HIGHLIGHTS

HOPE INTERNATIONAL   1992 - Present
Director, Donor Relations
World's second largest humanitarian organization and a non-political affiliate of the United Nations.

- *Reorganized the entire Donor Relations Department. Increased productivity levels while decreasing personnel by 18%.*
- *Created three major marketing campaigns that increased funds raised in first year by 24% with no increase in costs.*
- *Increased unrestricted funds collected by more than $12 million within first three years. Increased total donations from $86 million to more than $135 million.*
- *Cited by Executive Director as "the most valuable addition to the organization" during his tenure.*

HUMANITARIAN AMERICA   1984 - 1992
Director of Donor Relations - 1986 - 1992
Managed 18 regional offices nationwide of the nation's largest organization dedicated to relieving domestic hunger.

- *Increased donations in first year by nearly $1.9 million, while reducing operating and administrative expenses by 8.8%.*
- *Recruited more than 200 distinguished Americans to participate in press releases and public service announcements.*

Director of Corporate Relations - 1984 - 1986

- *Obtained overwhelming support for a new corporate program, "Care-A-Thon", increasing donations by 125%.*

EDUCATION

M.A. - Psychology - Boston University   •   **B.A.** - Humanities - Arizona State University

GENERAL MANAGER/SALES AND MARKETING FOCUS

CAROL ANNE WESLEY

216 West Juniper Avenue ✦ Clarksburg, OH 23622
709-559-3725 (W) ✦ 709-865-2298 (H)

Manufacturing executive with full P&L responsibility in sales and marketing management, manufacturing, operations and general management. Experienced in both consumer and industrial markets, and virtually every phase of plant operation.

✓ Led division to highest sales and profits in its history -- 27% R.O.I. compared to 6% under previous management.

✓ Negotiated 12 national contracts, increasing profits each year from less than 2% to 23.5% over a four year period.

✓ Took division with reputation for poor quality and service, to a position of quality and service above industry standards.

✓ Updated technology, improved maintenance programs, and increased sales in spite of eliminating two product lines.

Commended by C.E.O. as "the most capable" of his subordinates. Results-oriented leader committed to profit. Ability to remain calm and collected under the severest pressures. Accustomed to sophisticated controls and demanding standards.

══════ PROFESSIONAL EXPERIENCE ══════

MASTER MANUFACTURING CO. (A DIVISION OF WATSON INDUSTRIES)   1991 - Present
General Manager
Full P&L responsibility for a $27 million decentralized division distributing packaged consumer products.

* Took division from a subordinate group, furnishing the corporation with companion items, to a self reliant form.
* Increased profit from 2.5% of sales in the last fiscal year before assuming control, to 11% of sales within first two years.
* Decreased operating expenses 6% by revising advertising and promotion budgets, and by a consolidation of staff through reorganization.
* Improved gross profit by reducing costs, eliminating low profit lines, increasing prices of marginal lines, and the introduction of high margin lines.
* Introduced profit planning for the entire division. Appropriate corrective or opportunistic action by department heads became automatic in a results-oriented atmosphere.

CHEMICAL PRODUCTS, INC. (A DIVISION OF CHEMICALS INTERNATIONAL)   1982-1991
General Manager
Full P&L responsibility for a manufacturer of molded products and specialty plastic parts.

* Overcame backlog of more than 850,000 pieces and started shipping on schedule within five months.
* Reversed a 7% loss to a 5% profit with no change in net sales, an improvement of $700,000 in pretax earnings.
* Increased actual gross margins in two years from 19% to 34% with only a 10% increase in prices.
* Increased productivity from 70% of desired volume at costs of 18% above target, to 104% of production goals at costs 11% below target.
* Established seasonal sales projections which allowed sufficient inventory levels to meet customer orders as they arose. Net result was to double volume.

PRIOR EXPERIENCE: **Manufacturing Manager** for Stone Works Corp., manufacturers of molded products.
Operations Supervisor for Atek International, manufacturers of video and audio tape cassettes.

SUPPLEMENTARY EXPERIENCE: **Adjunct Faculty** for Columbia University teaching Operations Management.

══════ EDUCATION ══════

Executive Development Program - Harvard University

Master of Business Administration - Operations Management - St. John's University

Bachelor of Science - Industrial Engineering - New York University

HEALTH CARE EXECUTIVE

CAROL ANNE WESLEY

216 West Juniper Avenue
Clarksburg, OH 23622
709-559-3725 (W) • 709-865-2298 (H)

Senior-level executive experienced in developing and growing both health care facilities and home health care agencies. Extremely knowledgeable in program development, operations, strategic planning, administration, marketing and general management.

Top performer whose drive and leadership expertise produces results far exceeding normal expectations.

- Planned and directed the construction of a new intensive care wing, resulting in an increase of more than 2,300 annual visits.
- Tripled presentations to prospective clients, leading to a 63% increase in contracts signed over a 2 year period.

Disciplined professional with proven success in cutting costs and improving profitability.

- Reduced professional liability insurance by 6% and employee benefit insurance premium reserves by 14% while maintaining the same level of coverage.
- Increased annual revenues by $1.4 million in the first year through more efficient administrative practices.

Board Member, Home Health Care Foundation • Board member, Hospital Association of America
Appointed by the Pennsylvania Commissioners as a Member of the State Medical Authority

EDUCATION

Master of Science in Health Administration, University of Pittsburgh
Bachelor of Science in Business Administration, Duquesne University

EXPERIENCE

MEDICAL MANAGEMENT GROUP OF AMERICA
Executive Vice President   1992-Present
Direct all general operations for this Fortune 500 medical facilities management company. Manage a staff of 138 professional and non-professional support personnel.

- Increased the visit volume at two hospitals by 5.3% and 16.4% respectively, resulting in additional revenues of $5.6 million.
- Decreased operating costs for major metropolitan teaching hospital by 12% and exceeded budgeted productivity by 9%.
- Reversed 4 years of losses by cutting personnel and overhead in a major home health care agency, resulting in an 8% profit.

HOSPITAL CONSULTANTS
Vice President, Northeast Region   1989-1992
Established administrative and operational procedures for independent hospitals in an eight state region.

- Established a referral feeder system which generated more than $6.3 million in additional annual revenues.
- Reversed an excessive employee turnover rate by revising antiquated policies and stressing a participative management style.

Director, Consulting Group   1986-1989
Established the firm's first consulting group specializing in the home health care field. Grew division from $660 thousand in annual revenues to $5.2 million over a 3 year period.

- Conceived plan and negotiated terms that merged 3 home health care groups into a single entity, reducing overhead by 42%

Hospital Administrator   1980-1986
Assigned on an interim basis to manage all administrative activities of client hospitals while they were engaged in job searches to find full time administrators.

- Received 4 letters of commendation from client hospitals for significantly improving operations during interim assignments.

HIGH-END RETAIL SPECIALIST

FRED SMITH
1117 Morrison Drive
San Francisco, CA 94930

Qualifications:

- *Over 20 years retail experience, principally with major men's stores operations.*
- *Extensive knowledge and expertise in modern management systems and effective motivational sales techniques.*
- *Excellent interpersonal communication skills; establish and maintain rapport with major suppliers, customers, staff members and people from diverse backgrounds.*
- *Meet and exceed all sales goals; consistently achieve outstanding customer service and sales performance.*
- *Experienced in the hiring, training, motivating and supervising of management and sales personnel.*
- *Knowledgeable in market analysis and determining buying strategies essential for inventory and price point adjustments.*
- *Organized; able to handle multiple tasks, work on deadlines and in high pressure situations.*

Employment:

1984 to Present	Apparel Central	San Francisco, CA
	Area Manager	

Responsible for hiring, training, and developing sales personnel for multiple store locations. Monitor sales and customer service performance making sure all quotas are met and company standards adhered to. Oversee 30 day call, thank you notes, and effective usage of customer lists. Process bank deposits and requests from Headquarters. Handle the merchandising, overall visual presentations and displays. Perform demographic studies to determine customer demands, market trends and inventory requirements. Also manage tailor operations and quality of service.

Consistently increased sales volume by improving customer service and successfully analyzing customer need. *Developed enthusiasm and pride in the sales staff, raising the level of customer service culture throughout the stores.*

1976 to 1984	Benny and Bob	San Francisco, CA
	Vice President—Divisional Merchandise Manager	
	Men's Furnishing & Sportswear	

Responsible for the controlled buying, merchandising and profitability of 60 stores with over 200 employees. Analyzed customer demand, forecast market trends and prepared purchasing plans. Devised, instituted and implemented programs for each individual store designed to achieve the maximum sales turnover possible. Directed all divisional advertising. Also participated in acquisitions, liquidations and the overall administration. Hired as a Floor Salesman and was subsequently promoted through positions of increasing responsibility, becoming Divisional Merchandise Manager for five years before leaving Benny and Bob for two years. Returned to the same position and became Vice President-Divisional Merchandise Manager in 1979.

1974 to 1976	SuperWear, Inc.	San Francisco, CA
	President	

Organized and set up all aspects of this necktie and sport shirt manufacturing enterprise. Established effective policies, procedures and operations systems.

Brought sales volume to $750,000.

Education:

DeWitt College - Business Courses	San Francisco, CA
Various Industry Seminars	Sacramento, CA

(Note: Two stints each with Apparel Central [1978–1979 and 1984–Present] and Benny and Bob [1976–1978 and 1979–1984].)

HIGH-END RETAIL SPECIALIST

Fred Smith
1117 Morrison Drive
San Francisco, CA 94930

QUALIFICATIONS

- *Over 20 years retail experience, principally with major men's stores operations.*
- *Extensive knowledge and expertise in modern management systems and effective motivational sales techniques.*
- *Excellent interpersonal communication skills; establish and maintain rapport with major suppliers, customers, staff members and people from diverse backgrounds.*
- *Meet and exceed all sales goals; consistently achieve outstanding customer service and sales performance.*
- *Experienced in the hiring, training, motivating and supervising of management and sales personnel.*
- *Knowledgeable in market analysis and determining buying strategies essential for inventory and price point adjustments.*
- *Organized; able to handle multiple tasks, work on deadlines and in high pressure situations.*

EMPLOYMENT

1984 to Present   **Apparel Central**   **San Francisco, CA**

Area Manager
Responsible for hiring, training, and developing sales personnel for multiple store locations. Monitor sales and customer service performance making sure all quotas are met and company standards adhered to. Oversee 30 day call, thank you notes, and effective usage of customer lists. Process bank deposits and requests from Headquarters as well as associated customer purchases with sales slips. Handle the merchandising, overall visual presentations and displays. Perform demographic studies to determine customer demands, market trends and inventory requirements. Also manage tailor operations and quality of service. Originally hired as General Merchandise Manager (see below). Left the store and then returned as Store Manager. Subsequently promoted to positions of increasing responsibility.

- *Increased sales volume by 21% by improving customer service and successfully analyzing customer needs.*
- *Developed enthusiasm and pride in the sales staff, raising the level of customer service culture throughout the stores.*

1979 to 1984   **Benny and Bob**   **San Francisco, CA**

Vice President—Divisional Merchandise Manager
Men's Furnishing & Sportswear
Responsible for the controlled buying, merchandising and profitability of 40 stores with over 100 employees. Analyzed customer demand, forecast market trends, and prepared purchasing plans. Devised, instituted, and implemented programs for each individual store designed to achieve the maximum sales turnover possible. Directed all divisional advertising. Also participated in acquisitions, liquidations, and the overall administration.

Hired as a Floor Salesman and was subsequently promoted through positions of increasing responsibility, becoming Divisional Merchandise Manager for five years before leaving Benny and Bob for two years. Returned to the same position in 1979 and became Vice President—Divisional Merchandise Manager.

1978 to 1979   **Apparel Central**   **San Francisco, CA**
General Merchandise Manager
Responsible for merchandising mens clothing, sportswear and accessories for 120 stores throughout Southern California. Conducted market research and trend analysis, working with three buyers in purchasing stock and advertisements.

1976 to 1978   **Benny and Bob**   **San Francisco, CA**
Division Merchandise Manager
See above description

1974 to 1976   **SuperWear, Inc.**   **San Francisco, CA**
President
Organized and set up all aspects of this necktie and sport shirt manufacturing enterprise. Established effective policies, procedures and operating systems with other key stockholders. Directed all aspects of the operations and administration, including designing the entire line, purchasing materials, fabrication, sales of product and financing through credit and collections. Brought sales volume to $750,000.

EDUCATION

DeWitt College - Business Courses   San Francisco, CA
Various Industry Seminars   Sacramento, CA

HIGH-TECH EXECUTIVE

JOHN SMITH   555 MAIN STREET § FAIRFAX VA 22037 • (555) 338-0505

SENIOR EXECUTIVE - INTERNATIONAL

Software development / Technical operations / Marketing / Support and service
Hands-on, profit-driven senior executive with 12 years' proven performance leading high
growth and start-up software/information service companies to national and international
market leadership positions. Combine extensive technical ability and business acumen to
discover opportunities, penetrate new markets, and introduce technical innovations. Demonstrated ability to:

   ☆ Conceive, develop, and manage exceptionally successful large-scale projects throughout
      product design, development, documentation, delivery, and support processes
   ☆ Design/reengineer top-notch customer service and technical support operations
   ☆ Institute across-the-board cost-saving measures without downsizing
   ☆ Assemble, lead, and motivate high-caliber technical/professional teams
   ☆ Establish and manage cost-effective international sourcing and import/export operations
   ☆ Devise repackaging/bundling strategies to dramatically boost sales and profit margins

———————————————— **PROFESSIONAL EXPERIENCE** ————————————————

DATASCREEN COMPANY, Fairfax, VA   **1992–Present**

$25 million international market leader in development and installation of client/server
based travel industry accounting and administration systems.

Senior Vice President & Chief Technical Officer (1995–Present)

Vice President of Technical Operations (1992–1995)

With ultimate responsibility for customer satisfaction, direct staff of 90 in operation of all
technical functions including Development, Documentation, Product Management, Customer Service/Sales Support, MIS, and Internet Connectivity. Manage all personnel issues
including recruitment (50+ hired in only two years). Oversee existing software maintenance,
new version development, and porting to new environments. Discover, evaluate, and implement new technologies.

   • Key strategist in company's growth from $4MM in revenues/no profit to $17MM in revenues/$4MM profit in two years; projected revenues of $25MM for 1995.
   • Organized and led reengineering team in successful redesign of implementation process
      and organizational structure resulting in marked improvements in technical support
      and customer service.
   • Slashed 40% from corporate telecommunications costs by introducing alternative carrier
      and recharge system.
   • Created, proposed, and implemented innovative business strategy bundling hardware
      with software sales for 20% net income increase.
   • Enhanced corporate image and name recognition as keynote speaker, technical seminar
      organizer, and seminar instructor for four consecutive user group conferences.
   • Pioneered use of Internet's World Wide Web (WWW) as information delivery resource
      for customers.

111

STAMWAY COMPANY, Hartford, CT 1986–1992

International company specializing in software system solutions for executive search industry.

Managing Director

Reporting directly to Group Managing Director, directed all software development, support, and sales operations, with full P&L responsibility. Directed team of programmers and installers and supervised development of documentation and training materials. Served as primary architect of J-987 products running under Unix.

- Instrumental in company's growth from zero to position as leading provider of recruitment systems in Northeast Region and its sale to public company.
- Designed and wrote entire suite of software modules for company's primary product, ultimately transforming it into leading brand in eastern region.
- Sold $1/2 million system to international recruiting firm for installation at 7 sites.
- Pioneered use of text retrieval software linked to relational databases.

INFOSTATE CORPORATION, Bombay, India 1983–1985

National retail/wholesale operation specializing in home and small business computers and software.

Managing Director

As Founder and Partner, managed all financial, personnel, import, procurement, sales, and software development functions. Established wholesale outlets using internationally sourced imports for supply.

- Grew business from single one-room shop to wholesale distribution network with numerous outlets nationwide.
- Increased profits and expanded PC market by selling imported computers at low cost.
- Developed and successfully marketed first-ever PC real estate software package.

—————————————— TECHNICAL EXPERTISE ——————————————

Highly proficient in a wide variety of computer applications and platforms.

—————————————— PROFESSIONAL DEVELOPMENT ——————————————

Many professional seminars and courses in Programming, Networking, Database Administration, Object-Oriented Programming, and Professional Management.

HOSPITALITY EXECUTIVE

JOHN H. SMITH

316 Walnut Lane ◆ Media, PA 19063
610-444-2374

A senior- level executive with extensive experience in all areas of the hospitality industry. Expert in developing, renovating, and managing properties from 50 to 1,200 rooms.

Demonstrated success in turning around ailing properties, increasing sales and improving profitability.

- Achieved the property's highest gross and GOP, including two months of 100% occupancy, within five months of takeover in spite of a declining physical plant and the virtual lack of operating systems. Awarded "General Manager of the Year."
- Stemmed losses and achieved an operating break-even of $23,000,000 within six months of assuming control of a bankrupt convention center, office building and hotel facility.

Broad-based experience in the development, construction and renovation of major properties.

- Executed numerous renovation projects ranging from soft and hard goods replacement to complete room renovation in properties up to 900 rooms, all with no lost room nights.
- Managed new construction projects including site planning and selection, zoning, construction, pre-opening marketing, staff training and opening. Completed virtually every project on time and within budget.

Track record in achieving growth through franchised operations.

- Directed new franchise efforts, resulting in 16 new franchises within a one year period during a down economy.
- Revoked more than 50 franchises without litigation, while increasing profits of the remaining properties as much as 45%.

Innovator with keen sense of marketing and sales techniques for creating dynamic growth in revenues.

- Repositioned property from an inn to a conference center. Executed a complete marketing, advertising and sales campaign around the theme "The Center for Everything," resulting in an 18% increase in profits.
- Implemented new outlet concepts resulting in revenue increases up to 25%. Created "packaged" holiday and event banquets that more than doubled revenues.

Goal-oriented leader with the ability to manage and improve the performance of human resources.

- Established Human Resource Departments where none previously existed. Published new policies, overhauled compensation and benefit programs, improved employee relations, planned bargaining strategies, and ensured legal compliance.
- Initiated aggressive training activities in virtually every property managed. Requested to deliver similar programs throughout the orient.

Bachelor of Science in Hotel Administration, University of Miami

―――――――――――――――――― **PROFESSIONAL EXPERIENCE** ――――――――――――――――――

Executive Director THE HOSPITALITY HOUSE, Philadelphia, PA	**1995-Present**
General Manager WONDERLAND HOTEL AND CONVENTION CENTER, Clearwater, FL	**1992-1995**
Managing Director DAYTON CONVENTION PLAZA, Dayton, OH	**1990-1992**
Executive Vice President **Vice President - Operations and Development** **Director - Franchise Division** **Regional Director - Operations**	**1976-1989**

THE MAJOR HOTEL CORPORATION, Franchise Division, San Francisco, CA

HUMAN RESOURCE SPECIALIST

JOHN H. SMITH
316 East Walnut Lane
Media, Pennsylvania 19063
610-444-2374 • E-mail: jhsmith@greatnet.com

HUMAN RESOURCE GENERALIST
International . . . Domestic
Union . . . Non-Union
Multiple Location

A senior-level human resource generalist with exceptional strengths in each of the following areas:

- HR Policies, Procedures & Programs
- Forecasting & Succession Planning
- Employee & Labor Relations
- Information & Reporting Systems

- Training & Management Development
- Staffing & Expatriate Administration
- EEO & Legal Compliance
- Compensation & Benefits Administration

Disciplined professional with proven success at integrating HR programs with corporate objectives and strategic plans.

- Formalized the Human Resource Budget Planning and Forecasting System into an integrated corporate activity involving every function and operating level. Used the database to assess the effects of planned changes on the size, nature, and cost of the workforce during milestone growth stages of the "Ten Year Strategic Plan".

- Received mention in the annual report for large scale employee development program which combined participative management, marketing strategy implementation, and procedures training.

- Created an automated career profile and skills inventory system. Database was effectively used for career path assessment purposes and the identification of middle and senior management developmental needs.

Experienced in creating policies and procedures, managing diversified programs, and directing HR administrative functions.

- Led task team that created and implemented a strategic plan for compensation improvement which curbed inflationary salary growth and strengthened union-free posture. New compensation system reduced pay-related turnover by more than 80%.

- Overhauled the employee benefit program to create greater flexibility at a lower annual cost by instituting flexible spending accounts, wellness programs, 100% out-patient services, and cost containment features. Reduced insurance premium reserves by nearly 16%. Directed the installation and subsequent upgrade of a 401(k) program.

- Updated all expatriate policies, procedures and programs to meet both statutory requirements and customary practices on an individual country basis for 3,400 expatriates, nationals, and third country nationals operating in eight foreign countries.

- Orchestrated a two-third majority vote in an NLRB election covering 185 administrative and support personnel, thereby maintaining non-union status for the group.

_____ **PROFESSIONAL EXPERIENCE** _____

Vice President Human Resources   1990-Present
AMAZING COMPUTER COMPONENTS, Wilmington, DE
- Created a Human Resource Department and directed the installation of all policies, procedures and systems as the company grew from 135 to more than 1,200 employees at 16 locations over a 4 year period. Recognized by the CEO as one of the three most valuable managers during the company's rapid growth.

Director of Human Resources   1983-1990
MAZONT CHEMICALS INTERNATIONAL, Stamford, CT
- Played key role during the sale of the company by preparing a 5-year manpower projection and making several presentations to acquiring principals and investors from South Africa. Continued for six months after the sale to assure the smooth transition of departmental activities.

_____ **EDUCATION** _____

Master of Business Administration - Industrial Relations - Pennsylvania State University
Bachelor of Business Administration - Management - Temple University

INTERNATIONAL EXECUTIVE

MARTIN BELLINGHAM

934 Stevens Avenue
Boston, MA 01923
(555) 555-5555

Executive experienced in international business development, negotiations and finance who generated 63% first-year sales increase, despite strong competition, through expansion in Asian market.
Manages Asia-Pacific region and contributes to its growing profits by directing all business aspects of operation.

- *Built Chinese joint venture from ground up including identifying partner, hiring/training management and staff and developing business/marketing plan.*
- *$1 million in sales realized by building superior sales networks in China with quality representatives/agents.*
- *Penetrated untapped territory by developing/executing customer, marketing and advertising strategies.*
- *Prepared thorough financial analysis including cash flow, income statements and balance sheets.*
- *Managed business in Japan, Malaysia, Taiwan, Hong Kong, Thailand, Malaysia, Singapore and Indonesia.*

Skilled communicator able to eliminate cultural barriers and adapt to business protocols within global environment.

- *Negotiated up to $500K in contracts with key accounts considering cultural, economic and competitive factors.*
- *Resolved delicate issues between U.S. and Chinese partner. Built global reputation of integrity.*
- *Effectively interfaced with engineers, management and staff throughout all department levels.*
- *Swiftly built rapport based on customer trust through sincerity and product knowledge.*
- *Analytical thinker skilled in solving numerous problems by identifying source and charting logical course of action.*
- *Constantly focuses on company's best interests while negotiating with partners and customers worldwide.*

Fluent in English, Mandarin and Cantonese.   Open to international travel and/or relocation.

EDUCATION   MBA (International Business and Finance), University of St. Peter, Galveston, TX, 1989
Bachelor of Engineering, with honors, China University, Hong Kong, China, 1982

EXPERIENCE   *ABCD, Inc. (1989 to Present)*
(International co. selling instrumentation to oil & gas, petrochemical and process industries.)
ASIA-PACIFIC REGIONAL MANAGER Wichita, Kansas (1995–Present)

- Managed major projects in Asia. Coordinates efforts with engineering and contracting firms.
- Establishes customer commitments and develops strategies to ensure continued satisfaction.

MANAGER OF ASIA DEVELOPMENT, Chicago, Illinois (1993–95)

- Established joint venture with China and managed all phases of development including contract negotiations, financial analysis, budgeting, strategic planning, staff recruitment.
- Traveled extensively throughout China establishing contacts and developing new business.
- Member of joint venture Board of Directors.

APPLICATION ENGINEER, Chicago, Illinois (1990–93)

ENGINEER, ROSE, INC., New Orleans, Louisiana (1989–90)

- One of few selected to transfer with company. Managed engineering functions of international business. Selected most cost-efficient model to solve application requirements.
- Reduced time needed to complete wide range of applications from 3 hours to 20 minutes through design of computer program.

HARBOR PLANT ENGINEER, Malaysia (1982–86)

- Managed 10 technicians in ensuring quality control; maintained daily contact with customers.
- Solved wide range of technical problems utilizing process controls, analyses and tests.

INTERNATIONAL EXECUTIVE/OPERATIONS FOCUS

• MEL RYAN •
• 2352 Fifth Avenue • New York, NY 10011
• 555/555-5555 (phone) • 555/555-5556 (fax)

Multilingual Senior Executive experienced in international business development and management who simultaneously built 2 companies increasing sales from $4 million to $30 million (in 7 years) with $8.7 million profit.

- Achieved sales of $150 million with $13 million profit first year after merging 2 companies (1 with $65 million sales and $8.5 million loss, the other with $120 million sales and $6 million profit).
- Took sales from $150K to $9 million with $1.2 million profit by building sales organization for new subsidiary.

Experienced in achieving growth through mergers, start-ups, joint ventures and introduction of new product lines.

- Restructured European presence and maintained $100 million sales through new product introduction.
- 29% profitability achieved a chairman of joint venture start-up company.

20 years of progressive management experience with full P&L responsibility. Proven ability to build new organizations, reorganize troubled operations or expand into international markets.

Fluent in English, Dutch, and German. Proficient in French.

Extensive international experience. Lived and worked in Europe, South America, Australia, and Central America.

Currently based in New York. Willing to relocate internationally.

Masters Degree in Economics, University of Paris, 1971.

EXPERIENCE

AAA COMPANY
1993–Present

Vice President International Operations

Restructured company's European presence with headquarters in Amsterdam and offices in all major western European countries. Responsible for $100 million sales and $8 million profit.

SMITH & CO., USA, Germany, Netherlands
1983–1993

VP / General Manager, Springfield, MA, 1991–1993

Responsible for German and Central European consumer products operations and start-up operations in Russia.

Vice President / General Manager, France, 1990–1991

Restructured French companies following major acquisition. Maximized profitability by right sizing operations and creating 2 business units; consumer products and pharmaceutical.

Vice President International Operations, Springfield, IL, 1989–1990

Responsible for $100 million consumer/nutritional products.

General Manager, Sweden, 1983–1989

Built 2 companies (1 a start-up) with total P&L, marketing, sales, administration, medical affairs and business development responsibility. Took sales from $4+ million to $30 million.

VUMEN LTD, Paris, France
1975–1983

General Manager

Established subsidiary and introduced branded generic concept for pharmaceutical products in France.

SPARKWAY INDUSTRIES, Melbourne, Australia
1972–1975

Sales Manager

Progressed from Salesperson to Sales Manager. As Sales Manager, responsible for $6+ million in sales volume.

INTERNATIONAL GENERAL MANAGER

JOHN H. SMITH

316 Walnut Drive
Media, PA 19063

610-756-2300 (Bus.)
610-444-2374 (Res.)

International executive and general manager experienced in all phases of international operations, related planning and liaison. Experienced with major chemical and coating manufacturers in the U.S. and Latin America. Strengths include plant management, sales and marketing management, corporate re-organization, product diversification, and general management.

★ *Increased profitability by 18% in spite of a reduction in personnel from 1,150 personnel to 840.*

★ *Instituted systems, procedures, processes and diversification, which increased sales by more than 800%.*

★ *Restructured Chilean presence and increased sales by $18 million through new product introduction.*

Creative problem solver with knowledge of international statutory requirements and customary practices on an individual country basis. Proven ability to deal effectively with foreign nationals and resolve problem situations.

★ *Directed negotiations and reconciliation efforts of a long-disputed bank account with a foreign affiliate, resulting in a cash realization of $6.5 million.*

★ *Led a task force which successfully protected a $12 million receivable exposure of a Columbian subsidiary.*

★ *Cited by top management for expert management of crises situation arising from currency devaluations in Columbia, Chili and El Salvador.*

Fluent in Spanish, with some facility in Portuguese, French and German. Willing to relocate internationally.

EXPERIENCE

CONGLOMERATE INTERNATIONAL (LATIN AMERICAN GROUP)   1992 - Present
General Manager - Chilean Subsidiary
Full P&L responsibility for this five-plant $135 million chemical process business (ammonia, sulfuric acid, methanol, fertilizer, etc.).

★ *Developed two new chemical plants, achieving a diversification of products that improved sales by 700%.*

★ *Planned, justified and directed the construction of a modern $58 million engineering and test facility. Net result was the addition of $11 million in additional sales within 16 months.*

UNIVERSAL CHEMICALS & COATINGS   1981-1992
General Manager - Columbian Subsidiary - 1988-1992
Full P&L responsibility for the fourth largest chemical operation in South America (seven plants).

★ *Completely reorganized and revitalized chemical and industrial products manufacturing operation. Improved multi-plant efficiencies and profitability.*

★ *Renegotiated loans with two Columbian banks totaling $22 million at a full percent lower than original rate.*

Manufacturing Superintendent, Chemical Division - Miami, FL - 1983-1988
Directed all functions other than sales and finance for the manufacture of chemical coatings for the maritime industry.

Production Manager, Chemical Division - Dallas, TX - 1981-1983
General supervision for the manufacture and quality control of commercial paints and coatings.

EDUCATION

M.S. - Chemical Engineering - Brown University   ◆   **B.S.** - Chemical Engineering - University of California

INTERNATIONAL MARKETER

JOHN H. SMITH

316 Walnut Drive ■ Media, PA 19063
610-444-2374 ■ E-mail: jhsmith@greatnet.com

Travel sales and marketing executive with extensive contacts throughout the U.S., Europe and Japan. Skilled at identifying and closing new business, growing existing business by winning customer loyalty, and managing the sales force.

Maintained active business relationships with 1,783 travel agencies and corporations.

Increased agency/corporate market share by 46%, thereby securing high-yield business.

Led sales effort in new niche markets and secured incremental business.

M.B.A., Business Law • Chicago University ✦ B. A., International Affairs • Michigan Central University

――――――――――――――― PROFESSIONAL EXPERIENCE ―――――――――――――――

SEABOARD TRAVEL AGENCY, Philadelphia, PA   **1993-Present**
GENERAL MANAGER
Global travel management company, with $46 million annual sales and 36 offices worldwide. Develop and manage business relationships with all domestic/international airlines. Direct all sales activities including the "Customer Satisfaction" program. Evaluate competitor information on pricing, route structure and alliance issues.

- *Created the "Global Sales Program" with international offices to facilitate global sales growth.*

- *Re-established and maintained business relations with the City of Philadelphia, the City of Camden, the Philadelphia Convention Center, the Visitors Bureau, and the Chambers of Commerce for Philadelphia and Camden.*

- *Increased corporate clients by 300% resulting in $12 million in additional revenues.*

- *Built airline brand-awareness through a unique marketing communication plan.*

- *Directed a sales and marketing effort that reversed two years of losses in the Miami regional office and generated a profit of $75,000 in six months.*

WONDERFUL AIRLINES, Phoenix, AZ   **1984-1993**
REGIONAL SALES MANAGER - 1989-1993
Domestic and international airline with a 350-aircraft fleet, global route structure, and sales of $8 billion. Managed seven person sales team and directed all sales activities in a six-state region. Coordinated world vacation sales efforts for Dixie and Mid-Atlantic Airlines. Developed and administered key business programs, including Travel Agency Council.

- *Increased Dixie and Mid-Atlantic World Vacation Program revenues by 60%.*

- *Effected a substantial increase in market share through the use of sales-effective override and incentive contracts.*

- *Developed a highly differentiated in-house automated client database system that was used to strengthen Wonderful Airlines' reputation as an industry leader through specialized mailings and personal contact.*

MANAGER, NATIONAL SALES - 1985-1989
Managed a six-person "key account" sales team. Managed and developed a $68 million territory. Negotiated group, meeting and convention fares, corporate agreements, and tour operator programs. Created and managed all marketing and promotional activities.

- *Selected to personally manage the company's largest customers. Grew sales volume by 60% over four year period.*

- *Implemented and supported the first car rental and Amtrak programs.*

MEMBERSHIPS

Corporate Travel Managers Association ✦ ASTA ✦ Philadelphia Travel Managers Association

118

INTERNATIONAL MARKETER

JOHN SMITH
777 Main Street, Salem, MA 01970
555/555-5555

CAREER PROFILE

International Marketing & Sales Management

Seasoned international marketer with over 12 years' experience in Australian market specializing in high tech and mechanical products. Expertise encompasses all aspects of import/export process including market research and development, contract negotiation, international finance (letters of credit, creditworthiness evaluation, payments, delivery). Skilled manager of large marketing and field sales organizations through both distributor networks and direct with full P&L responsibility. Key contributor to corporate strategic planning process.

Key Strengths

- *In-depth knowledge of Australian market, culture, mentality, and business practices*
- *Special facility with languages and cross-cultural communication*
- *Skilled in developing and leading aggressive sales strategies in competitive markets*
- *Readily inspire and motivate marketing/sales force through creative leadership*
- *Skilled and savvy negotiator in the international marketplace*
- *Dedicated to customer satisfaction and prompt and amicable problem resolution*
- *Solid technical knowledge base facilitates thorough product familiarity, understanding of production and delivery constraints, and communication with potential clients*

PROFESSIONAL HIGHLIGHTS

Marketing / Sales Management

SWEETCO, Melbourne, Australia   1990–Present
Representative Engineering Agent—U.S.

As President of Service Partnerships, Inc. (American-based company created for export purposes), negotiate export contracts with American manufacturers and distributors. Develop and implement new product sales strategies in Australia. Oversee all aspects of resulting business including pricing, invoicing, and delivery.

- *Significantly reduced time required for quoting/purchasing/delivery process.*
- *Lowered costs and increased reliability of service by increasing base of suppliers.*
- *Introduced new products resulting in 18% Australian sales increase in 1993.*
- *Negotiated exclusive distribution contracts from American and Taiwanese manufacturers.*

NEW PATH INDUSTRIES, Melbourne, Australia   1982–1990
General Manager Marketing / Sales & Operations (1985–1990)
Directed operations, managed sales/marketing department, and supervised technical staff.

- *Based on market research, totally reorganized plant's infrastructure to fabricate technologies new to Australian manufacturing; seized considerable tax advantages in process.*
- *Implemented marketing strategy resulting in a 70% market share within 1 year.*
- *Increased revenues by 290% in three years while operating below budget.*

119

Engineering Management

NEW PATH INDUSTRIES, Melbourne, Australia   1982–1990
Plant Manager (1982–1984)

Implemented QM concepts to direct, organize, and establish priorities for engineering department, improve inventory planning and manufacturing schedules.

- Increased production output by 22% first year through automation and equipment layout.
- Lowered costs and improved quality, reducing scrap from 15% to 3%.

BEACON CORPORATION, Melbourne, Australia   1979–1982
Production and Control Manager

Developed and managed aggressive multi-product schedules and capacity plans.

- Inspired exceptional teamwork resulting in enhanced quality and efficiency.
- Increased production output, reduced costs, and shortened time to market.

EDUCATION AND TRAINING

M.S. Mechanical Engineering Candidate   December 1995
Massachusetts Technical College, Boston, Massachusetts

B.S. Physics   December 1993
Westerly University, Anaheim, CA

Business Administration   1982–1984
University of Melbourne, Melbourne, Australia

TECHNICAL SKILLS

Machines—lathes, grinding, milling, production machinery

Computer Hardware—IBM and Macintosh systems

PROFESSIONAL AFFILIATIONS

Member, Association of Mechanical Engineers (ASME)

INTERNATIONAL AND U.S. REFERENCES FURNISHED UPON REQUEST.

INTERNATIONAL MARKETER

JOHN H. SMITH

316 Walnut Drive • Media, PA 19063 • 610-756-2300 (W) • 610-444-2374 (H) • E-mail: jhsmith@greatnet.com

Senior-level sales and marketing professional with 15 years national and international experience.

Opened more than 75 accounts in one year with sales in excess $1.25 million.

Reduced turnover of key sales personnel by 84% through an innovative incentive program.

Recipient of one "Gold Key" and two "Platinum Key" sales awards over three consecutive years.

Developed a new sales training program that was duplicated and introduced to every division in the company.

Strengths include the ability to reorganization and revitalize stagnate marketing and sales efforts, develop strategies for new product introduction, and manage the continued growth of both national and international accounts.

M.B.A. - Wharton School of Business - University of Pennsylvania • B.A. - Psychology - University of Texas

PROFESSIONAL EXPERIENCE

HOLLY PRODUCTS, INC., Cherry Hill, NJ **1991-PRESENT**
VICE PRESIDENT, SALES
Direct all marketing and sales activities for the northeastern territory of an $80 million industrial products company.

- Established the first distributor network system, creating an additional $4.5 in sales in the first year.

- Introduced a new aluminum stamping machine and exceeded the market penetration plan by 38%.

- Created a new marketing campaign for a stagnate product that achieved 34% of total market share within 18 months of its introduction.

- Convinced a major international account to renew its business relationship after being lost due to blunders by previous management. Sales will exceed $45 million over a three year period.

EASTERN HOTEL CORPORATION, Dover, DE **1987-1991**
GENERAL SALES MANAGER
Managed all sales efforts for seven resort hotels located in Florida, Texas, California, Arizona and the Caribbean.

- Reorganized a slumping sales effort, placing the primary emphasis on increasing bookings of corporate sales meetings and retreats. Effort led to a 38% increase in sales in the first year.

- Devised a "singles" package that nearly doubled revenues at two facilities, and accounted for more than $52 million corporate-wide.

- Honored by the National Resort Association as one of the ten most successful sales managers in the U.S.

BETTER SOFTWARE CORPORATION, New Hope, PA **1983-1987**
SALES ASSOCIATE
Developed new and serviced existing accounts for a software development company serving a three state area.

- Refined an existing telemarketing program which led to an overall increase in client leads by more than 40%.

INVESTMENT/BROKERAGE EXECUTIVE

JANE SMITH

537 Redway Lane
Hartford, CT 06831
555/555-5555

Objective   Seeking a position in Business Development and Client Services

Qualifications

- Over 9 years experience as a senior level Executive in the financial field.
- Successfully built both brokerage and investment advisory firms.
- Knowledgeable in investment and production technology, compliance issues, marketing, endowments/foundations. Taft-Hartley Plans, sub-advisory, due diligence, trading, soft dollars, prime brokerage, etc.
- Established and maintain a comprehensive list of resources and contacts.
- Proven troubleshooting skills; identify problems and implement appropriate solutions.
- Experienced in motivating personnel, fostering team work among employees, and negotiating contracts.
- Organized with the ability to handle multiple tasks such as budgeting, forecasting, business and growth planning implementation.
- Wide range of capabilities in all aspects of the marketing process, from product creation to developing new markets and client relations.
- Computer literate on Instant, Bloomberg, Bridge, MAS90, Advent, Microsoft Work, Exell, Telemagic.

Employment

1988 to Present   **International Portfolio Services, LLC**   **Hartford, CT**
President/Chief Executive Officer/Chief Financial Officer & Co-Founder

Oversee all aspects of operations and administration for this multimillion-dollar investment advisory firm. Develop key retail and institutional client relationships. Responsible for marketing; compliance; legal and financial issues. Recruit and supervise up to 35 employees.

- Oversaw the firm's growth from $5 million to $480 million in 3 years.
- Successfully initiated mutual fund sub-advisory relationship and was instrumental in growing the firm's assets to $480 million.
- Developed on/offshore limited partnerships.
- Member of investment policy committee, encompassing performance attribution review, investment flow, portfolio construction, sell discipline, monitor and control over portfolio management and analysis.
- Perform as Chairman of Management Committee: Engineered product development, marketing plan, and client service standards.
- Implemented numerous operational enhancements including compensation strategies, system upgrade, and increased interdepartmental coordination.

122

1990 to 1993	**Northern Securities** *Managing Director*	Hartford, CT

Responsibilities included overseeing all daily operations including handling mutual fund, equity and bond trading and research; hiring, training, compliance, managing 8 employees. Initiated clearing arrangements with major clearing firm. Produced financials and in-depth business plan which included due diligence procedures for an alternative manager data base, soft dollar programs for institutions, short interest rebates, and prime brokerage clearing for hedge funds. Built two companies simultaneously.

- Successfully turned a $1.0 million loss into a $2.0 million gain in 1-1/2 years.
- Developed investment manager/broker-wrap programs and compliance procedures for retail brokerage and order room.
- Personally responsible for $80 million in client assets and growing firm to $6.8 million in annual revenue.
- Initiated strategic plans to redirect the firm's focus.

1988 to 1990	**Brave Financial** *Vice President/Operations & Partner*	Hartford, CT

Oversaw broker/dealer clearing agreements with major clearing firms. Organized the trading room, administered compliance issues, and handled finance. Supervised and trained 8 employees.

- Performed focus 1 & 2 calculations.

1984 to 1987	**Borne Securities** *Registered Representative*	Hartford, CT

Sold securities to private individuals and businesses.

- One of Top 25 Brokers every year.

Education

Connecticut State University, Hartford Bachelor of Science, Finance	Hartford, CT

Licenses

NASD Series 7, 63, 24, 65

Special Distinctions and Memberships

Connecticut State Task Force

- At the request of Governor, served on the 9-member task force that recommended new investment guidelines for local and state investment practices. Reviewed the policies and procedures related to the Orange County bankruptcy case and reported to Governor and the California Legislature, recommending findings for possible investment, as well as guidelines to be considered for the future.
- At the request of State Treasurer, served on Connecticut Advisory Commission

Memberships

AIMSE
Hartford Financial Advisory commission
Hartford Society of Financial Analysts

LOGISTICS SPECIALIST

BARBARA NELSON

321 West Street
Minneapolis, MN 55202

Senior Manager with US and international experience in logistics, maintenance and safety management who effectively managed a logistics/supply work system with $1.5 million budget and $150 million inventory system.

Top performer whose diligence and leadership expertise yield results far exceeding company averages.

- 40,000 accident-free hours achieved spanning 12 years—longest safety record in company history
- .043% inventory shrinkage vs. 1.56% district average—#1 of 15 stores.
- $2K inventory in return to vendor items vs. $8K district average—#1 of 20 stores.
- 94% score on corporate shipping/receiving audit vs. 75% company average.

Disciplined professional with proven success in expanding operations, cutting costs and meeting tight deadlines.

- 90% availability of work centers attained (from 60%) through hands-on process management.
- 6-year track record of savings while managing annual budgets of $450K+.
- Coordinated 12 aircraft/15 trucks for worldwide mobilization with as little as 5 days notice.

Open to relocations in US and abroad. Married.

Working knowledge of Spanish and Arabic languages. Extensive experience in Far/Middle East.

EDUCATION

MBA candidate, Jones School of Management, Minneapolis, MN
MS, General Administration, Kansas University, 1986
BA, Political Science, Arkansas University, 1979

EXPERIENCE

COPY CITY   Minneapolis, MN   1993–Present
Regional Receiving Manager

- Responsible for shipping/receiving in $9.5 million group of office supply store/copy centers.
- Controlled inventory losses to $13.5K vs. $60K national average.
- Manage 50-mile delivery area shipping $35K inventory weekly.
- Acting Store Manager for largest sales day in store history.

REDWAY COMPANY   Hutchinson, MO   1992–1993
Receiving Manager

- Managed shipping/receiving department with 7 trucks/6 trailers for 6-state area with $9 million inventory.

UNITED STATES AIR FORCE   1979–1991
Safety Manager (1989–1991)

- Directed safety program to longest safety record in history through diligence and standardization.
- Received Safety Award 2 consecutive years.

Logistics/Maintenance Manager (1979–1988)

- Managed $1.5 million budget and $150 million inventory system.
- Supervised scheduling, training and productivity for companies in excess of 300 employees.
- Coordinated all transportation requirements throughout the US and Far/Middle East.
- Achieved 95% grade on maintenance audits.

124

MANUFACTURING EXECUTIVE

CAROL ANNE WESLEY

216 West Juniper Avenue ✦ Clarksburg, OH 23622
709-559-3725 (W) ✦ 709-865-2298 (H)

Strong background in equipment manufacturing for the direct mail marketing, graphic arts, and exhibit design industries. Experience includes operations, sales, new business development, strategic/operational planning, and HR development.

✓ Played key leadership role in changing from a centralized structure to decentralized production teams. Change significantly increased production leading to substantial sales revenue growth.

✓ Evaluated and implemented a computerized job costing system. Linked electronic timekeeping, purchasing, estimating, and job costing. System allowed departments to be charged for 100% of their costs.

✓ Negotiated the first cost plus contract with a major client. Directed contract audits and resolved all issues to the satisfaction of the customer's audit team.

✓ Supervised the capital expenditure budgeting process. Played lead role in the acquisition of assets from an exhibit company, and their subsequent resale at a $135,000 profit.

Have developed marketing communication strategies which resulted in a stronger image and greater positive community awareness. Skilled administrator. Maintain favorable relationships with all organizational levels.

PROFESSIONAL EXPERIENCE

GRAPHIC PRODUCTS CORP., Dayton, OH 　　　　　　　　　　　　　　　　　　　1991 - Present
Resource Director
Manage resource allocation for custom exhibit and point-of-purchase display production teams. Responsible for production planning and coordination between teams, departments and functional areas.

- Set-up Manufacturing Test Department by transferring work formerly done by Design Engineering. Group grew from 2 to 11 technical employees.

- Participated in the development of budgeting and profit planning programs; guided functional groups in the implementation of these programs.

- Developed and implemented a Key Account Strategy Program. Retained all key accounts and increased number from three to seven.

CHATWOOD GRAPHICS, Dayton, OH 　　　　　　　　　　　　　　　　　　　　1982-1991
Regional Sales Manager - 1988-1991
Managed sales and direct marketing for a $40,000,000 commercial printer. Trained and expanded sales force from two to seven. Increased revenue from $6,500,000 to $26,000,000. Seven-figure operating budget responsibility.

- Opened more than 80 new accounts with a 78% retention rate.
- Reduced annual sales staff turnover rate from 60% to less than 10%.
- Increased revenue by 15% in first year, and 127% over three years.

Director of Planning (Chatwood Graphics) - 1984-1988
Managed the development and implementation of the firm's first Strategic and Operational Planning Process.

- Facilitated the executive management group through the strategic planning process. Facilitated the operations management group in the development of annual operational plans. The combined planning process led to the successful execution of strategic growth objectives of more than 14%.

EDUCATION

Bachelor of Arts - Sociology - Boston University

MANUFACTURING EXECUTIVE

JOHN SMITH

§ 122 Long Lane § Salem MA 01970 §
Voice Mail: (555) 222-2222, Ext. 22 § Residence: (555) 222-1111

SENIOR EXECUTIVE

Manufacturing § Marketing § Product Development § R&D for Medical/Healthcare & Critical Industrial Environment Product Industries

Dynamic executive with 25+ years' proven success delivering record-breaking cost, quality, and profitability improvements to multi-million dollar domestic/international manufacturing operations. Special expertise in medical/industrial garment production, PVC sheet extrusion, and medical manufacturing. Keen intercultural sensitivity and business sense with global experience throughout USA, Europe, and PacRim. In-depth knowledge of international regulatory requirements as well as manufacturing and management processes including TQM, JIT, SPC, Benchmarking, Total Productive Maintenance, Total Employee Involvement.

Demonstrated Abilities To:

- Translate corporate vision and mission into concrete, feasible strategic plans and provide strong leadership for their implementation
- Identify and capitalize on market opportunities for increased profitability
- Recognize organizational strengths and weaknesses, making tough people and process decisions necessary for long-term improvement
- Serve as catalyst for adaptations needed to meet needs of changing global market
- Utilize in-depth understanding of processes to elevate management from an art form to a scientific approach, identifying root causes of deficiencies in quality, service, and efficiency

PROFESSIONAL EXPERIENCE

BENET HEALTHCARE   1976–Present
Manila, the Philippines (1991–Present)
Vice President/General Manager, Philippines Operations

Manage major medical/industrial garment manufacturing operation, with full P&L responsibility for multiple sites employing 4,000+, as well as all aspects of international marketing, product development, and R&D. Concurrent responsibility for strategic planning, budgets, financial reporting, staffing, and quality control. Established both short-term goals and long-term vision, marshaling united team with highly focused approach to day-to-day business operations.

Top Quality Award: Facility Winner, 1995; Senior Examiner, 1994; Facility Finalist, 1993

- Analyzed operations, developed and won approval for multi-faceted initiative to improve budgetary control, financial reporting, and staffing procedures.
  Result: Reversed negative cash flow to positive position in only one year.
- Evaluated staffing requirements and reduced expatriate staff from 5 to 2, reassigned underperforming staff to more suitable positions, and recruited highly qualified local staff.
  Result: Saved $750,000 annually and produced significantly more efficient and effective team.
- Identified root causes of quality defects and benchmarked competitors, with goal of being the best.
  Result: Improved quality 500%, reducing defects from 13,000 per million to 2,000 per million.
- Recognized local technical strengths and advocated locally managed R&D effort to management.
  Result: Established R&D effort which cut product-to-market time two-thirds from 18 to 6 months.
- Demonstrated superior local ability to relate to customers in Hong Kong, the Philippines, and India.
  Result: Customized marketing strategy for PacRim, producing significant increase in regional sales.
- Examined operations and developed cost reduction strategies sustainable for the long-term.
  Result: Reduced production costs by 22% over four years.

126

CHICAGO, ILLINOIS   **(1990–1991)**
Plant Manager, Specialized Medical Garments Division

Requested to take short-term assignment to evaluate viability of operation and provide recommendations regarding its retention or disposal. Managed all aspects of OEM marketing and manufacturing of medical and industrial garments.

- Analyzed staffing requirements across-the-board and implemented changes indicated.
  Result: Lowered personnel costs by reducing staff count 40% and hiring temporaries at lower rates.
- Examined production floor activities and devised improved, more efficient processes.
  Result: Reduced production costs by 30% within the first year.
- Trained management team in theory and practical applications of process changes.
  Result: Produced management team capable of sustaining reduced costs, improved quality and efficiency.
- Championed reestablishment of industrial customer as well as medical customer.
  Result: Introduced a significant new profit center to the operation.

SAVANNAH, GEORGIA   **(1976–1990)**
Plant General Manager, Plastics Operation (1980–1990)

Directed 50 million pound annual PVC production operations employing state-of-the-art extrusion and blending equipment to produce blood and IV solution containers to stringent quality standards.

- Lowered operational costs by $10 million over period of ten years.
- Improved product quality 100%.
- Converted entire operation from manual to automated systems, using highly sophisticated, leading edge equipment to reduce costs while improving quality.
- Earned three Technical Awards for Processing, Special Machinery, and Design in recognition of innovative contributions to cost reduction and quality improvement.

Human Resource Manager (1976–1980)

Held comprehensive responsibility for human resource functions for 2,500 population plant, managing recruitment, salary administration, AAP, EEO, workforce strategic planning, terminations, training and executive development, and plant safety.

- Conducted in-depth analysis and revision of position descriptions and rankings, implementing new system in tandem with campaign to ensure understanding and acceptance by both management and staff.
- Introduced Quality Improvement Process System emphasizing training and leadership.
- Facilitated availability of up-to-date, timely information for senior management through development and implementation of routine communication package.
- Pioneered Executive Development Program which evaluated management team and set in motion succession planning process.

EDUCATION

B.S. - Business & Accounting, Harvard University

PROFESSIONAL AFFILIATIONS

Board Member, Association of Philippines Medical Suppliers
Board Member, American Trade Council

MANUFACTURING EXECUTIVE

JOHN H. SMITH

316 Walnut Drive ◆ Media, PA 19063
610-444-2374 ◆ E-mail: jhsmith@greatnet.com

An experienced division manager with superior strengths in production, operations, scheduling, material handling, purchasing and general management. Complete P&L responsibility in a variety of production environments.

Superior knowledge of sophisticated manufacturing and control techniques in demanding environments. Demonstrated success at turning around stagnant operations, increasing both sales and profitability.

Took specialty products plant from a $1.7 million loss to a $1.4 million profit over a 16 month period.

Increased plant availability from 62% to 93% by instituting a structured production planning program.

Grew new division from $2.4 million to $46 million and from 1 to 6 products in 4 years.

Bachelor of Science • Drexel University • Industrial Engineering
Graduated Magna Cum Laude

PROFESSIONAL EXPERIENCE

1983 to Present   **REAL WORLD CORPORATION**
VICE PRESIDENT - PLASTICS DIVISION - West Chester, PA (1995 to Present)
Full P&L responsibility for three plants manufacturing reinforced plastic materials. Implemented an entrepreneurship mentality so that action becomes automatic in a results-oriented atmosphere.

- *Revitalized poorly performing plants, increasing revenues from $47 million to $54 million in 1 year.*
- *Developed a quality control program with tracking procedures that reduced customer complaints from 13% under previous management to less than 2%.*
- *Introduced new scheduling techniques and automated equipment, increasing overall productivity by nearly 21% and eliminating backorders that exceeded 1.2 million pieces.*

GENERAL MANAGER - PROTECTION PRODUCTS DIVISION - Scranton, PA (1991 to 1995)
Full P&L responsibility for Protection Products Division. Brought in to turn around a poorly operated facility and return to profitability. Assignment was accomplished in 16 months.

- *Achieved #2 in market share and took sales from $14 million to $46 million during 4.5 year tenure.*
- *Received "General Manager of the Year" award after increasing production by 17% and plant availability from 74% to 92%.*

PLANT MANAGER - MOLDED PRODUCTS DIVISION - Binghamton, NY (1987-1991)
Directed all production and plant operations. Selected for position before more senior managers due to proven ability to correct production problems and improve productivity.

- *Developed and executed a production plan that increased output from 46,000 to 64,000 units per month with less than 3% in additional manufacturing expense..*
- *Initiated a public auction method for obsolete vehicle and equipment disposal. Increased salvage value more than 400% over previously used "sealed bid" method.*

PLANT MANAGER - CABLE AND APPARATUS DIVISION - Altoona, PA (1983-1987)
Responsible for all production, quality control, material control, and equipment/tool maintenance.

- *Implemented systematized procedures for purchasing which achieved economies of more than 3 times any previous efforts. Improved safety record by reducing on-the-job accidents by 74%.*

1979 to 1983   **BAYSIDE CORPORATION**
OPERATIONS MANAGER - SAFETY PRODUCTS GROUP - Orlando, FL
Developed/executed annual and long-range production plans, and assured a smooth manufacturing operation.

- *Maintained consistent flow of raw materials and subcontracted components during an energy crisis.*

128

MARKETING EXECUTIVE

FREDERICK KIDD

987 Anderson Hill, Boston, MA 02127

CAREER OBJECTIVE

Senior Vice President of Sales and Marketing, Palmby Industries

PROFESSIONAL SUMMARY

Eleven years of proven success in sales and marketing for industry leaders in the computer accessories and communications equipment fields.

EXPERIENCE

Marketing Manager, VirusFree Products, Melrose, Massachusetts (1989–Present)

* Recruited and trained all-new sales team
* Led this team to #1 rank in organization within 18 months
* Accepted CEO's challenge to "implement all-new strategies and completely re-organize" sales offices
* Increased annual revenues from $500,000 to $18 million over four years as a result of this reorganization campaign
* Created powerful advertising and merchandising campaigns credited with 43% increase in percentage of market share.
* With Head of Engineering, chaired committee charged with overhauling price structures
* Resulting price lists led to single most profitable year in company history
* "Jump In" campaign for new line of virus detection software won major industry award (1994)

Marketing Associate, Plax Corporation, Billerica, Massachusetts (1988–1989)

* Launched most successful new product line in company history.

Account Executive, VendWay, South Boston, Massachusetts (1988)

* Met one-year quota within four months of accepting the job.

EDUCATION

Bachelor's degree in politics from August College, Stratford, Connecticut (1987)

MARKETING EXECUTIVE
EXECUTIVE SUMMARY FOR MEL JONES

To: Mel Jones
Fr: Anita Smith

It was great to talk to you recently. Here are some of my career highlights.

You mentioned that you are looking for someone who is "comfortable operating in a high-growth environment and making contributions almost immediately."

- **I OFFER:** 17 years of executive, marketing and sales experience for companies that grew from as low as $1 million to as high as $46 million; skilled at training employees, building sales territories and negotiating profitable contracts.

You mentioned that you are looking for "a hands-on problem-solver."

- **I OFFER:** Deep experience in setting up procedures, organizing nationwide subsidiaries and boosting bottom line profits at 39% margins.

You mentioned your organization's "broad base and far-flung operations:"

- **I OFFER:** Experience in directing up to 610 employees in fifteen locations throughout eight states.

Anita Smith • 765 Main Street • Salem, MA 01970 • 555/555-5555

MARKETING EXECUTIVE

Jane Smith § 888 School Street § Wilmington, DE 19898 § 555/555-5555

SALES & MARKETING MANAGEMENT EXECUTIVE

Therapeutic Equipment and Instruments for the Health Care Industry

20+ years of demonstrated success generating marketshare, growth, and profits for nationwide sales and service organizations, including over 16 years in the health care industry. Specialist in pressure reduction and relief products; co-inventor of patented pressure reduction device. Accustomed to full P&L responsibility and management of multi-million dollar sales budgets, supervision of up to 50 employees, and management of dealer networks up to 400.

Management Approach

- Strategic view of the marketplace utilizing in-depth understanding of marketing/sales and precise positioning of programs and products to achieve results.
- Strong focus on teamwork and performance-based compensation and recognition.

Demonstrated Ability To:

- Ignite stagnant operations; mobilize sales force/dealer network with performance incentives.
- Pioneer innovative and profit-producing promotions and sales training programs.
- Build strong business partnerships, maximize account retention, earn customer loyalty.
- Control costs and produce tremendous savings through insightful market analysis, adept handling of dealer receivable problems, minimizing employee turnover, and integration/streamlining of functional areas.

PROFESSIONAL EXPERIENCE

CAMUNET CORPORATION   1991–Present

$28 million medical device manufacturer specializing in blood pressure and sterilization monitoring equipment.

National Sales Manager

Direct and motivate staff of 4 regional managers, 40 hospital sales representatives, and 4 alternate site specialists; manage and coordinate nationwide 400-dealer network. Responsible for U.S. domestic sales budget of over $23M, dealer promotions and trade show coordination, annual sales forecasts, and national account performance. Coordinate all activities with operations, corporate management, and marketing.

- On First Day of Hire: Saved company $320,000 by providing unique marketing information.
- Instituted highly successful "put it in writing" sales representative quota system requiring 95% or better performance to earn bonus; established company's first performance and sales force recognition policy; initiated company-wide consultative selling training program. Resulted in:

  - **1st Qtr. sales increase of 22%, highest percentage increase in company in 10 yrs.—1995**
  - **$2MM sales increase (10%)—1994**
  - **$1.2MM sales increase (7%)—1993**
  - **$2MM sales increase (13.7%)—1992**
  - **$1.7MM sales increase (11%)—1991**

Gross margin jumped from 52% to 59% from 1993 to 1994.

- Accomplished singular $600,000 sales increase for 1992 as direct result of convincing management to allow entire sales force to sell all products.
- Established greater accountability and better reporting at regional and representative levels through creation of automated field sales reporting system and new target account system.

– Enhanced customer feedback and satisfaction by creating President's Advisory Council.
– Dramatically improved dealer relations and sales.
– Established Camunet as a key supplier vs. larger companies throughout network.
– Pioneered new company promotions with distributors in hospital/alternate site markets.
– Created and implemented first major dealer incentive programs.

FREEMAN RESOURCES, INC. (purchased by Cyclodex in 1993)   1990–1991

$35 MM company offering a full line of anesthesia and respiratory disposable products.

Eastern Area Sales Manager

Directed and motivated staff of 7 sales representatives with budget of $9 million.

– Region of Year in 1991.
– Hired and coached two over-quota performers; kept 5 of 7 territories on quota.
– Settled two $1 Million+ dealer receivable problems within 30 days by communicating directly with accounts, helping them rectify internal computer system problems responsible for delays.

TRAMWELL, INC.   1987–1990

$240MM supplier of kinetic therapy equipment including therapeutic beds and devices for low air loss and profusion therapy for pain relief in multiple trauma patients. Significant contributor to volume explosion from $58MM at hire.

District Sales Manager

Managed staff of 37 sales/clinical consultants and service technician personnel within 3 service centers, with full responsibility for P&L and coordination of technicians and contracts.

– Directly negotiated 19 new accounts within 90 days of hire for new volume of $1.8M.
– Grew district sales volume from $2 MM to $9 MM within 2 years.
– Achieved lowest turnover of personnel nationally, 1989–1990.
– Boosted sales 58% first year despite loss of largest billing account to national contract award.

HIGHLIGHTS OF EARLIER EXPERIENCE

VEERO MEDICAL PRODUCTS   1979–1987

Area Sales Manager: Led all other sales areas in average percent to quota performance and gross margin dollar average from July 1981; average increase of 24% per year. Area of Year 1984; Runner-Up 1982. Pioneered programs to integrate sales and service companies in region.

BARBER LABORATORIES   1978–1979

Territorial Manager: Converted King Hospital account to Bybend product; converted Bickford ER to total use of IV catheter (annual volume $200K) and UDW Solution (annual volume $500K).

AMBER COMMUNICATIONS & ELECTRONICS, INC.   1974–1978

Zone Sales Manager: Best Annual Quota Performance—150% (1975); Salesman of the Month, January 1976; Best Performance for Service/Maintenance Contract Sales from 1975–1978.

EDUCATION

B.S. Political Science, California State University
Sales Management and Prospecting Course, FFG Sales Training Systems

MARKETING EXECUTIVE

JOHN SMITH
456 Main Street
Farmington, CT 06156
555-555-5555
555-555-6666

Senior marketing professional with a proven record of superior results.

OBJECTIVE: Obtain a position as Vice President of Marketing for Kansas Technologies.

CAREER KEYS:
- Highly skilled in sales and marketing management.
- 16 years of experience as a Manager and Director of Sales, Operations and Marketing for companies with annual revenues ranging from $5 million to $4 billion.
- Praised as "marketing genius" by *National Retailer* magazine (July 16, 1994).
- Particularly adept at new consumer product development - assisted in the development of 34 new consumer products yielding a total of $120 million in revenue over the past nine years.
- Personally conceived and launched new line of household cleaning products with revenues totaling $62 million annually.
- Launched effective market research campaigns for over two dozen projects.
- Skilled at cross functional team leadership.
- Have supervised sales forces ranging in size from 7 to 35.
- Named "Sales Manager of the Year" in 1986.
- Gifted (and self-taught) graphic artist.
- Created six award-winning product and/or package designs.
- Praised by Mel Harper, president of Isley Associates for "consistent ability to establish products as market leaders in particular segments."

EMPLOYMENT HISTORY:

1992–Present   BJ Consumer Products, Hartford, Connecticut—Director of Marketing

1986–1991   Isley Associates, Boston, Massachusetts—Director of Sales, Operations, and Marketing

1983–1986   Mimeo Tech Services, Peabody, Massachusetts—Sales Manager

1981–1982   List Services Associates, Danvers, Massachusetts, Sales Representative (promoted to Sales Manager after only six months)

EDUCATION: B.A. in English, John Quincy Adams University, Quincy, MA (1979)

M.B.A., Melvin Business School (1981).

MARKETING EXECUTIVE

ELLEN MARKWAY
18 Craigie Street / Cambridge, MA 02139
555/555-5555 (days) / 555-555-5556 (evenings)

Areas of Expertise:

12 years of experience in developing important new markets for multi-million-dollar technology and business equipment companies. Proven expertise in sales and marketing management with particular skills in:

•Territory development •Sales force training
•Advertising •Trade shows •Customer service

Professional Experience:

HANDIWAY DATA SYSTEMS, Norwood MA, 1986–Present.
Recruited as salesperson; named VP of Sales in 1988.
  • Responsible for marketing operations in 9 territories, doubling sales and achieving company's top profit ranking.
  • Personally led three-rep team in closing Heritage Days Amusement Park sale, representing 375 customized point of purchase cash management systems. Worked with senior management to develop terms and system configurations that overcame bid of a major competitor. Deal represented $3.5 million in revenue.
  • Praised by (now-retired) predecessor for "superior customer service, training, and territory development skills."

ROCKINGHAM BUSINESS EQUIPMENT, Cambridge MA, 1985–1986.
Account Executive. Exceeded quota each year.

PLAZA SYSTEMS, Melrose MA, 1985.
Named "Rookie of the Year." Developed new data entry system to track prospects; this was adopted company-wide within three months.

Education:

Bachelor's degree in Business Administration Spellman College, Benton, NE.
Graduated 3rd in 158-person class. Carried 3.82 grade point average.

Business Computer Applications:

MS Word, Excel, Lotus 1-2-3, Netscape, PalmPilot, etc.

MARKETING EXECUTIVE (SUMMARY FORMAT)

BOB SMITH
786 Melody Way, Dallas, Texas 75265
* 555/555-8772 (days) * 555/555-9122 (evenings)

BRIEF RESUME HIGHLIGHTS

Carwell Industries seeks a "Tested Marketing Professional."

BOB SMITH:

19 years of experience in marketing, direct sales and executive management in both start-up and Fortune 1000 environments.

Carwell Industries seeks a "senior marketer" with "background in electronics and computer sales."

BOB SMITH:

Record of superior results at Deaton Data Systems and Berrigan Group. Skilled in marketing and selling manufactured consumer products and representing multiple manufacturers; special focus on electronic, mechanical, computer and high-tech products and services.

Carwell Industries seeks a marketing professional willing to "lead our team to deliver superior results to customers and stockholders."

BOB SMITH:

Oversaw marketing and sales team of professionals with $45 million in annual sales.

RECOMMENDATION:

We should meet to discuss this position.

MARKETING AND MEDIA EXECUTIVE

JANE SMITH

62 Essex Street, Boston, MA 02127
555/555-5555 (Business)
555/555-6666 (Message)
555/555-7777 (Home)

SENIOR EXECUTIVE

Sales & Marketing / Media Services

Customer-focused, profit-driven executive with 14 years' distinguished success leading entrepreneurial-spirited company from start-up to $25MM in annual sales in fiercely competitive market. Proven performance in strategic planning, business development, new product roll-outs, and establishment of brand/name recognition and loyalty for diverse industries. Versatile and innovative problem solver who views thorough research of customer's needs in relation to company's products and services as key to success.

"The practical man is the adventurer, the investigator, the believer in research, the asker of questions, the man who refuses to believe that perfection has been attained... There is no thrill or joy in merely doing that which anyone can do... It is always safe to assume, not that the old way is wrong, but that there may be a better way."—Henry R. Harrower

DEMONSTRATED CAPABILITIES TO

- *Maintain competitive edge by continuously defining and updating knowledge of the customer.*
- *Translate research insights into creative and highly effective marketplace applications.*
- *Build long-term customer bonds to brands and services.*
- *Galvanize sales teams; devise and implement unique ways to support field sales force.*
- *Define the value/function relationship for media and marketing investments.*
- *Expand lines, launch new products, penetrate new markets, and boost bottom line profits.*

PROFESSIONAL EXPERIENCE

WESTON CORPORATION, Weston, MA   **1980–Present**

Executive Vice President

Launched media service with goal of refining marketing disciplines utilized by large national advertisers and advertising agencies for retail-oriented needs of local and regional companies. With full responsibility for all company operations inclusive of strategic planning, business development, finance, sales, and account management, grew sales from zero to $25MM annually and established industry trademark of service, brand building, and consumer recognition.

- *Built diverse client base spanning retail, pharmaceutical, entertainment, publishing, gaming, food and beverage, packaged goods, travel, and political advertisers.*
- *Transformed ABC's PermaDee brands from sporadic spot TV advertiser to substantial network marketer and planned successful roll-out of three new OTC brands.*
- *Delivered 50% increase in business for American Financial Corp., championing switch to radio advertising from print to promote 50+ services.*
- *Completely reorganized management of VeriBrite Brands' media buying effort and rolled out East Coast program, increasing business there by 200%.*

136

- *Introduced Betterway brand to broadcast promotion with such exceptional results 1996 broadcast budget and market list have been doubled.*
- *Negotiated regional cable sponsorships for CleanCare, enabling them to utilize major sports associations on local basis without funding exorbitant commercial TV costs, garnering 60% increase in brand recognition, and competing successfully with BGE Services in specific merchandising categories.*
- *Authored introduction and roll-out plans for Cedex's retail stores, exceeding all sales and traffic projections for each month of test and earning letter of commendation from client.*

COMMUNICATION CORPORATION OF AMERICA, INC., New York, NY   1977–1980

Vice President - Media Planning & Sales
Directed media planning and buying services for assigned accounts, developed planning strategies for new business presentations, and acted as liaison to advertising agency clients. Guided diverse accounts including RAVEN Group, Time Partners, and 1180 Products in media placement as primary investment within advertising plans expected to contribute substantially to sales and profitability.

- Authored strategy for and executed most successful roll-out in sweetened cereal category history, spurring MegaMill's purchase of ChewyGrain brand from Toro Group.

BERRIGAN ADVERTISING, Los Angeles, CA   1975–1977

Associate Media Director
Participated in new business development efforts and led team of 12 broadcast buyers. Developed management skills, gained experience with national retail accounts and exposure to promotional needs of corporate sales organization which could be tied into traditional media strategies.

- Ensured clients maintained competitive position with their advertising budgets, executed plans efficiently, and delivered results in terms of sales increases and profitability.
- Negotiated network television schedules for American Garments and Taco Planet.
- Performed all media planning functions and sports promotions for Northern California SipWay Bottlers.

CRENWAY ADVERTISING, Los Angeles, CA   1972–1975

Media Planner
Worked with United Foods and Consumer Products performing media research and planning with emphasis on development of objectives, media execution strategies, and rationales for media selection.

EDUCATION

B.A., University of Massachusetts, Amherst

MARKETING/OPERATIONS DIRECTOR

RICHARD J. BORARDI
889 Gates Avenue
San Francisco, CA 94930
(555)-555-5555

Executive experienced in general and sales management, sales marketing, strategic planning and new business development.

Doubled revenue (from $50 million to $100 million) in 12 months during flat market.

Increased financial performance from 32% to 101% of plan in 6 months.

Doubled revenue (from $30 million to $60 million) in 2 years.

Demonstrated success in take development and implementation of new processes that improve efficiency and productivity.

> *$2+ million annual savings achieved by restructuring specialist sales force.*
> *$150K (50%) reduction in base cost of region achieved within 1 year.*
> *Increased productivity 50% by reorganizing sales force.*

Recipient of numerous stock options, sales and management awards including 4 quarterly Top Manager Awards (#1 of 12 regions), Group Management Awards and #1 of 21 zone offices of 11 consecutive months.

Innovative leader adept at building teams with the ability to think creatively and design profitable organizational changes. Keen understanding of customer needs and optimal work environment to ensure maximum performance from employees.

B.S., Marketing, Chicago University, 1982.

Numerous management courses including 2-month VVM Global Management Development.

Age, 37. Hobbies include tennis, sailing, skiing, and martial arts.

PROFESSIONAL EXPERIENCE

UNITED CIRCUIT PRODUCTS (Present)
Director, Northern United States, Boston, MA (1996–Present)
- Manage sales, marketing, operations ad engineering functions for 23 states, staff of 70 in $250 million business.
- Created game changing processes for sales, operations and strategic marketing teams.

Region Manager, Medical Management Group, San Francisco, CA (1995–1996)
- Directed $100+ million sales in Southwest Region (largest in US).
- 50% reduction in customer disputes achieved through cross functional team ownership.

Regional Product Manager, Medical Management Group, Los Angeles, CA (1993–1995)
- Managed 22 technical sales specialists in support of sales and marketing functions for western US.
- Created and implemented complete marketing plan for product launch.

Zone Sales Manager, Medical Management Group, Dallas, TX (1990–1993)
- Managed culturally diverse sales force and service managers/administrative personnel for $60 million sales.
- Achieved Top 20% of zones and exceeded targets in 1991 and 1992.

Product Specialist, Medi Management Group, Boise, ID (1989–1990)
- #2 of 24 specialists in the US for computer topography (CT)/magnetic resonance (MR) products.

CORWAY CORPORATION (1983–1989)
Southwest Region Sales Manager, Houston, TX (1986-1989)
- Presidents Club, 1988 (required 130%+ performance, 2 10 12 regions qualified).

Systems Specialist, Roanoke, VA (1981-1982)
- #1 of 9 system specialists in the US, Presidents Club, 1985.

Sales Representative, Pasadena, CA (1983-1984)
- #2 of 60 sales representatives in the US for division, Presidents Club, 1984.

138

MEDIA AND MARKETING SPECIALIST

BILL JOHNSON
78765 Greenway Avenue
Los Angeles, CA 90022
555/555-5555

CAREER GOAL   Director of Communications and Media Relations for Bullin Corporation

SUMMARY

Superior problem-solving, training, and writing abilities.

Adept at media relations, with a deep contact base of print and broadcast journalists both nationally and in regional (West Coast) markets.

Skilled in organizational operations, fund-raising and public relations, with particular skills in corporate training, staff supervision and media-related coaching and consulting.

AWARDS

+ Bode Award for Excellence in Copywriting.
+ Selected as "Speaker of the Year," Northern California Speaker's Assembly.
+ Named "Top Presenter" at conclusion of 1996 Direct Marketing Society conference.

EXPERIENCE

14 years of experience (1984-present) as Associate, Executive Vice President, Consultant, Marketing Director and Executive Director for Mann Associates (Pomona, CA), a for-profit direct-marketing firm specializing in contract work for major philanthropic and charitable organizations.

Hailed as a "miracle worker" by National Direct Mail Foundation's in-house publication (July, 1995) for resuscitation of Verron House Outreach Center fundraising operations after negative media attention focused on past problems.

Developed compelling written appeals for major nonprofit organizations, one of which set an organizational record for response rate by a direct-mail piece within its field.

As a consultant, responsible for regional campaign operations for Save the Forests, Inc., supervising a staff of 33 personnel and raising public donations of $35 million.

MEDIA MANAGEMENT

A seasoned, experienced developer of positive press attention with specialty in crisis management.

Instrumental in development of balanced and positive press coverage for clients.

Media campaign for United Minority College Council described as "virtually flawless" by The New York Times *(11/13/96).*

Personally conducted press conferences and developed balanced press releases during negative press cycles, leading to positive outcomes for: American Hospital Guild, Green Group, and the American Library Foundation.

BOOKS

Author of six published books, including:

+ *Media Relations, 101* (Hangworth Publications, 1996)
+ *Dealing with Difficult Media* (Hangworth Publications, 1994)
+ *Media Crisis Management* (Cashman Press, 1990)

EDUCATION

Bachelor's degree, English, Central Illinois College (1983)

Member, American Society of Journalists and Authors

MEDIA RELATIONS

JOHN H. SMITH

316 Walnut Lane ◆ Media, PA 19063
610-444-2374

An increasing track record in sales, public relations, broadcasting, and general operations in professional baseball. A tireless worker accustomed to varied responsibilities, long hours and short deadlines. Proficient in developing excellent relationships with players, management, support personnel, press and fans.

Sales, public relations, and game-day promotional activities.

- Top salesperson on a 5 person staff. Helped increase spring training ticket sales by 4%. Increased annual "day camp" revenues by 100%.
- Created weekly press releases featuring player profiles and stats for local newspapers. Arranged all player promotional interviews for the Texas Rangers farm system.
- Arranged all player appearances at promotional and community events for the Texas Rangers top prospects.
- Planned and conducted on-field presentations and pre-game promotional activities involving regional corporations and youth softball/baseball leagues.
- Conceived and implemented the first "kids run around the bases" during the annual day camp celebration. More than 1,000 kids and faculty participated in the promotion.

Broadcasting baseball games and post game radio programs.

- Announced 70 home games for the Charlotte Rangers without missing one game.
- Recognized in the Charlotte Sun Herald as "a very professional (PA) announcer" for the Rangers.
- Hosted the weekly "Rangers Roundup Show" broadcast by two Charlotte radio stations.

Operations intern with the Philadelphia Phillies and the Clearwater Phillies.

- Assured that broadcaster, media and press boxes were prepared and organized for broadcasts during all of the Philadelphia Phillies spring training home games.
- Developed knowledge of spring training ticket sales, met with media during game day, and assisted broadcasters with statistical information.

Record of conscientious applications, reliability, and loyalty in past positions. Possess a high-energy level, with an ability to organize work and resolve problems which arise in day-to-day activities.

EDUCATION

Bachelor of Science, Public Relations, Plymouth State College, Plymouth, New Hampshire

PROFESSIONAL EXPERIENCE

Director of Media Relations/Public Address Announcer
CHARLOTTE RANGERS, April 97 to Present

Operations Intern
PHILADELPHIA/CLEARWATER PHILLIES, January 97 to March 97

Customer Service Representative
WILSON'S DEPARTMENT STORE, June 96 to January 97

MEDICAL EXECUTIVE

JOHN SMITH

888 Southlane Road
Chicago, IL 60609
(555) 555-1111—Home
(555) 555-2222—Business
(555) 555-3333—Mobile Phone

SENIOR EXECUTIVE Medical and Orthopedic Products Industries

Dynamic start-up, turnaround, and acquisitions specialist with proven track record delivering increased sales, profits, and shareholder value to organizations throughout U.S., Europe, and the Pacific Rim. Expertise spans Sales/Marketing, Finance, Operations, Human Resources, R&D, Regulatory Compliance, and Inventory/Quality Control. Proficient in international business practices and regulations; conversant in French.

Demonstrated ability to:

Implement aggressive reorganization, expansion, and management initiatives to turn around declining or stagnant operations and produce record sales and profits

Identify and capitalize upon market opportunities to reposition companies via expanded and restructured product lines, creative pricing and bundling strategies

Develop lucrative international networks and strategic alliances, open new markets

Introduce innovative training programs to ignite sales organizations to peak performance

Foster a customer-focused organizational culture of responsiveness and productivity

Improve bottom line by maximizing efficiency and quality while minimizing costs

PROFESSIONAL EXPERIENCE

BASIL, INC., Chicago, Illinois   1994–Present
$48+MM international manufacturer of reconstructive instruments/implants/sterilization cases.
Vice President

Recruited to spearhead turnaround of corporation by planning an Acquisitions Strategy and reorganizing Marketing, Sales, R&D, and Customer Service functions. Concurrently charged with laying groundwork for and implementing new international division.

- Grew company to $48MM from $12MM in three years and established Basil as global competitor.

- Developed effective pricing strategy to accomplish the following in first year:
  - *Tripled operating income from $700K to $2.3MM.*
  - *Converted net operating loss of $54K to net income of $1MM+.*
  - *Boosted sales 50% from $12MM to $18MM; doubled orders from $12MM to $24MM.*

- Repositioned company and expanded both present opportunities and future potential:
  - *Initiated successful IPO effort with Wall Street; company will go public within two years.*
  - *Transformed from an order taker to an aggressive marketing organization composed of several companies providing large and small instruments in Reconstructive, Trauma, Arthroscopy, Spinal, and sterilization cases.*
  - *Developed contacts with international companies in joint effort to put a manufacturing plant overseas.*

- Implemented initiatives to streamline inventory management and restructure product lines:
  - *Reduced inventory by 22% through elimination of obsolete items and converting customers to quarterly vs. monthly ordering schedule.*
  - *Discontinued unprofitable product lines; launched five major instrument systems.*

- Enhanced corporate image and customer relationships:
  - *Developed customer-focused key account strategy from R&D to product release.*

141

- *Remodeled offices and support materials to project company in, not going out of, business.*
- *Completely revamped customer interface in one year.*

MARQUETTE, INC. (ESSEX CORPORATION), San Francisco, CA   1992–1994
$600MM international orthopedic products company.
Director/General Manager, Medical Products Group
   Hiring in to head up Custom Products division, quickly launched seven new implant product lines and reduced inventory by 30%, earning fast-track promotion in five months to Director, New Products. Transformed division into new working group, which was $225,000 ahead of plan at departure. With P&L responsibility for $80MM:

- Boosted sales 25% from $64MM to $80MM in two years, operating income by 30%.

- Pioneered numerous sales and pricing innovations including:
  - *Bundling survey program yielding product groupings for conceptual sales.*
  - *Creative sales tools including techno-marketing support, sample cases, product profilers.*
  - *Completely reorganized and updated sales training program.*
  - *Creative pricing programs designed to facilitate winning National Account contracts.*

MEDIDEX, INC., Los Angeles, CA   1987–1992
$1.1 billion international company marketing trauma, powered instruments, soft goods, spinal, reconstructive, arthroscopic, and suture anchor products.
Marketing Manager
   With P&L responsibility for $30MM, traveled to Europe to launch products globally. Developed surveys and bundling programs. Declined promotion to Director to complete MBA.

- Consistently surpassed plan and delivered 20%+ annual sales and gross profit increases.

MULTI MEDICAL, INC., Austin, TX   1986–1987
$30MM international general medical products OEM supplier to Barber, Medical Arts, Burbank Technologies, etc.
Director of Marketing
   With full P&L responsibility, directed all marketing efforts and conducted international negotiations in Australia and New Zealand. In only one year, boosted Operating Income 23%:

- Grew sales 34%, including major OR contract yielding $1 million.

- Introduced disposable shoe cover line bringing in $500K first year at 45% GP.

EARLY EXPERIENCE HIGHLIGHTS

Lines Industries, Director of Corporate Marketing: As youngest Corporate Director in company history, increased sales 24% and GP from 22 to 35%; reduced costs by 17%.

Invall Industries, Regional Sales Manager: Increased sales 24%+ every year, surpassed all quotas.

HospiTex, Sales Representative: Quintupled sales and initiated Textile Cost Management program introducing "conceptual" selling to dramatically increase sales.

EDUCATION

M.B.A.—Parker Graduate School of Management, Indianapolis, Indiana 1991
M.A.—Audiology, Illinois University, Chicago, Illinois, Full Scholarship 1978
B.A.—Speech and Hearing, Chicago University, Chicago, Illinois, 1977

PROFESSIONAL AFFILIATIONS

Illinois Medical Manufacturing Council
Board Member of Essex Center

MORTGAGE BANKER

CAROL ANNE WESLEY

216 West Juniper Avenue ■ Clarksburg, OH 23622
709-559-3725 (W) ■ 709-865-2298 (H)

Experience manager in mortgage banking, including loan processing, closing and underwriting. Knowledgeable in conventional, VA, FHA, FHLMC, FNMA, prime and subprime markets, retention and credit risk scoring.

Broad background working with retail, broker, wholesale and conduit operations.

Characterized as being an analytical planner, possessing superior customer sensitivity, interpersonal and communication skills. A quality- and detail-oriented manager capable of assessing problem situations and implementing corrective actions.

PROFESSIONAL EXPERIENCE

NATIONAL MORTGAGE SERVICES   1988 - Present
Manager, Residential Loans
Manage Underwriting, Retention, and Subprime Loans (a-c paper) Departments. Direct staff of 38 with responsibility for all credit decisions on residential transactions in accordance with FNMA, FHLMC, VA, and FHA guidelines for purchases and refinances in all 50 states. Have loan approval authority for up to $4 million.

- *Exceeded unit goals by nearly 20% and reduced turnaround time on pre-approvals from 24-48 hours to 6-12 hours in home equity underwriting.*
- *Developed a "Credit First" underwriting function within the sales department which permitted loan officers to take more efficient applications and decreased customer fallout by more than 10%.*
- *Implemented new procedures for processors, allowing processors to handle in excess of 100 loans with an average of 90% being turned around within 30 days.*
- *Led multi-departmental task team for a FHLMC reverification project which prevented the company from having to repurchase approximately 180 loans from the agencies which were involved. Savings exceeded $4.7 million.*

TAMPET FEDERAL SAVINGS BANK   1978-1988
Loan Manager
Responsible for the processing of applications from origination through loan approval. Assured compliance with appropriate underwriting agency guidelines. Coordinated activities with customers, brokers, and settlement companies to expedite the loan process and settlements.

- *Increased funding in the closing department by streamlining the process into three main functions -- pre-settlement, scheduling and packaging.*
- *Developed a follow-up procedure for processors which reduced cycle time from 120 days in process to 45 days to approval.*
- *Received "The President's Award" two consecutive years for the most outstanding individual performance and highest departmental productivity level.*

EDUCATION

Master of Business Administration - Finance major - Ohio State University

Bachelor of Business Administration - Business and Economics - Ohio State University

SELECTED TRAINING PROGRAMS

Introduction to Fair Lending/Diversity Training ■ Advanced Workshop on the Self-Employed Borrower FHLMC
Credit Score and Layered Risk FHLMC ■ Loan Prospector Training ■ Underwriting Flexibilities FNMA

MULTI-INDUSTRY SENIOR EXECUTIVE

JANE JONES
456 Main Street, Ipswich MA 01938
555/555-5555

Proven leader with demonstrated ability to achieve results, develop subordinates and motivate employees.

QUALIFICATIONS

15 years experience in positions as President, General Manager, and Director of Marketing for corporations with between $20 million and $220 million in annual revenue.

Supported domestic and international pharmaceutical, publishing, and consulting operations.

EMPLOYMENT

1993–Present

Mellison Pharmaceuticals, St. Louis, MO
President
Took over troubled company following tampering incident and attendant negative media coverage. Increased revenue from $160 million to $220 million. Led firm to an operating profit for the first time in three years; not a single year in the red under my tenure.

1991–1993

Comway Publishing, Chicago, IL
General Manager
Promoted from Director of Marketing. Developed successful direct mail campaign that increased company revenues by 41%. Eliminated underperforming editorial positions; reduced personnel expenditures by 37% while increasing revenues from $11 million to $20 million.

1982–1991

Porter Group Consulting, Chicago, IL
Partner
Offered acquisition and business advice to clients in a variety of industries, including publishing, metals fabrication and processing, and pharmaceuticals. Recommended acquisition of underperforming aluminum plant that went from $2 million loss to $8 million profit in three years. Offered support and logistical advice on Masser Corporations acquisition of Ellis Publishing. Led partners in annual billings for three consecutive years, and seven out of ten overall.

**EDUCATION
AND HONORS**

Leslie Collins College (Smalltown, IL), 1979
Bachelor's degree in Business Administration
Furillo University (Brooklyn, NY), 1981
M.B.A.

Local Chairman, Minority Business Council.
Named "Executive of the Year" by *Pharmaceuticals Today* magazine.

OTHER

Married (11 years); three children. Avid horsewoman.

NATIONAL SALES MANAGER

JOHN SMITH

123 Main Street
Boston, MA 02127
555-555-5555

Objective: To become National Sales Manager for RightCo.

OVERVIEW

Skilled in all areas of business operations, planning and management with particular skills in sales, marketing, personnel management, contract negotiations and customer relations.

Owned and operated an athletic equipment operation with $12 million annual sales that employed a 35-member sales force. (Sold the business in 1992.)

Over fifteen years of experience as a sales manager and entrepreneur. Excel in transforming mediocre performers into polished, persuasive contributors.

SALES MANAGEMENT ACHIEVEMENTS

- Hired team of overachievers at underachieving athletic equipment firm that led to three record-breaking years in a row (after seven below-quota years under previous management).
- Trained each member of my 35-member sales force.
- Taught effective prospecting skills to both new and old hires on an ongoing basis; monitored progress toward predetermined prospecting goals.
- Selected external training programs for sales force; negotiated favorable contracts with these vendors. Mentored three entry-level salespeople whose incomes eventually exceeded $125,000 per year. Proficient in Microsoft Office, Lotus 1-2-3, ACT!, and other popular computer programs.

ANALYTICAL STRENGTHS

Skilled at planning, forecasting, and policymaking. Named "Most Efficient Executive of the Year" at Beeson Associates. Trained in business forecasting, statistical analysis, and performance analysis through management programs at FirstCo.

ORAL AND WRITTEN COMMUNICATIONS

Exceptional in-person presentation skills. Comfortable in coaching, counseling, and assisting others in career turnarounds. Skilled at establishing workable written and electronic record systems.

EMPLOYMENT HISTORY

Throughout career, have exceeded expectations and specialized in the overattainment of important organizational goals.

REEGO ATHLETIC, New York, New York (1993–1997), Owner and Operator

BEESON ASSOCIATES, Chicago, Illinois (1991–1993), National Sales Manager

FIRSTCO, New York, New York (1983–1991), Senior Sales Manager

HOLMS AND WATERS TRAINING, New York, New York (1981–1983). Sales Associate

EDUCATION

B.A., Politics, Proselli University, Somerville, Massachusetts, 1981.

NATIONAL SALES MANAGER/TRAINER

BILL SMITH
981 Church Street
Oak Brook, IL 60609

Objective: To become Vice President of Sales Management for Purchase Communications.

Summary of Qualifications Fifteen years experience in the development of motivational training services and executive leadership programs for major companies and charitable organizations. Currently ranked first out of 24 company trainers nationwide in total annual billings. Expert at leading and motivating employees, utilizing interpersonal bonding skills to make compelling presentations, and negotiating large domestic and international contracts.

PROFESSIONAL EXPERIENCE

1982–Present: <u>MGV Enterprises</u>, Oak Brook, IL
(Promoted in 1990 to:) Senior Trainer and Sales Consultant

I currently serve as the lead trainer and motivational speaker for this dynamic, high-growth communications and training firm.

Share national sales management responsibilities with company's founder and president, Melvin Forrest.

Deliver between 75 and 125 in-person presentations annually in the Midwest and Northeast, addressing paying audiences of between 50 and 500.

Personally responsible for sales of motivational seminars within my territory, and for delivering dynamic in-person presentations to decision makers.

Delivered total billings of $2.4 million in most recent fiscal year.

Have trained 17 of current 24 company trainers.

Described by seminar participants (including high-level executives within organizations) in written evaluations as:
* Dramatic * Exciting * Outspoken * Energetic * Powerful * Career-changing * Compelling
* Entrancing * Highly Motivating

1981–1982 <u>Joplin Magazine Group</u>, Chicago, IL
Sales Associate

I was the youngest Most Valuable Player in the history of the organization.

Education: B.S. in Communications, Mellini University, Chicago, IL, 1981.

OPERATIONS EXECUTIVE

John Smith
3165 Beacon Street
Boston, MA 02127
555/555-5555 (Home)
555/555-6666 (Business)

SENIOR EXECUTIVE: OPERATIONS / SALES / DISTRIBUTION / SERVICE & SUPPORT

High-energy executive with over 12 years' success optimizing operations, increasing revenues, reducing costs, and positioning communications systems company for worldwide leadership in fiercely competitive, rapidly evolving marketplace. Proven ability to expertly handle full P&L responsibility for multiple business units and guide strategic planning for multi-million dollar organizations. Recognized expert in development and implementation of successful operations systems.

Management Style focuses on interdepartmental teamwork and clearly articulated mission and values for buy-in of staff, field sales-support-installation force, and management at all levels.

Demonstrated Capabilities To:

★ Operationalize corporate vision and implement systems to manage explosive growth

★ Develop massive, nationwide installation/service networks in impossibly short timeframes

★ Exploit computer technology to maximize accessibility and usefulness of information

★ Create and implement comprehensive strategies to roll out innovative marketing concepts

★ Identify, recruit, and train potential leaders who consistently move into management

---

PROFESSIONAL EXPERIENCE

COMMUNICATIONS TECHNOLOGIES, Boston, MA   1983–Present
$250MM manufacturer and distributor of communications equipment.

Vice President of Operations (1995–Present)
Reporting to Senior Vice President of Sales and Distribution, lead team of seven regional Operations Directors in all aspects of distribution, installation, and management. Concurrently serve as Vice President of Eastern Region Operations, Vice President of Operations (national installation network), and Director of joint venture with antenna manufacturer.

★ Developed systems to handle 182% increase in sales revenues from 1995 to 1996:
  • Designed retailer commissions program interfacing three databases and bar code system.
  • Instituted sales reporting procedures for tracking by dealer, zip code, etc.
  • Implemented procedural systems for all sales channels including consumer electronics retailers, direct marketers, and regional telephone operating companies.

★ Held operating expenses to 82% of budgeted projections:
  • Implemented comprehensive system to manage purchasing function.
  • Analyzed operations and eliminated costly, inefficient ways of doing business.
  • Computerized and automated functions where applicable.

★ Took company from start-up to installation presence in 36 major U.S. markets:
  • Developed nationwide network of company-owned as well as subcontractor facilities.
  • Trained and motivated team of seven regional Operations Directors.

Vice President, Sales & Operations - Communications Local Outreach
(subsidiary of Communications Technologies) (1992–1995)
Reporting directly to President, managed company's $100MM revenue plan as well as Cleveland distribution facility's $25MM plan, with additional responsibility for various other business units within company. Coordinated national sales and marketing activities.

★   Expanded sales revenues on average by 20% per year:
   • Introduced first-ever revolving charge plan to dealer base, making $5K+ systems affordable with payments as low as $30 per month.
   • Launched frequent buyer program offering deeper discounts for dealers along with additional service perks.
   • Expanded marketing plan from strictly inbound 800# sales to an aggressive plan employing a nationwide force of outside sales representatives.

★   Limited operating expenses to 90% of budgeted projections and expanded net income by 11%.

Divisional Vice President—Eastern United States (1989–1992)
Reported to Vice President of Operations with full responsibility for $60MM revenue plan, management training program, and strategic planning for achievement of annual goals and objectives.

★   Led Eastern Region to become highest revenue producer in Corporation for 1992.

★   Exceeded budgeted revenue projections for both 1990 and 1992.

★   Developed high-caliber Directors through training and mentorship in leadership, decision-making, managerial style, techniques, and accountability.

Director of Operations—ST Denver (Subsidiary of Communications Technologies)
(1984–1989)
Recruited, trained, motivated, and supervised 6 middle managers and a staff of 30, with direct accountability to Divisional Vice President and oversight of 5 departments. Participated extensively in strategic and budgetary planning as well as financial controls and review.

★   Led division to position as highest revenue-producing operation in country.

★   Developed system of operational standards for implementation company-wide.

EDUCATION

B.S. Business Administration & Economics, University of Massachusetts, Amherst, June 1981

TECHNICAL SKILLS

MS Windows '95, Lotus 1-2-3, Excel, Wordperfect, Word, Powerpoint,
various database systems including Access

OPERATIONS EXECUTIVE

MELANIE GREEN
123 Main Street
New York, NY 10001

Operations Management Executive experienced in multi-plant manufacturing who achieved $2 million in annual cost savings, transferred 100K annual hours of assembly labor to Mexico and improved productivity 10%.
- Improved on-time delivery from 39% to 92% through capacity planning, computerized forecasting, cycle time reduction and JIT supplier program.
- Attained 98% stockroom cycle count accuracy and eliminated need for physical inventory.
- Increased production rate 10-fold to 420 units per year while converting to new products.

Turned around ailing Field Service business with very high level of employee and customer dissatisfaction.
- 64% increase in sales to $15 million. Improved margin to 36% (5% above industry average).
- Reduced turnover from 40% to 6%.

Hands-on development of quality management. Initiated TQM program with goal of being 6 sigma by 1994. Developed goals, measurement and feedback loop to Quality Action Teams for continuous improvement.
- 75% reduction in outgoing defect rate.
- 30% reduced installation time through development of quality feed-back system.
- 15% increased productivity through improved training and methods.

Experienced in planning and construction of new manufacturing and corporate facilities. Relocated to new facility while maintaining continuous production.

Transitioned company from organized to non-organized labor environment.

M.S. in Management, California Technical Institute, 1980. BSIE, University of New York, 1970.

PROFESSIONAL EXPERIENCE

FORWAY CORPORATION, New York, New York 1989–Present
$60 million high volume manufacturer of RF connectors and cable assemblies.
> **DIRECTOR OF OPERATIONS**
> Responsible for materials, manufacturing engineering, and multi-plant production including South American assemble operation.

REDEX INTERNATIONAL, New York, New York 1982–1989
$75 million privately owned manufacturer of computer systems and high resolution film recorders.
> **VICE PRESIDENT OF OPERATIONS, 1985–1989**
> **DIRECTOR OF MANUFACTURING, 1982–1984**
> Created full manufacturing function during transition from manufacturer to independent corporation. Developed and staffed purchasing, production, materials, quality assurance and manufacturing engineering.

AMERICAN INDUSTRIAL COMPANY, New York, New York/Boston, Massachusetts, 1970-1982
Equipment Products Department
> **MANAGER SHOP OPERATIONS, 1980–1982**
> Supervised scheduling, cost forecasting, production, process engineering, and maintenance of Piezoelectric Ceramic Operation producing 50K units annually.

Drive Turbine Department
> **MANAGER OF MAIN PARTS BEARINGS AND PACKING, 1977–1980**
> Responsible for high precision shop operation machining high pressure castings, exhaust fabrications, bearings and packing. 70 employees.
> **MANAGER OF MATERIALS, 1975–1977**
> **MASTER SCHEDULING SPECIALIST, 1973–1975**
> **BUYER, 1973**
> **MANUFACTURING MANAGEMENT PROGRAM, 1970–1973**

OPERATIONS EXECUTIVE

Melvin Jones
873 Fischer Court, Beverly, MA 02127 555-555-1345

Offering nine years of progressive business experience in both entrepreneurial and corporate settings; a seasoned contributor who is adept at helping organizations manage change and achieve maximum profitability.

SPECIFIC AREAS OF STRENGTH

Statistical analysis   *Information systems management*
Financial and accounting reporting *Capital and operational budgeting*
Project management   *Operational management*

EMPLOYMENT

Senior VP/Operations:
GLENNWAY CONSTRUCTION, Beverly, MA (1995–Present)

Overhauled personnel, sales, and bidding systems, resulting in $32.5 million in new contracts with organizations who had never done business with us in the past.

Directed successful strategic planning efforts to resurrect this once-struggling construction operation, leading the way for it to thrive in highly competitive market—despite two straight years in the red before my arrival.

Oversaw, at CEO's (founder's) request, transition from family-owned and operated business to shareholder-owned business.

VP/Manager:
TESSEDINE LEASING, Boston, MA (1993–1995)

Developed commercial leasing strategies for retail developments in six eastern states.

Identified growth opportunities in down market, delivering 6% growth while industry as a whole was in steep decline

General Manager:
PAINTPRO CORPORATION, Hartford, CT (1991–1993).

Recruited by founder to help run this start-up house-painting franchise operation; revenues rose from $0 to $3 million.

EDUCATION

Bachelor's degree in Public Management from Hartford College; M.B.A. from University of Albany.

OPERATIONS EXECUTIVE

JOHN SMITH
123 Beacon Street ▲ Boston, MA 02127
555/555-5555 (daytime)
555/555-5556 (evenings)

Objective: To become Vice President of Operations for Beacon Group, and use my 15 years of experience in administration and general management to fulfill important corporate goals for that organization.

QUALIFICATIONS

15 years of experience in Administration and General Management. Proven track record of turning around troubled operations, establishing successful accounting and management procedures, restructuring organizations and training employees.

General Manager for General Pathways Corporation, Wayland, MA (1994-Present)

Head of Operations for Oregon Restaurant Technologies Group, Portland, OR (1991-1994)

Manager and Regional Manager for Freedonia Restaurant Systems, Portland, OR (1983-1990)

EXPERIENCE

▲ Boosted monthly sales for an underperforming sales office from $30,000 to $500,000 as General Manager for General Pathways Corporation.

▲ Brought that #37 office to #1 status in 18 months.

▲ Personally trained salespeople in new prospecting and interviewing techniques.

▲ Developed new computerized sales prospect follow-up system that resulted in 28% higher close ratios on annual basis.

▲ Developed new purchase tracking procedure that eliminated $115,000 in unnecessary purchases as Head of Operations for Oregon Technologies Group.

▲ Managed a $4 million dollar budget with "ruthless efficiency and unparalleled people skills." (Quote from Bert Greenson, president, Oregon Restaurant Technologies Group.)

▲ Hired and motivated staff as manager and regional manager for Freedonia Restaurant Systems.

▲ Named "Regional Manager of the Year" at Freedonia on three separate occasions.

▲ Instituted new safety procedures that resulted in 11% reduction in insurance rates chainwide.

▲ Trained selected managers in restaurant operations and overall personal productivity.

▲ Cited for "intensity, originality, and effectiveness" of managerial training program by regional vice president.

▲ Superior analysis, problem-solving, and people skills.

▲ Excellent computer skills; proficient in Microsoft Office, with particular strength in Word, Excel, Access, and PowerPoint; Lotus 1-2-3; and Internet access software.

▲ Skilled in both Windows and Macintosh environments.

EDUCATION AND AFFILIATIONS

B.A. Degree, Government, Wadsworth University, 1982
   Member, National Association of Minority Business Leaders
   Member, Operations Professionals Association
   Regional Chairman, Boy's Clubs of Boston

OPERATIONS EXECUTIVE

Jane Smith•425 Derby Street•Dallas, TX 75265•555/555-5555

Objective: To become Vice President of Business Operations for Collins Industries.

QUALIFICATIONS

Nearly two decades of experience as a senior operations professional for major commercial organizations. Skilled in all areas of executive business operations. Highly organized, technically skilled, and capable of delivering solutions for both large and small work groups.

EDUCATION

Recipient of a B.A. (1977) and an M.A. (1979) in Economics, both from Ivytown University. Graduated fifth out of a class of 722 in 1977, and carried a 3.85 grade point average.

EXPERIENCE

McBurger, Incorporated, Dallas, Texas (1994–present)

Senior Operations Planner: Reviewed and updated all company information systems. Selected hardware and software vendors. Streamlined communications between regional offices; developed faster and more accurate company-wide monthly reports that led to reduced delays and better management decisions. Consolidated data systems for two neighboring regions, resulting in an annual savings of $3.7 million.

Wellstone Securities Systems, Houston, Texas (1991–1994)

Vice President of Management Information Systems: Developed systems that synchronized reports on activities in sales, marketing, operations management, customer service, design, business analysis and planning. Contributed to weekly executive committee meetings. Evaluated suppliers at all levels and delivered one-year savings of $5.2 million.

Hartwell Cable, Atlanta, Georgia (1978–1990)

Project Manager (1978-1979) and General Manager (1979-1990): As General Manager, Responsible for the General Management of a corporate branch office with 62 employees, realizing $5.5 million in annual sales and increasing revenues by 51% in 19 months.

Proficient in Windows, Macintosh, and mainframe computer environments.

152

PROCESS REENGINEERING—CHANGE PROGRAMS

John Smith
135 Beechbrook Lane • Chicago, IL 60609
(555) 555-5555

EXECUTIVE MANAGEMENT

Operations • MIS • Supply Chain/Marketing • Business & Manufacturing Process Reengineering
Proven leadership with over 9 years of success delivering innovative solutions to complex strategic, supply chain, information technology, and organizational issues on an international scale across multiple industries. Diverse executive level consulting experience with over Fortune 1000 companies analyzing operations, identifying reengineering benefits, and designing change programs which deliver quantum leap improvements in business performance and profitability.

MANAGEMENT STYLE

Contagious enthusiasm quickly mobilizes high-performing teams in innovative motivational environments which take into account organizational culture and resources. Readily facilitate buy-in at all levels of management and understanding across multiple companies, industries, and issues.

DEMONSTRATED CAPABILITIES TO

* Design and implement comprehensive change programs, strategies, processes and systems
* Successfully integrate acquisitions and orchestrate large-scale reorganizations spanning business processes, organizational structure and culture
* Develop comprehensive market approach for diverse products and services
* Identify supply-side management opportunities and devise programs to capitalize on them
* Analyze and develop strategies for improvement of process manufacturing supply chain
* Discern/address implications of regulatory and environmental changes to business processes

PROFESSIONAL EXPERIENCE

INTERWAY GROUP, Chicago, IL   1990–Present
Recruited as Consultant, assumed key executive role as principal in this international consulting firm in 1995.
Principal/Senior Consultant
Lead global organizational analysis and change program projects across multiple industries and countries, spearheading activities of Global Analysis & Design and Information Management teams of up to 20. Full responsibility for engagement vision and design, client executive management, people development, margin management, and program design and start-up. Sample deliverables include:

* Identified supply-side management opportunities in U.S., Asia, and Europe for international, multi-business chemical company. In first five months of project:
  – *delivered $2MM of "quick hits" and thoroughly analyzed all procurement activities*
  – *outlined "as is" organizational capabilities and "to be" requirements*
  – *prepared organization for change*
  – *developed design of 18-month program to deliver up to $200MM in spend improvements*

* Designed comprehensive change program for one of Asia's largest process manufacturing companies:
  – *developed strategies, processes, and systems to transition to profitability and global competitiveness*
  – *balanced need for organizational growth and development with broader cultural and sociological issues, garnering critical union support*

* Analyzed complex process manufacturing plant producing pharmaceutical, medical, and commodity chemical products:
  – *provided analysis of critical quality control/assurance processes required for compliance with regulatory agency mandates*
  – *designed program to align plant vision, manufacturing processes, and organizational culture*

153

* Developed detailed program to integrate two competitive laboratory chemical companies as result of acquisition. Leveraging international expertise in M&A management:
  - *delivered $1MM in benefits over 12-week effort as well as 9-month program to deliver benefits while maximizing combined business value*
  - *developed market approach for product co-branding and manufacturing site rationalization*
  - *devised plan for creating top level as well as full organization for integrated company*

* Developed multiple strategic, competitive, process, organization, and systems scenarios for large telecommunications client:
  - *predicted implications of regulatory environment changes and convergence of content, cable, and telecommunications*
  - *enabled company to drive industry change, assume position as innovative leader, and maximize shareholder value in industry shake-out*

* Analyzed consumer product company's supply chain from promotion design and execution through manufacturing to order fulfillment and accounts receivable:
  - *developed 14-month program to re-engineer key processes and systems and redesign market approaches with emphasis on "leapfrogging" competitive initiatives*

* Designed end-to-end business model for large energy company:
  - *defined strategic, process, and organizational changes, driving a large-scale reorganization*
  - *defined leading edge systems development process to leverage object-oriented technology*

ENERGEX, Houston, Texas   1988–1990
Manager Implementation Services
Charged with full responsibility for implementation of GIS (Geographical Information Systems) worldwide for utility, government, and oil and gas companies. Concurrently managed all U.S. operations including project design and proposal development.

* Instrumental in tenfold revenue increase (from $300K to $3MM), growth from 5 to 13 consultants.
* Designed and implemented graphic design system for Central Mapping Agency in Toronto which was adopted as base for all fire, ambulance, engineering, and police activities.
* Developed and implemented oil and gas lease management system.

REDPATH ENERGY, Houston, Texas   1983–1988
Systems Manager—Southwest Division (1987–1988)
As manager of GIS systems, led all application development and system management activities.

* Implemented GIS system including all procedures and standards.
* Established development program for new GIS applications.

Programmer Analyst (1983–1987)

* Key participant in development of state-of-the-art system and business processes for exploring and producing oil and gas.

EDUCATION

B.S.E. Honors—*Mineral Engineering Mathematics*, Colorado School of Mines, Golden, Colorado, 1983

COMMUNITY INVOLVEMENT

Chairman, *Fundraising Committee*, Regional Multiple Sclerosis Association

PRODUCT MANAGER

JANE SMITH 60 Brown Avenue, Springfield, MA 09851 555/555-5555

MARKETING/BUSINESS/DEVELOPMENT/PRODUCT DEVELOPMENT MANAGER

Dynamic management career spearheading market and business development programs nationwide. Expertise in strategic market identification and penetration, sales and staff development. Participative leadership style with skill in cross-functional team building that generates revenue and promotes efficient and profitable operations. Strong experience in all aspects of direct marketing.

PROFESSIONAL EXPERIENCE

1987–Present INFORMATION COMPANY BOSTON, MA
PRODUCT MANAGER

Manage product development, promotions, pricing strategies and positioning for existing and new products. Develop and deliver new product training.

Achievement

Turned non-profitable product into profit center by increasing number of units sold by 50% and by decreasing costs by 10%

MANAGER, CUSTOMER ACQUISITION

Part of management team that launched INFORMATION COMPANY onto the World Wide Web with PHONELOG.

Developed and implemented sales channel and customer acquisition strategy

Assumed sole responsibility for sales collateral program for product launch and promotion

Nurtured relationships with strategic marketing partners to ensure campaign success

Achievement

PHONELOG is the #1 WWW yellow page service as a result of successful launch

Established, trained and managed national reseller network of 100

Recruited and supervised telemarketing service bureau and in-house staff that succeeded in generating 95% of total revenue

MARKETING MANAGER

Implemented national marketing plan for INFORMATION COMPANY CD-ROM directory products.

Oversaw new product introductions

Identified target markets; managed database marketing efforts and list selection

Hired and managed outside advertising agency that created numerous promotional campaigns; selected multimedia and placement and public relations activities

Managed the development of effective promotional materials and product packaging in conjunction with copywriters, photographers, printers, vendors and/or in-house staff

Identified, evaluated and selected 25 trade shows annually; responsible for all logistics, participation and content

Achievement

IMMY awarded in national recognition of two direct mail pieces (1st and 2nd prize)

Recipient of Vice President's Quality Award for successful new product launch

Premier directory used by government agencies, law enforcement organizations and fortune 100 corporations

1984–1986 PATCO, INC. TEANECK, NJ
SALES MANAGER

Managed sales in excess of $18 million; developed cross-sell strategy and sales training program that increased sales volume by 15%

EDUCATION

1979 MADISON UNIVERSITY NEW YORK, NY
Bachelor of Science Major: Business Management—Cum Laude.

PRODUCT MANAGER

JOHN H. SMITH

316 Walnut Drive ♦ Media, PA 19063
610-756-2300 (W) ♦ 610-444-2374 (H)

Major product manager with more than 12 years of progressive experience in sales and marketing for the Food Product Division of a $3.7 billion consumer products company.

Achieved record sales/earnings for major product line. Attained 23% average annual growth rate vs. industry average of 11%. Restructured product mix. Eliminated low margin items and introduced a new product, resulting in 18% higher net earnings. Created new packaging for slumping product and an aggressive advertising campaign, yielding a 46% increase in market share.

KEY FUNCTIONAL STRENGTHS INCLUDE:

- Profit and Loss
- Sales Forecasting
- Pricing and Margins
- Strategic Product Planning
- Advertising and Promotion
- Distribution
- Market Research
- Operational Planning
- Product Development/Improvement

Equal success at developing creative marketing strategies for the introduction of new products or revitalizing/repositioning stagnate product lines.

- Directed the successful introduction of a new butter spread product achieving a 17% market penetration in 1 year.

- Repositioned a failing confectionery line and increased sales by 235% in a two year period.

- Created and implemented a novel advertising strategy for a stagnate product line accounting for a 32% increase in market share. Received mention in the Company's annual report and Creative Advertising magazine for this creative effort.

Successful at improving product quality, creating effective marketing campaigns, meeting/surpassing sales targets, improving operations, and reducing operating expenses.

- Directed a product improvement effort and corresponding marketing campaign that increased sales by $2.7 million in 9 months.

- Implemented a new computerized shipping system which reduced freight costs by 18%, yielding $730 thousand in annual profit.

- Exceeded sales targets each year by an average of 13%. Received special bonus award for this achievement.

One of six Food Product Division managers selected to address the Board of Directors regarding current performance and the direction of future marketing strategies and objectives. Received commendation letters from both the CEO and Chairman of the Board for effort.

EDUCATION

M.B.A. - Marketing - UCLA, Los Angeles, CA ♦ **B.S.** - Marketing - University of Kansas, Lawrence, KS

PROFESSIONAL EXPERIENCE

1986-Present NATIONAL FOOD PRODUCTS, St. Louis, MO
PRODUCT MANAGER, FOOD PRODUCT DIVISION - 1992-PRESENT
Develop and implement marketing policies and strategies for 6 major product lines totaling $358 million annually. P&L, market research, margins, pricing, quality, packaging, advertising and distribution.

MARKETING MANAGER, FOOD PRODUCT DIVISION - 1988-1992
Managed the implementation of strategic plans and marketing strategies. Prepared sales forecasts, supervised new product development, and coordinated activities with salespersons throughout the division.

MARKETING RESEARCH ANALYST, FOOD PRODUCT DIVISION - 1986-1988
Developed market research and market evaluation studies for the Food Products Division. Directed initial marketing studies to determine product acceptance among consumers.

PRODUCTION EXECUTIVE

JAMES JONES

7832 CreedyWay
Chicago IL 60609
555/555-5555 (days) or 555/555-6666 (evenings)

Objective: To become Vice President of Production of Expertway Corporation.

Key Skills: Proven strengths in all phases of production and operations management; with particular skills in planning, budgeting, pricing, contract negotiations and quality control. Skilled at development of efficient, highly targeted plans, and in developing responsive teams to carry them out.

Adept at:

Design review	Planning
Analysis	Records management
Resource development	Training

Awards: 6 Operational Excellence Awards; 3 Ferretti Awards for Excellence in Operations Management; 2 Benton Awards for Quality Control. Named "Regional Leader of the Year" by national headquarters office.

Work Experience: *Senior Production Analyst*, SpinCom, Chicago IL (1989–Present)
VP/Production, Extel, New York, NY (1988–1989)
Regional Director, Outlook Group, Flushing, NY (1987–1988)
Production Assistant (promoted to) Production Manager, Rannikin Corporation (1984–1987)

- Established award-winning quality control systems that were praised by users and senior executives alike.
- At SpinCom, built production from start-up to $40 million in volume in 7 years.
- Beat aggressive 45-day schedule by 3 days on rollout of Interroad Navigational System, making prescheduled national promotional campaign possible.
- Supervised staffs of between 16 and 30 personnel.

Other: Volunteer with wife of 10 years at Mercy County Hospital fundraisers since 1993.

Education: Bachelor's degree in Mathematics, Beltway College, Washington D.C., (1983).

Honors: Member, American Society of Production Professionals.

PROPERTY DEVELOPMENT EXECUTIVE
(SUMMARY FORMAT)

RESUME SUMMARY FOR:
Mary Wilson, President, Acme Development

FROM:
Brian Welsh 567 Benson Street Chicago, IL 60609 (555-555-5557)

YOU NEED:
"A senior property development professional with at least 10 years' experience."

I OFFER:
18 years of experience in office building and shopping center leasing. Handled executive-level tenant improvement, leasing and property management responsibilities for 4.2 million square foot Betterway Business Park located in Oak Park, Illinois. Conducted negotiations with dozens of Fortune 250 companies.

YOU NEED:
"Solid record of achievement in negotiating and property analysis."

I OFFER:
A superior record in analyzing and negotiating leases, and expansion/contraction, remodeling and lease extension agreements for local tenants (Better Bargain Outlets) and national companies (Mandrake Industries, RDR Industries).

YOU NEED:
"Demonstrated ability to manage costs."

I OFFER:
Savings of over $1.5 million over the eight-year life of one lease for the corporate headquarters of the nation's 3rd largest consumer electronics chain.

YOU NEED:
"Superior oral and written communications skills."

I OFFER:
Record of strong team-first achievement as a consultant (BHE Partners) and manager (Sweetwater Management Group), and excellent communication skills on all levels. Accomplished public speaker.

158

PUBLIC RELATIONS SPECIALIST

CAROL ANNE WESLEY

216 West Juniper Avenue ◆ Clarksburg, OH 23622
709-559-3725 (Bus.) ◆ 709-865-2298 (Res.)

Senior-level Public Relations Officer for major publisher of industrial trade journals. Experienced in dealing with media relations, stockholder relations, employee communications, and public/community relations.

Received the prestigious Andrew P. Johnstone Award for the best public relations brochure from the American Association of Public Relations. Selected from more than 2,000 finalists.

Significantly reduced the use of outside public relations firms by bringing most activities in-house. Resulted in annual savings of more than $450,000.

Wrote all executive speeches for investor meetings, prepared promotional materials, and directed all media, employee, and public relations matters during the successful bid for a management buy out of the company.

Prepared all written materials for management in concert with the corporate labor attorney during a national labor union's unsuccessful attempt to organize 135 telemarketers.

Prepared the company's first international promotional and public affairs materials for Spain, Germany, France and Japan. Received mention in the President's Quarterly Review Report for its quality and effectiveness.

PROFESSIONAL EXPERIENCE

BUSINESS PUBLICATIONS, INC.   1983-Present
Vice President, Corporate Affairs - (1991-Present)

- Develop strategy and direct the ongoing communications effort with stockholders, the media, employees and the general public to present the company's objectives, plans, prospects and activities.

- Produce quarterly and annual reports for shareholders. Manage the annual stockholders meeting and serve as company spokesperson with the financial and trade media.

- Write speeches for and provide communications counsel to the CEO and the Chairman of the Board. Develop guidelines for corporate donations, write all major press releases, and handle national media inquiries.

- Earned 14 awards including the Freedom Foundation award and three citations from the International Council of Public Affairs. Published more than 50 articles in trade journals. Twice honored by Toastmasters International.

Manager, Employee Relations - (1983-1991)

- Created, implemented and managed employee communications programs. Served as corporate spokesperson with the local media. Created and managed special events for employees.

- Created and produced the first employee quarterly newsletter. Assisted in the development of program themes and content for management presentations, including the preparation and production of speeches and slide presentations.

- Designed, wrote and taught a course on creative communications for all middle and senior management staff. Served as liaison between corporate offices and field offices.

EDUCATION

M.S.J - Northwestern University School of Journalism ◆ **B.S.J.** - Northwestern University School of Journalism

"Outstanding Journalism Graduate" - Awarded Sigma Delta Chi Special Award

RETAIL AND MANUFACTURING CONSULTANT

JANE SMITH • 123 Main Street, • Hanover, MA 01123 • 555-555-5555

SUMMARY

Retail and manufacturing consultant for clients in the men's, children's, and bridal industries. Over 20 years entrepreneurial experience as the owner/operator of renowned Boston retail/manufacturing businesses. Comprehensive sales and marketing abilities.

QUALIFICATIONS

Extensive sales, marketing and management experience
Skilled in classification buying as well as in developing and implementing effective marketing and advertising campaigns
In-depth knowledge of small retail/manufacturing ventures including plans and strategies for start-up and early stage retail/manufacturing ventures
Expertise in lease negotiation, financial statement analysis, store construction and in-store department build-out

EXPERIENCE

1993–1996   MARGARET'S   Providence, RI
National Sales Manager
After sale of business, full responsibility for over 200 wholesale accounts representing over $3 million in sales. Prepared for and participated in national trade and trunk shows.

1987–1993
Chief Operating Officer
Assumed full responsibility for family retail/manufacturing business with combined sales of $5.5 million. Development of and creative placement of $250-400 thousand annual advertising budget. Developed point of sale advertising and sales tools for both retail and wholesale aspects of business. Responsible for pricing and merchandising of three product divisions as well as managing 80 employees in the manufacturing plant. Opened three retail stores and two in-store shops across the country as part of a successful expansion plan. Complete responsibility for sales and presentations to 200 wholesale accounts.

1973–1993   WILLIAM LORD   Providence, RI
Chief Operating Officer
Established and built men's clothing store. Expanded business to include a women's store and sportswear store with a total volume of $1.3 million. Responsible for all aspects of business including: buying, maintaining appropriate inventory levels, anticipating customer needs, advertising and merchandising. Trained over 30 sales associates in effective sales techniques.

EDUCATION

BOSTON COLLEGE   Boston, MA
Bachelor of Arts

RETAIL EXECUTIVE

JANE SMITH
443 South Street
Boston, MA 02127
555/555-5555 (Business)
555/555-6666 (Message)
555/555-7777 (Home)

SENIOR EXECUTIVE: RETAIL SALES/OPERATIONS MANAGEMENT

Dynamic, highly creative executive with 14 years' experience in corporate and entrepreneurial settings maximizing sales and bottom line profits for retail consumer product and business-to-business service organizations. Combine solid educational background including M.A. Public Affairs/Business Administration with uniquely broad hands-on experience in operations, sales/marketing, customer service, contract negotiations, space design, purchasing/inventory control, finance, and information systems.

Key strengths include abilities to:

*Apply strong customer focus, target market instincts, and design sense to create positive
retail environment conducive to customer loyalty and increased sales*

Identify market needs, develop a concept, and take business from idea stage to profitability

*Implement custom-tailored policies, procedures, and information systems to manage diverse functions including
marketing, customer service, accounting, AR/AP, inventory control*

PROFESSIONAL EXPERIENCE

GREAT LOOKS, Boston MA   **1989–Present**
Retail children's specialty store with $1 million in annual sales specializing in high-end layette, clothing, furniture, toys, and bedding as well as custom room design services.

PRESIDENT

Launched highly successful self-financed venture to fill identified marketplace need. Built operation from ground up including site selection and negotiation, space and display system design and build-out, marketing/advertising, hiring and training of six associates/design personnel, finance/accounting, customer service, purchasing and vendor relations, and inventory control. Grew business to efficient and profitable operation with first year sales of $700K, minimal end-of-season inventory (5% remainder donated to charity), and loyal customer base providing $1MM in annual revenues by:

- Establishing nationwide reputation as one-stop shop with unique, high-quality product line.
- Offering and implementing ironclad 100% customer satisfaction guarantee.
- Maintaining fresh, exciting inventory replenished and changed weekly to sustain interest.
- Designing innovative space and display system with well-received whimsical "rainbow" theme.
- Emphasizing diversity, flexibility, and completeness of customer service including 7-day hours, shop-at-home, gift registries, corporate baskets, customization, and special orders.
- Instituting policies and cost controls to provide highly responsive yet "bare bones" operation.
- Launching aggressive marketing program including mailers and media advertising.

SUSSEX ENTERPRISES, Chicago, IL   **1984–1989**
$40 million financial and property management services firm specializing in tax shelters and securities.

VICE PRESIDENT OPERATIONS

Recruited as Office Administrator, advanced quickly to VP position with 25 direct reports and 75 indirects and responsibility for marketing programs, operations, computer systems, recruitment, site selection, budgets and forecasting for seven offices in as many states.

- Developed and implemented marketing strategies which facilitated multi-state expansion.

161

- Designed and developed state-of-the-art computer operations including leading edge modem-based network system; one of first to implement use of fax machine technology.
- Structured multiple major partnership deals requiring months of meticulous preparation; e.g., multi-million dollar shopping center limited partnership.

LEE CORPORATION, Chicago, IL   1981–1984
Small, family-owned credit and collections firm connecting clients with attorneys in local jurisdictions, providing monitoring service, and serving as intermediary between attorney and client.
   VICE PRESIDENT
      Hiring in as Account Executive, earned fast-track promotion in only six months to VP with oversight of diverse areas from marketing to computer systems.
- Selected and managed conversion from manual to computerized system, running both in parallel for one year to ease transition.
- Launched aggressive attorney recruitment program, expanding attorney pool from 12 to over 3,000 dispersed nationwide; resulted in significantly improved service to clients and increased sales.

EDUCATION

UNIVERSITY OF CALIFORNIA AT BERKELEY
M.A. Public Affairs, Minor: Business Administration   May 1981
B.A. Political Science, Minor: Public Administration   May 1979

COMMUNITY INVOLVEMENT

Member, Greater Boston Chamber of Commerce.

RETAIL EXECUTIVE

JANE SMITH / 888 Third Avenue, New York, NY 10000 / 555/555-5555

Responsibilities:

18 years of experience as a Vice President of Sales and Purchasing, General Manager and Retail Store Manager for Zap!, the nation's third largest personal electronics retailer.

* Drafted organization-wide purchasing guidelines.
* Developed core ideas for highly successful national consumer campaigns.
* Provided initial ideas for new product launches via in-house brand lines.
* Established and continually updated guidelines for store layout that maximized sales revenue through intelligent management of store traffic.

Achievements:

A demonstrated record of success in ...

SALES AND MARKETING

An innovative, driving force in retail store management and product management.

* Significant product development skills (concept through marketing); contributed directly or indirectly to 22 successful new product launches.
* Developed initial manufacturing and promotional concepts behind Schedule-Minder personal data management accessory—the most successful new product introduction in company history. (Revenue over first 3 years: $8.5 million.)
* Skilled in retail store operations, purchasing, training, inventory and vendor contracts.

STORE AND DIVISIONAL OPERATION

Proven aptitude as a leader and self-starter; capable of hiring, organizing, and motivating effective team members at all levels, and establishing workable systems.

* Responsible for opening and operating the company's first two stores and growing the business to 25 outlets with $65 million in sales.
* Established guidelines for personnel evaluation and overall motivation; kept absenteeism and tardiness to levels significantly below industry averages.
* Awarded "Silver Star" for operational excellence by National Association of Consumer Retailers, 1995

PRODUCT DEVELOPMENT

Skilled in market analysis, design consultation, and product launch activities. In addition to ScheduleMinder (see above), successful new Zap! products developed include:

* ScanMaster (personal business card scanner)—total revenues approximately $6.4 million.
* FoodMate (personal calorie counter)—total revenues to date approximately $4.7 million.
* MemoMate (personal voice recorder)—total revenues to date approximately $3.3 million.

Employment:

Zap! Stores, Cupertino, CA (Headquarters), 1979–present. Currently Vice President of Marketing. (Began as store manager of two-store chain.)

Education:

B.S. in Business Administration (Truman College, Independence, MO) and an M.S. in Business Education (College of the West).

SALES AND FINANCE EXECUTIVE

John Smith

2875 Elworth Avenue
Boston, MA 02127
555/555-5555 (days) or 555/555-6555 (evenings)

Professional Summary:

A seasoned sales and finance professional with a demonstrated track record of success in sales and marketing management. Significant skills in business planning and development, financial analysis, market research and contract negotiations. Accomplished sales leader familiar with proven strategies for rapid, high-level growth.

Significant Work History and Accomplishments:

Holm Radio Systems, Boston, MA - Senior Sales Manager - 1994–Present
- Head up dynamic for sales organization with over $300 million in revenue.
- Supervise 3 sales offices on rotating basis, visiting each office at least once per week.
- Developed 21 account executives who exceeded yearly sales targets by an average of 161%.
- Conducted weekend training seminar for new hires praised by president of Heritage as "stellar" during annual achievements banquet.

GlobalComm, Worcester, MA - Account Executive, Sales Manager - 1985–1993
- Developed successful promotions that highlighted GlobalComm products, including a charity fundraiser, eighteen youth sports league affiliations, and a radio tie-in. Sales in my territory rose 34% in just six months.
- Used creative techniques to reach top decision makers.
- Upon promotion to Sales Manager, trained reps in community involvement, contact methods, and phone techniques, leading to biggest yearly sales increase in company's history.

Education:

B.S. in Sociology (Kettering University, 1980)

SALES AND MARKETING EXECUTIVE

JOHN SMITH 500 MILLER STREET, BOSTON, MA 01920 617/555-5555

QUALIFICATIONS
Marketing, sales, and managerial expertise, aptitude for integrating technical information and market trend data into new product development: follow through from inception to product roll out - on time and within budget
Excellent communication skills in solving problems, building consensus, coordinating interdepartmental resources and nurturing partnerships with customers and colleagues

EXPERIENCE

1988 to Present
MORAX INCORPORATED   Boston, MA
DIRECTOR OF PRIVATE LABEL SALES DIVISION, Hair and Skin Care Products
Responsible for direct sales, marketing and administration of all O.E.M. sales activities
Oversee 23 active accounts generating $84 million in annual gross sales; manage sales associates
Develop niche products; thus far have introduced 35 new products
Lead cross-functional team from R&D, production, finance and legal departments to ensure that product roll-out occurs within agreed upon specifications, costs and timeframe
Achievements
Increased gross profit by 5% to 33%, thereby earning the highest gross and net profit margins of any division in the company
Increased customer base by 16% over 5 years

MANAGER OF CUSTOMER SERVICE
Conducted on-line order entry, processing and expediting for four product lines generating $80 million annually; supervised staff of 5
Coordinated efforts of sales, purchasing, production and shipping departments to ensure quality services
Evaluated promotional programs to determine viability, recommended modifications

SALES PLANNER, PRIVATE LABEL SALES DIVISION
Maximized sales via product development and new markets
Translated sales projections into master production and shipment schedules
Achievement
Selected to develop international business plan which led to significant growth and market penetration

1986 to 1988
MORTON INCORPORATED   Boston, MA
PRODUCTION PROGRAM PLANNER, Electronics Systems
Established time and action production schedules to meet customer demand
Directed group leaders on implementation of work schedule; worked with engineering and purchasing to incorporate design changes into master production schedule
Coordinated all floor production from sub-assembly to final test and burn in for avionics and communication system.
High government security clearance due to multifaceted responsibility of coordinating with various departments in developing prototype blueprints and schematics

PRODUCTION CONTROL GROUP LEADER
Responsible for the operational implementation of plan schedules in four areas of manufacturing; managed 5 control coordinators
Oversaw materials handling; analyzed production throughout to target inefficiencies and maximize output

PRODUCTION CONTROL COORDINATOR
Prioritized production schedules for two shifts, work force of 65
Provided daily throughput status reports as well as weekend production analysis

EDUCATION
1980-1984   UNIVERSITY OF MASSACHUSETTS   Amherst, MA
                                     BACHELOR OF SCIENCE DEGREE, Major: Education

SALES AND MARKETING EXECUTIVE

JOHN SMITH 68 Wilson Street, Salem, MA 01970 555/555-1234

Dynamic sales and marketing management career. Expert qualifications in increasing market penetration and capturing market opportunities by converting market data into successful strategies. Proficient at motivating sales teams as well as implementing systems and procedures that establish accountability and increase productivity and sales.

PROFESSIONAL EXPERIENCE

1996–present

Music, Inc.   Milford, MA
REGIONAL SALES MANAGER, Diagnostic Equipment Service
  Manage sales force of 4 and 15 technologists; operate within $4.5 million budget
  Provide value-added service to corporate clients; negotiate contracts
ACHIEVEMENTS
  Generated contractual agreements within 8 months with 6 new accounts valued at $1.2 million
  Produced sales of $3.3 million in year 1: became leading sales director in the region

1990–1996

Medical Assessments   Boston, MA
REGIONAL SALES MANAGER, U.S. Managed Care
  Led 5 marketing representatives in MA in setting and achieving goals
  Responsible for direct sales, marketing and administration
  Trained sales team to develop partnerships with medical and insurance professionals; practiced continuous follow through and prompt response
  Identified markets, developed strategies and qualified leads
  Conceived and developed marketing tools; hired and worked with promotional companies
  Interfaced with upper management in developing new markets and investigating other managed care opportunities
ACHIEVEMENTS
  Consistently ranked #1 or #2 in sales as part of a national team of 27
  Performed 125-180% above quota for 8 consecutive years
  Selected to establish PA territory; handled logistics of setting up 3 offices, hired and trained staff of 21 including a sales and support team of 13 as well as contract physicians
  In MA, achieved sales of $2 million within 18 months; set company record for developing profitable operations in this new territory on time and within budget
  Simultaneously increased sales in PA to $4 million by further penetrating competitive market and cultivating established account
  Within first year increased sales volume in PA by 50%

1987–1990

Biological Training Programs   Nashua, NH
DISTRICT MANAGER
  Provided direct sales, marketing and administration for 7 offices
  Hired, trained and evaluated 8 sales representatives
ACHIEVEMENTS
  Increased sales volume from $1 million to $2.5 million within 2 years
  Developed and implemented format and marketing material that led to 30% increase

1986–1987

U.S. Balance Company   Boston, MA
ADJUSTER
  Processed and investigated workers' compensation claims

EDUCATION

1986   Cambridge, MA
Harvard University
Bachelor of Science, Major: Business Management

SALES AND MARKETING EXECUTIVE

DAVID SMITH
800 Westway Road
San Francisco, CA 94930
555/555-5555

Executive experienced in sales and marketing management who consistently achieves record sales and profits.

#2 ranking out 42 regions, achieved 153% of quota, $78 million sales.

#3 ranking out of 35 regions, achieved 151% of quota, $47 million sales.

#1 ranking of 40 districts, achieved highest profit contribution of any U.S. district.

Demonstrated success in turning around stagnant districts, increasing sales and profitability.

* Revitalized poorly performing district, increased revenues from $12 million to $66 million in 1 year.
* Added $2 million to bottom line in one transaction through aggressive negotiations.

Experienced in opening new markets, introducing new products and training sales force on marketing strategies.

* Opened new marketing areas throughout U.S.
* Member of 5-person team responsible for major new product introduction.
* Recognized as #2 rated speaker among 32 in Executive Briefing Program.

Goal-oriented leader with high degree of business acumen and ability to manage multiple functions simultaneously.

M.B.A., Marketing, Minnesota State University, 1978. B.A., Business & Economics, Eton College, 1974.

Willing to relocate. Married, 1 child. Age, 43.

PROFESSIONAL EXPERIENCE

ABC CORPORATION, San Francisco, CA 1985–Present
Regional Director, San Francisco, CA 1993–Present
Direct sales and marketing in 6 southeastern states with $47 million to $93 million annual sales. Supervise 14-person staff. In 1995, Crenway account was reassigned following territorial changes and corporate restructuring.

* Finished within top 5% of all company regions in 1993, 1994, and 1995.

District Sales Manager, Charleston, SC, 1991–1993
Managed 3-state area. Responsible for sales, technical leadership and development of customer/executive relationships.

Corporate Account Executive, Burbank, CA, 1990
Responsible for development and implementation of financial upgrade strategy from current product line to new product line. Team member for major new product introduction.

National Product Manager, San Diego, CA, 1989–1990
Managed storage products line including marketing, product requirements, forecasting and presentation to executives.

Sales Representative, Phoenix, AZ, 1985–1989
Sales for high-volume territory consisting of commercial, state and municipal government accounts.

MULTIPLE COMPUTERS, Hills, MD, 1984–1985
Sales Representative
Sold large systems to local utility and state/municipal government accounts in Michigan territory.

COM CORPORATION, New York, NY, 1978–1984
Sales Representative
Responsible for sales to health, education and government accounts. Secured only new account in branch office in 1979.

SALES AND MARKETING EXECUTIVE

JOHN H. SMITH

316 Walnut Drive • Media, PA 19063 • 610-756-2300 (W) • 610-444-2374 (H) • E-mail: jhsmith@greatnet.com

A goal-oriented, self-starter in sales and marketing management who consistently achieves record sales and profits.

Exceeded sales projections each year, including 114% of sales budget in 1996.
Opened three national chain accounts in twelve months, increasing sales by $1,800,000.
Increased national sales by 18% in the first year, and 20% in the second year.

Demonstrated success at developing market strategies for new product introduction, building strong customer relations and managing the continued growth of both regional and national accounts.

Bachelor of Business Administration • Marketing Major • Stanford University

PROFESSIONAL EXPERIENCE

WONDER PRODUCTS, INC., Philadelphia, PA   **1992-PRESENT**
REGIONAL SALES MANAGER
Direct all sales, marketing and technical development activities for both the northeastern and mid-Atlantic territory.

- Increased territory sales from $1,800,000 in 1992 to its current level of $3,900,000.

- Introduced a new insulating foam product and exceeded market penetration plan by 50%.

- Established a new consumer product with an industry leader within two months of its introduction. Achieved 68% of total market share within 18 months of introduction.

AMERICAN PRODUCTS CORPORATION, St. Paul, MN   **1989-1992**
NATIONAL ACCOUNTS MANAGER
Managed 30 manufacturers' representatives in 25 states. Formulated all advertising, promotion and merchandising for key accounts. Recruited, trained and directed sales team.

- Recruited and trained three new sales agencies (12 salespeople) leading to an increase in sales of approximately 15% over the previous year.

- Conceived a targeted promotion campaign for a new kitchen fixture, increasing sales of the line by more than 10%.

PACIFIC FINANCIAL COMPANIES LTD., San Francisco, CA   **1987-1989**
ASSOCIATE
Determined financial needs of business owners with a net worth in excess of $10,000,000. Acted as liaison between the client and tax attorneys, Certified Public Accountants, and other senior financial planners.

- Achieved President's Club status for three straight years by consistently placing in the top 10% of more than 2,000 sales associates nationwide.

- Refined an existing telemarketing program used to assist new associates in gathering leads. This effort led to an overall increase in client leads by more than 30%.

CENTURY HOME PRODUCTS, INC., San Francisco, CA   **1984-1987**
SALES ASSOCIATE
Managed all manufacturers' representatives and agencies throughout the U.S. Hired, trained and directed all sales representatives. Established marketing strategies and designed advertising campaigns for the entire residential line.

- Marketed a new adhesive product to the home center industry within three months of the product's introduction.

SALES AND MARKETING EXECUTIVE

Jane Jones ■ 123 Main Street ■ Chicago, IL 60609 ■ 555/555-5555

Objective: To become Vice President of Marketing for Healthway, Incorporated.

**Highlights of
Qualifications:** 24 years of experience in sales and marketing management for wholesale and distributor organizations of over-the-counter consumer health products.

**Relevant
Experience:** A seasoned professional with deep experience within the industry who boosted annual sales by $9.2 million in the most recent fiscal year. Skilled at:
- New product introductions.
- Development of incentive programs.
- Recruiting.
- Directing personnel—managed up to 25 employees (including district managers).
- Interacting with distributor staffs.

**Managerial
Background:** Accomplished motivator and trainer. Highlights in this area include:
- Evaluated and refined cross-departmental team ideas for new merchandising initiatives; chaired monthly meetings.
- Resulting campaigns included three of the most impressive performers of the year: promotions through Personal Health Book Club, company World Wide Web site, and targeted radio promotions.
- Chose all in-house and out-of-house training programs.
- Personally trained team members in distributor management and personnel issues.
- For past seven years, personally conducted annual "Where We Are, Where We're Going" retreat for top management.

**Employment
History:** Freedom Vitamin Products, Hartford, CT, 1983—present. Currently National Marketing Director.
Breenway Products, Ellsworth, VT, 1981–1983. Merchandise Manager.
Super G, Breen, MA, 1975–1980. Sales Manager.

**Education and
Training:** B.S. in Marketing and graduate studies in brand management at the University of Hartford.

SALES AND MARKETING EXECUTIVE

CAROL ANNE WESLEY

216 West Juniper Avenue • Clarksburg, OH 23622
709-559-3725 (W) • 709-865-2298 (H)

Sales/Marketing executive with more than 15 years hands-on managerial experience. A self-starter with strengths in market analysis, developing market strategies for new product introduction, identifying customer needs, building strong customer relations, strategic planning, forecasting for budget, and managing the continued growth of major accounts.

Self-starter whose drive and leadership abilities produce results far exceeding normal expectations.

- Doubled presentations to prospective clients, leading to a 63% increase in sales over a 12 month period.

- Conceived and led a multi-function "Business Development Group" that established an international sales effort more than two years ahead of projections.

Creative professional with the ability to evaluate situations and develop effective actions to improve sales and profits.

- Developed "cross-selling" program that helped take new product to the number three market position within 18 months.

- Evaluated pricing alternatives and their impact on sales volume and revenues. Effort led to an additional $3.75 million in sales during first six months.

Secretary, National Association of Marketing Executives • Board member, Marketing Association of America

EDUCATION

Bachelor of Science, Business Administration, West Chester University • Phi Beta Kappa

EXPERIENCE

KLONE ENTERPRISES, INC.
Regional Vice President   1989-Present
Manage a $13.5 million territory selling high-end computers to distributors, wholesalers and retailers.
- Initiated the first trade programs that resulted in three of the largest month's sales volumes on record.
- Managed team that achieved market share gain on a mature product, the first growth in more than three years.
- Devised plan to creatively utilize excess inventories, reducing storage expense and creating $1.1 million in revenues.
- Installed a planning model to aid in forecasting sales and market trends, providing 96% on-time delivery.

WEBSTER MARKETING
Sales Manager   1986-1989
Heavily involved in sales planning, promotion, pricing and advertising for this marketing services firm.
- Designed and administered a comprehensive sales development program, contributing more than $200K in earnings.
- Achieved 115%, 138%, and 156% of quota during three consecutive years.

GREEN CONSULTANTS
Account Executive   1981-1986
Sold sophisticated management information systems software to service companies of all sizes.
- Directly contributed to the threefold growth of the client base and 700% increase in gross revenues.

SALES AND MARKETING EXECUTIVE
(SUMMARY FORMAT)

CONCISE EMPLOYMENT SUMMARY
prepared for Jane Norman

Mel Smith • 123 Front Street • New York, NY 10000

Objective: An executive position in sales or marketing with Ellison Industries.

Ellison requirement: "Successful applicant will possess at least 10 years of sales and marketing experience in high-level corporate environments."

Mel Smith offers: 11 years of experience in sales and marketing for $6 million to $1.5 billion organizations.

Ellison requirement: "We seek a team-first motivator who can take charge, produce results in short order."

Mel Smith is adept at: organizing a sales team, creating advertising and merchandising campaigns, establishing product pricing and successfully selling products.

Ellison requirement: "We're looking for someone with a demonstrated track record of marketing and sales achievement."

Mel Smith: Increased annual revenues from $6 million to $35 million by reorganizing existing sales and marketing teams at Holly Industries, Incorporated.

SALES AND MERCHANDISING EXECUTIVE

JOHN SMITH
123 Main Street
Boston, MA 02127
555/555-5555

SUMMARY:

An experienced senior executive with significant skills in:
- Retail management.
- Personnel administration.
- Merchandising.
- Systems control.
- Recruitment and training.
- Customer service.
- Loss control.

ACCOMPLISHMENTS:

12 years of experience in sales management and operations for a $6 billion company.
- Responsible for $3 million in annual sales.
- As store manager, consistently guided facility to top-five finishes nationwide (out of 300 chain operations in system).
- Managed and directed up to 300 employees.
- Skilled in inventory management; reduced lost sales arising from shortages by an estimated $2.5 million over three years.
- Named "Store Manager of the Year" (twice) and "Divisional Manager of the Year" (once).
- Youngest Sales and Merchandising Director in history of organization.
- Developed innovative theft-prevention program adopted throughout 300-store chain.

EMPLOYMENT:

Creedee's Discount House, headquarters in Greenwich, CT, 1986–present. Currently Sales and Merchandising Director for Northeast Region. (Began as clerk in Hartford, CT store.)

EDUCATION:

B.S. Business Administration, Connecticut State College (1985).

AFFILIATIONS:

Member, American Association of Retail Executives.

SENIOR ACCOUNTING SPECIALIST

Victor A. Sabatini, C.P.A.
(718) 975-6520

503 Gilbert Place
Manhattan, New York 11030

SUMMARY OF KNOWLEDGE AND EXPERTISE

MANAGED HEALTH CARE / WORKERS' COMPENSATION
OVERSIGHT / SHORT - LONG RANGE PLANNING
CASH / FINANCIAL CONTROLS
ADMINISTER COMPENSATION CONTRACTS
EFFECTIVE ORAL / WRITTEN COMMUNICATION SKILLS
INVESTMENT FUND MANAGERS SUPERVISION
RE-ENGINEER / INTEGRATION OF BUSINESS SEGMENTS
FINANCIAL CONSULTANT TO SENIOR MANAGEMENT
EXPERIENCED IN IDENTIFYING STRATEGIC OPPORTUNITIES

BUSINESS MANAGEMENT
FINANCIAL FUNCTION EVALUATION
DETAIL / RESULTS ORIENTED
SKILLED NEGOTIATOR
COST / GENERAL ACCOUNTING
FINANCIAL / OPERATIONAL AUDITS
BUDGET / FORECASTING FUNCTION
CAPITAL APPROPRIATION PROCESS
EXCELLENT TEAM PLAYER

ACCOMPLISHMENTS AND ACHIEVEMENTS

VIKIN HEALTH SYSTEMS:
- **Increased** revenue from $25 million to $120 million through acquisitions and internal consolidations.
- **Re-engineered** and integrated all business segments resulting in administrative expense reductions of 10%+.
- **Re-negotiated** contracts to eliminate low margin or unprofitable business and divested business segments successfully to align with parent company long-term strategic direction.
- **Implemented** cash and financial controls for Vikin's newly established international business.

GREEN CROSS:
- **Reduced** administrative expenses by $75 million by implementing control procedures and significantly enhancing all financial reporting mechanisms. This included reducing staff levels by 25% over a two year period.
- **Negotiated** large financial agreements with managed care vendors which included strict performance penalties. Eliminated several other long standing vendor agreements which were not profitable.

PARKER & TIMMONS SECURITIES:
- **Established** policies and procedures with regard to forecasting, budgeting, management reporting and statistical analysis for $150 million in employee benefit costs.
- **Reduced** employee benefit expenses by over $15 million through negotiations with insurance carriers.
- **Implemented** a strategic planning, budgeting and capital appropriation request process for a newly formed division.

PROFESSIONAL HISTORY

1994 - 1996   **SENIOR VICE PRESIDENT & CHIEF FINANCIAL OFFICER**
Vikin Health Systems, New York
Provided expertise in overseeing the Vikin Health Systems Group Division. Organized, planned, directed and evaluated the financial functions of company consisting of 1200 employees in 30 locations, representing annual revenues of $120 million. Performed oversight and long range strategic direction, managing budget process, administering compensation contracts, overseeing consulting relationships and negotiating customer pricing agreements.

1989 - 1994   **ASSISTANT VICE PRESIDENT / FINANCIAL PLANNING & CONTROL**
Green Cross, New York, New York

1980 - 1989   **DIRECTOR, EMPLOYEE BENEFITS FINANCIAL ADMINISTRATION**
Parker & Timmons Securities, New York, New York
Employed in March, 1980 as **Senior Corporate Auditor** and promoted through the ranks as follows:
- **SENIOR CORPORATE AUDITOR** - Supervised auditors in complete financial and operational reviews of Parker & Timmons.
- **FINANCIAL MANAGER / FINANCIAL SERVICES INDUSTRY GROUP** - Directed financial management functions of newly formed Parker & Timmons division.
- **DIRECTOR EMPLOYEE BENEFITS FINANCIAL ADMINISTRATION**

EDUCATIONAL HISTORY / LICENSES

Fordham University, Bronx, New York   B.S. Accounting

New York State Certified Public Accountant   1981

SENIOR ENGINEER

PEG VESSEY
76 Vine Street
Cincinnati, OH 45202

Objective: To become Senior Quality Operations Engineer for Conroy Computer Corporation

QUALIFICATIONS

Award-winning production process specialist with strong entrepreneurial focus. Over a decade of steadily more rewarding experience with Mitsohita Engineering USA, an $8.5 million oilfield equipment operation. Deep familiarity with computer-based design applications, including ION, PlanPro, and CorrectPlan systems, as well as spreadsheet, data management, and word processing software. Highly skilled in such diverse areas as:

Production control

Computer-assisted design

Marketing

Forecasting

Production-line preventative maintenance standards development

Product quality assurance

Management information systems

Sales

Budgeting

EDUCATION

Bachelor's degree in Mechanical Engineering from Bentworth College (1978)
M.B.A. from Bayton University School of Business (1981)

EXPERIENCE HIGHLIGHTS

Mitsohita Engineering USA (Cincinnati, OH)
Senior Quality Assurance Specialist

- Developed spin-off maintenance and repair consultation company with 7 employees and earnings of $2.4 million in the first year.
- Established quality control standards embraced systemwide and praised as "exemplary" by president of US operations.
- Implemented complete redesign of defective coupling device; personally detected flaw before shipment, saving company an estimated $340,000 in recall expenses.
- Named to team that developed CheckList (TM) Production System Analysis software for use by mid-sized manufacturing businesses; conducted initial market research, developed first-round technical specifications, and assisted in development of sell sheets, catalog text, and advertising copy. This application has resulted in over $750,000 in annual revenues for Mitsohita Engineering USA.
- Received Golden Signet Award for superior achievements in low-error-tolerance systems development.

OTHER EXPERIENCE

Vessey Technologies (Bakersfield, CA), Senior Design Analyst
Crowell Products (Orange, CA), Product Engineer

SENIOR EXECUTIVE, REAL ESTATE

MARK JONES
P.O. Box 1027
Boston, MA 02127
555/555-5555

Senior Executive experienced in P&L management, strategic planning, mergers/acquisitions, real estate development and sales, marketing, property/facilities management and real estate workouts.

- Added $20 million to bottom line annually through commercial real estate transactions and development of 10 projects.
- Sold out $2 billion portfolio at or above book value within 3-1/2 years, over $150 million in profits to company.
- Managed $125 million workout of defaulted mortgages on diverse-use REIT properties, saving over $30 million
- Doubled company size through strategic planning and merger.

Broad-based background in negotiations, operations, cash flow management, and reorganizations.

- Led major financial institution to $1+ billion in real estate sales in 2,500+ transactions within 3-1/2 years.
- Negotiated $60+ million in office and retail space leases.
- Developed $500+ million, 1.5 million-sq.ft. office space in downtown Boston; leased 500,000 sq.ft. before breaking ground.

Track record in productivity, management, and technology improvements.

- 20% increase in sales productivity through new sales incentive programs.
- Streamlined MIS reporting to control losses, sales strategies and compliance; saved thousands of report hours.
- Established 120-person department to sell and manage $1+ billion in product.
- Directed day-to-day operations, 150-person staff for multiple-building property management/development company.

Results-oriented team leader adept at problem solving, market analysis and managed risk taking. Strong listening, communication and interpersonal skills. Keen sense of bottom-line profitability.

Management Internship Program (MBA Equivalent), American Management Association, Boston, MA 1969–1970
B.A., Marketing, St. Peters University, 1977
Certified Property Manager (CPM), Institute of Real Estate Management, 1978

Willing to relocate

PROFESSIONAL EXPERIENCE

Owen Smith, LLC, Springfield, MA 1995–1996
Consultant/President
Developed strategic plan to grow company; acquired company that doubled size and initiated MIS reporting system.

Acme Management Corp. / Reston Financial Group, Springfield, MA 1992–1995

Senior Vice President / Division Head
Directed workout of $2 billion portfolio for FDIC with $150+ million profit in less than 4 years.

Marrison Properties Incorporated, Springfield, MA, 1983–1992
Senior Vice President / Senior Development Officer, Marketing, Property Management, Sales
Started Boston office, developed projects totaling 2+ million sq.ft., added over $200 million to bottom line. Hired and trained a staff of 20 real estate professionals. Consulted on other real estate and development projects throughout the U.S.

Landway Incorporated, Boston, MA 1982–1983
U.S. Vice President / Senior Development Officer
Managed and restructured various real estate operations/properties, saving $200+ million. Developed and implemented strategic plans.

Yale Properties Incorporated, New York, NY 1978–1982
Assistant Development Project Manager / Property Manager
Established leasing/property management program for Happyland USA property; turned around and totally leased complex within 2 years. Team member (1 of 3 assisting company president) on 2.5 million-sq.ft. Square Two project in New York.

Prior Commerce Real Estate Experience, 1970–1978
SDCI Mortgage Corporation, SDCI Properties Incorporated, A.B. Payne Company, Incorporated

SENIOR GENERAL MANAGER

JOHN H. SMITH
316 East Walnut Lane
Media, Pennsylvania 19063
610-444-2374 • E-mail: jhsmith@greatnet.com

SENIOR GENERAL MANAGEMENT
Consumer . . Industrial
Domestic . . . International
Service . . . Manufacturing

Senior general manager with full P&L responsibilities. Experienced in all phases of management including Manufacturing, Engineering, R&D, Operations, Financial, Product Development, Sales, Marketing, General Management and Service.

Reversed five years of financial losses ♦ *Increased sales by more than 60%* ♦ *Reduced inventories by 60%*

Improved bottom-line profit by $3.3 million ♦ *Reduced production time by 28%*

Improved product reliability 25% ♦ *Raised output 40% while reducing staff 14%* ♦ *Reorganized core business*

Expert at improving employee performance, increasing sales/profits, and reducing operating overhead/expenses.

- Tripled productivity without substantially changing facilities or personnel, reversing three years of operating losses.

- Improved quality rating 60% through the use of new standards, better training techniques, and strict quality assurance.

- Tripled output of high-tech manufacturing division by introducing a state-of-the-art robotic manufacturing operation.

- Recommended plant closing which reduced assets employed by $4.5 million and improved annual profits by $1.2 million a year.

- Monitored and negotiated the final closing on a $46 million cash acquisition.

Track record of growing companies by means of sound fiscal policies and a marketing-driven emphasis.

- Negotiated and secured loans with two major banks totaling $35 million, virtually eliminating high-interest credit line debt, resulting in savings of nearly $250 thousand per year.

- Achieved an upgrade of the company's commercial paper from A2 to A1 by Standard and Poor.

- Revamped and restaffed the marketing department leading to a 65% increase in dollar sales, and 35% in unit sales during first year with the company.

- Negotiated extended credit lines with vendors to double accounts payable level without serious adverse reaction.

- Installed a centralized budgetary program and reporting system to provide effective control of product line profits and manufacturing costs.

PROFESSIONAL EXPERIENCE

President and Chief Operating Officer   1990-Present
MOORE INDUSTRIES, King of Prussia, PA
Selected by the Board to succeed the previous president of this $335 million, five division company. Expert in establishing and implementing strategic plans, revitalizing stagnate operations, and turning operating losses into profits.

President   1981-1990
WESTERN FOODS (Division of Moore Industries), Denver, CO
Complete P&L responsibility for a $68 million processed and frozen foods division. Directed the operations of three plants and a national sales network.

EDUCATION

Master of Business Administration - Finance - Purdue University

Bachelor of Business Administration - Management - Emporia University

SENIOR PROJECT MANAGER

JOHN H. SMITH

316 Walnut Drive • Media, PA 19063
610-444-2374 (Res,)

Sixteen years experience managing residential, multi-family, and commercial construction projects. Exceptional strengths dealing with owners/investors, bankers, inspectors, sub-contractors, HUD, and salaried/hourly employees.

Demonstrated success at completing projects on time and under budget, managing multiple projects, scheduling, material/labor cost control, quality control, initiating OSHA safety requirements, and negotiating sub-contracts.

Brought in 126,000 sq. ft. office building 18 days ahead of schedule and $174,000 under budget.

Designed OSHA safety program, reducing small citations by 80% and major citations by 100%.

Completed 346 unit apartment complex 58 days ahead of schedule and $227,000 under budget.

Built 156 houses in one year, saving more than $170,000 while employing only 3 punch-out persons and 2 laborers. Maintained a customer rating of 8.6 out of a possible 10.

Awarded "Superintendent of the Year" two consecutive years and "Project Manager of the Year" three out of four years.

PROFESSIONAL EXPERIENCE

EASTERN SHORE CONSTRUCTION CO., INC.   **1994-PRESENT**
PROJECT MANAGER
Manage multiple jobs, hire superintendents, negotiate sub-contracts, coordinate operations with owners, develop and manage operating budgets, prepare schedules, maintain quality control, and general management.

- *Manage multiple projects including large apartment complexes, shopping centers, motels and hotels.*

- *Cut budgeted expenses by more than $280,000 during FY97 by implementing a strict cost control program, storing materials in secured areas, and employing company material handlers.*

- *Saved up to $80,000 per job by negotiating stricter terms with sub-contractors (i.e., doing their own clean-up, supplying their own nails and glue, etc.)*

WASHBOW GENERAL CONTRACTORS   **1981-1994**
PROJECT MANAGER
Managed new residential, multi-family dwellings, and commercial projects, as well as the renovation of existing buildings. Coordinated activities with owners/investors, architects, engineers and inspectors.

- *Managed residential projects exceeding 550 homes,   sq. ft. commercial buildings, as well as apartment complexes, shopping centers/malls, motels/hotels, and multi-family complexes.*

- *Saved $3,100,000 over a six-year period by implementing a strict quality control program and by completing projects on or before completion dates.*

- *Recognized for ability to complete quality projects under budget: Cinema $31,000 savings ◆ State building $52,000 savings ◆ Corporate headquarters $192,000 savings ◆ Shopping center $128,000 savings.*

SENIOR PROJECT/PLANT MANAGER

FRANK SMITH
9987 Beach Street
San Diego, CA 90002
555/555-5555

Five+ years senior project/plant manager who reduced capital costs and turned one existing manufacturing plant losing $1.5 million into $10 million profits in less than two years. Track record of bringing complex new plants from conception to production within budget and on time. Full responsibility for the design, construction, commissioning, start-up and operation of new manufacturing facilities.

Upgraded existing staffs, upgraded morale, reduced costs and produced substantial profits even in declining and competitive markets. Molded professional project teams with diverse technical, cultural and language backgrounds to complete tasks on budget and on time.

Twenty-four years progressive plant management/construction experience with Glycon with budget responsibility up to $250 million. Left Glycon despite their strong efforts to retain employment because wife desired return to states for the time being after six years of foreign assignments.

1965 B.S. in chemistry and physics from University of Texas. Will relocate.

EXPERIENCE:

GLYCON COMPANY, San Diego, CA 1966–1991
Plant Manager (Malaysia 1988–1991)
* Full responsibility for design, construction, commissioning, start-up, and operation of $225 million manufacturing facility.
* Reduced capital requirements $30 million without reducing capacity or efficiency.
* Negotiated $55 million tax incentives from Malaysian government.
* Reduced liaison team by 30%, saving $3 million.

Plant Manager (Peru 1986–1988)
* Negotiated $60 million in governmental investment incentives.
* Developed site selection guidelines and selected site for major mining operation.
* Implemented project commissioning program that saved $1 million.
* Developed project execution plan.
* Managed $250 million budget.

Plant Manager (Mexico 1984–1986)
* Full management responsibility for Depot's largest manufacturing site in Brazil.
* Eight fold improvement in safety; 30% improvement in productivity.
* Turned $1.5 million per year loss into $10 million per year profit.

Maintenance/Operations Manager (Savannah, GA 1980–1984)
* Improved process time 20% through improved maintenance procedures.
* Developed self-managing work teams; implemented multiple-skill mechanical training.

Environmental Coordinator (Wilmington, CT 1973–1980)
* Developed and executed environmental, engineering and operational plan for "green field" manufacturing plant. Developed major public support through community contacts.

Manufacturing/R&D/Maintenance Supervisor (Sacramento, CA 1966–1973)

PERSONAL: Born 8/6/44 in Frenchtown, MI. Married, 1965; no children.

SOFTWARE PROGRAMMER

ANTHONY MARCELLUS

2914 Willow Brook Road
Dayton, OH 45301

513-876-1654 (W)
513-743-9433 (H)

Computer Programmer with more than 12 years experience in the U.S. Air Force. Skilled in the design and development of large-scale software applications. Skilled technician with the ability to adapt to a variety of working environments.

Experience includes systems analysis and programming in a wide range of computing environments.

Expert software trainer with strong interpersonal and communication skills.

Knowledge of 43XX, OS/MVS/XA, DOS/VSE, COBOL, PASCAL, BASIC, CICS, DL/1, VSAM, ICCF, ROSCOE, EASYTRIEVE, SORT/MERGE, MSA, A/P,TSO/SPF, EDGAR, VOLLIE, C, C++, Ada, etc.

Experienced in the use of CASE and other information engineering tools.

PROFESSIONAL EXPERIENCE

Computer Programmer - McGuire Air Force Base, NJ   1994-Present

★ *Developed custom software applications using 3rd and 4th generation programming languages (e.g., C, C++, Ada, and COBOL).*

★ *Maintained the Integrated Financial Information System. Resolved software problems, coded and installed software modifications.*

Systems Analyst - Lackland Air Force Base, TX   1990-1994

★ *Wrote specifications for the design of a large-scale system that was to provide automated support in the logistic area.*

★ *Modular, top-down design enabled a team of programmers to concurrently work on different portions of the system. Credited with saving more than $65,000 in development costs by using this approach.*

★ *Involved in the development of Financial Software. Wrote applications for product creation and index processing.*

Computer Programmer - Lackland Air Force Base, TX   1988-1990

★ *Participated in design and programming for Financial Reporting System. Programmed for Computer Assisted Appraisal and Elections application. Wrote user guide for data entry (COBOL).*

★ *Analyzed, coded, and maintained COBOL and CICS Command Level programs.*

Computer Programmer - Travis Air Force Base, CA   1984-1988

★ *Designed and developed COBOL software applications that increased the efficiency of processing personnel records. Programming was completed on an IBM 3090 mainframe running MVS/TSO.*

★ *Received official commendation for efficiency and cost savings resulting from application.*

EDUCATION AND TRAINING

B.S. - MIS - University of Delaware   ♦   **A.A.** - Computer Programming - College of the Air Force

Courses on Systems Analysis, Database Manipulation Language, Transaction Programming Language, SCIP/SCOP, BASIC, ASSEMBLER, MS-DOS, Database Design Assembly Language Programming, Systems Support Programming, etc.

SUPPLY/LOGISTICS EXECUTIVE

John Smith
999 Main Street • Denver, CO 80202 • (555) 555-5555

SENIOR EXECUTIVE: SUPPLY/TRADING & LOGISTICS MANAGEMENT
High caliber supply/trading, logistics, and risk management strategist with over 25 years' experience controlling supply and transportation costs, establishing supply sources, and delivering increased growth and profitability to major players in the domestic and international oil markets. Special expertise in developing financial partnerships and joint ventures, as well as identifying target companies for acquisition. Solid reputation in industry for honesty, integrity, and straightforward manner. Key contributor to strategic planning, budgeting, and optimization of corporate operations.

SPECIAL ABILITIES TO:
- Structure, organize, and build supply networks for maximum growth and profitability
- Utilize innovative pricing formulae and risk-management knowledge to deliver multi-million dollar cost savings
- Exercise control over variable costs to maintain or increase competitive market advantage
- Analyze political climate and potentially destabilizing events in international arena and devise systems to minimize potential adverse effects of unforeseen price spikes
- Generate profits through highly developed expertise in speculative trading
- Deal with people of varied backgrounds and cultures worldwide and within organization

PROFESSIONAL EXPERIENCE

VORRIO ENERGY SYSTEMS, Denver, Colorado   1995–1996
Senior Vice President—Supply
Recruited to reorganize, restructure, and rebuild refined products network for adequate, dependable, and economical supply to 250+ active accounts with total forward demand in excess of 135 million barrels. With a staff of seven professionals directly reporting, managed purchase, sale, distribution, and delivery of 80,000+ barrels of refined products per day to commercial account base. Actively participated in development of short- and long-term business plans, budgets, and risk management procedures.
- Expanded supply network over 100% from 80 to 164 terminals spanning 35 states.
- Reduced inventory levels and monthly storage charges to less than one-fifth previous levels, from $260,000 to less than $45,000 within first six months.
- Reduced costs across-the-board by over $1.2 million within first six months.

SMO CORPORATION, New Orleans, Louisiana   1984–1995
Manager—Product Supply and Trading
Managed and participated in trading of approximately 100,000 barrels per day in petroleum products and feedstocks to geographic area spanning North and South America and the Caribbean. Directed staff of five trading, marketing, and risk-management professionals in trading activities including pipeline, cargo, barge, futures, options, and swaps. Coordinated with company offices in Paris, Geneva, Chile, and Singapore to exploit interregional trading opportunities and place equity crudes as requested.
- Personally negotiated company's first products contracts with various national oil companies in South America, enhancing company's trading presence in the United States.
- Delivered positive speculative trading results for 9 years out of 11.
- Completely revamped marine insurance program for $1 million cost savings in first full year of implementation.

MARKETCO, Denver, Colorado   1983–1984
Vice President—International Trading
Managed staff of seven professionals in geographically dispersed offices with responsibility for trading of approximately 110,000 barrels per day of various refined petroleum products and feedstocks in international markets including U.S. East and Gulf Coasts, Latin America, and Europe.
- Enhanced presence and increased sales in U.S. market by negotiating acquisition of fuel oil trading company.

PETROLINK, Houston, Texas   1980–1983
Vice President—Supply & Distribution
Managed acquisition, distribution, and trading of approximately 50 million barrels per year of products with market value in excess of $1.2 billion. Held direct responsibility for consummating supply and trading arrangements with domestic refiners and national oil companies throughout the world. Managed tidewater and inland terminal distribution system spanning 11 states with aggregate storage capacity in excess of 11 million barrels, as well as all marine transportation activities.
- Established and supervised Denver office.

OILWAY PARTNERSHIP, New Orleans, Louisiana   1980
Manager—Gulf Coast Supply & Trading
Recruited to organize and staff New Orleans supply and trading office to complement East Coast refining and marketing activities.
- Increased profitability of supply and trading activities, necessitating staff increase from 2 to 12.

EARLY CAREER HIGHLIGHTS

Manager—ABC Refining, New Orleans, Louisiana
- Negotiated several crude oil processing arrangements with refiners to establish trading base in markets where company had no previous presence.

General Manager—Supply & Trading, Merton Sales Corporation, Richmond, California
- Participated in studies leading to development of company's 40,000 barrels per day refinery.

SPECIAL SKILLS

Languages: Read and write English, Spanish, and French fluently.
Proficient in WordPerfect, Word, Lotus 1-2-3, Windows 95

EDUCATION

B.A., Economics, University of Denver, May, 1970
Petrolink Management Development Course

TRAVEL/TOURISM EXECUTIVE

JOHN SMITH   (555) 555-5555
260 Dixey Drive
Boston MA 02127

SENIOR EXECUTIVE
Product Development / Strategic Marketing
15 years of global corporate and consulting success developing innovative products,
researching and penetrating new markets, delivering increased market share, and extracting
greater margins through strategic partnerships. Special expertise in travel/tourism industry
and application of information technology. Multilingual, persuasive communicator with
cross-cultural business experience in all major international markets. Skilled start-up,
joint venture, and merger/acquisition strategist who built two successful operations
from scratch, including a complete tourism destination.

DEMONSTRATED CAPABILITIES TO:
- Position existing and start-up companies for aggressive growth and market dominance
- Identify market opportunities and conceptualize innovative products to capitalize on them
- Build dynamic teams, galvanize to action in environment of participative teamwork
- Develop and implement comprehensive market strategies for diverse products and services
  including direct/wholesale/retail channeling, and packaging, promotion, merchandising
- Maintain profitability and equity value despite fiercely competitive conditions and industry
  downturns utilizing strategic partnering and strict budgetary/overhead control
- Exploit opportunities created by Internet and emerging information technology

PROFESSIONAL EXPERIENCE
STREET AND HOWE, INC., Boston, MA   1994–Present
Management consulting firm providing strategic marketing services to tourism industry, air-
lines, hotels, and others.

President/CEO
Founded company to advise and assist select travel/tourism clientele focusing on new product development and distribution opportunities presented by rapidly evolving information
technology. Develop direct marketing channels, promotional materials, and merchandising
strategies, as well as identify potential for and promote joint venture partnerships.

- Built prestigious client base including publicly traded companies such as airlines, hotel
  chains, Liaison International, and the Billy Mason Company.
- Created innovative network marketing platform for major hotel and cruise vendors utilizing sophisticated database modeling techniques to provide direct marketing services
  to an independent travel agent network.
- Conceived, proposed, and developed adventure travel product line for Billy Mason,
  bringing strategic operating partner on board for scheduled launch in 1997.
- Increased profitability over 35% on its investment conferences by providing complete
  package of marketing and conference management services.
- Developed U.S.-based joint venture partners for private/state-backed consortium in
  Hong Kong targeting development of cellular communications network, airport renovation, import/export transaction financing, and natural resource development in main-
  land China.

SUNWAY, INC., Miami, FL   1982–1993
International tourism operation operating lodges in Jamaica and the Dominican Republic as well as a wholesale marketing concern in Miami.

President (1989–1993)
Charged with directing sales/marketing and operations via two separate and geographically diverse management teams with full responsibility for marketing channels and alliances, cost containment, and market share. Managed all aspects of sale to European Hotelier in 1992 and continued supervision of North American sales and marketing activities after sale.
- Strategized and executed merger which increased equity value 50% through addition of additional properties and positioned favorably for sale.
- Established company as dominant tourism operation in Jamaica.
- Positioned operation as Caribbean-bound tourism leader with 45% market share.
- Slashed marketing overhead from 8% to 5% of sales while dramatically increasing exposure by forging marketing alliances with airlines and hotels.
- Increased equity value tenfold in four years prior to sale.
- Cut operating and marketing costs 28%, maintaining profitability during industry-wide downturn.

Executive Vice President—Marketing & Sales (1982–1988)
Recruited by owners to establish U.S. marketing operations with full responsibility for marketing and sales development.
- Grew sales by factor of 9 in 7 years.
- Strategized purchase of overseas operating units.
- Significantly improved market profile/positioning through airline/hotel strategic partnerships.
- Developed new market segments including not-for-profits and special interest groups.
- Established targeted travel agency channels including database and marketing strategies.

DAYCO., London, England   1978–1980
Economic Analyst: Provided world and regional economic analysis to support management of $2 billion+ portfolio focused on technology and commodities.

EDUCATION
THE UNIVERSITY OF MANCHESTER   Manchester, England
   Master of Business Administration (MBA), 1981, Graduate School of Business
   B.A. (Honors) Economics 1977; B.A. , 1976

LANGUAGES
   Fluent in English, Spanish, and French.

TURNAROUND EXPERT (SUMMARY FORMAT)

JAMES SMITH ○ 123 Main Street ○ Salem, MA 01970 ○ 555/555-5555

EXECUTIVE SUMMARY: General Technologies is searching for "powerful and effective contributors to its new management team."

JAMES SMITH is an expert in manufacturing processes and domestic/international marketing with 17 years of experience in turning several underperforming domestic and international operations into successful and profitable outfits.
Past companies have ranged in size from $4 million to $50 million; names and provided on request.

Skilled at:
○ Refocusing unproductive teams
○ Establishing new domestic or international market goals and territories
○ Reducing expenditures
○ Taking charge and utilizing exceptional leadership skills to make profitability a reality

Highlights: Turned a $10 million losing operation into an organization with $1.35 million annual profits; developed an international operation that grew into a $45 million business within three years.

TURNAROUND SPECIALIST

Jane Smith § 714 Elwood Road § Phoenix, AZ 85004 § (555) 555-5555

SENIOR SALES / MARKETING / OPERATIONS EXECUTIVE

Multi-skilled, high-energy executive with strong entrepreneurial bent, keen financial acumen, and focus on results. Fast-track success with proven transferability to broad spectrum of industries. Combine high-caliber analytical and strategic planning skills with outstanding business development and marketing expertise applicable to both national and international business arenas. Exceptional mastery of marketing, motivational, and sales principles developed under mentorship of authorities in these fields. Thrive on challenges which may be daunting to others.

TARGET: Hands-on, leadership role with aggressive company positioned for growth.

EXECUTIVE PROFILE

Demonstrated Capabilities to:

Achieve stunning turnarounds for severely troubled organizations
Cut through the clutter of information to core problems and root them out
Develop and implement strategies to spur phenomenal growth in profits and market share
Bring start-up, growth, and established organizations alike to the next level of profitability
Raise millions of dollars in capital needed to weather reverses and fund growth

Key Strengths:

Extraordinary motivator and rapport-builder—readily ignite stagnant or failing operations
Skilled motivational speaker accustomed to addressing assemblies of 5,000+
Talent for locating and recruiting top-notch executives, managers, and staff
Personally recruited several Fortune 500 executives
Have selected and built high-caliber staffs for diverse organizations from scratch

ACHIEVEMENT HIGHLIGHTS

Vice President—Sales & Marketing/Recruitment
Wheeling Securities, Phoenix, Arizona 1993–Present
Multi-million dollar firm specializing in institutional, civic, and corporate investors. Recruited on contingency basis by this organization experiencing financial crisis to conduct an in-depth analysis of structural and operational flaws and devise/implement solutions. Starting at zero with a telephone and fax:

- Conducted intensive examination of company through incisive, in-depth interviews with CFOs over two-week period.
- Recruited and trained top-quality staff of 34 brokers within 16 months.
- Developed aggressive marketing and sales strategies.
- Trained, motivated, and empowered sales staff in marketing strategy implementation.

Results:

- *Raised over $4 million to capitalize company within only three months.*
- *Rescued organization from imminent bankruptcy, moving within two years to a firm financial footing boasting a solid multi-million dollar account portfolio.*

185

President/Principal
PeoplePower, San Francisco, CA 1989–1992
Started, developed, and managed executive recruiting firm serving international corporate clientele.
- Grew firm from its initial capitalization phase to a successful 16-employee operation.
- Managed all financial, human resources, and administrative aspects.

Results:
- *Built income from zero to annual revenues topping the $1.4 million mark.*
- *Personally recruited 11 top-level executives for clients including AceWater, Moore Hotels, and BBM.*
- *Staff collectively placed over 100 executives over four-year period.*

Sales Manager
SweetWater Title Insurance, Des Moines, IA 1985–1991
Fast-track promotion record from initial hire as sales representative trainee through Assistant Sales Manager to Division Sales Manager for this large nationwide insurer of commercial real estate.
- Managed staff of 12 sales representatives.
- Developed staff and maintained high morale through intensive program of sales meetings and motivational seminars.

Results:
- *Top Sales Manager within 14 months.*
- *#11 in organization nationwide.*

Cruise Director
Ocean Cruises, Miami, FL 1981–1985
Working on a contract basis during academic breaks, rapidly earned promotion from entry level position to Cruise Director, overseeing a staff of six in management of all entertainment and recreational programs. Developed and coordinated all passenger activity programming and served as Master of Ceremonies for all events. Gained considerable international background throughout travels.

CIVIC INVOLVEMENT

- Leader, Cub Scout Den 4, Pack 73, Phoenix, AZ
- Director, City Council, Phoenix, AZ

EDUCATION & PROFESSIONAL TRAINING

Business Management / Marketing—University of Arizona

TURNAROUND SPECIALIST/HIGH-TECH FOCUS

BERT POWER
987 Wellington Avenue, Ft. Lauderdale, FL 32098
555/555-9817

"In mighty enterprises, to have willed success is essential."—Sextus Propertius

SUMMARY

Proven track record in executive manufacturing, marketing, and operations positions for high-technology firms.

EXPERT AT

Turning around troubled teams and divisions
Streamlining companies
Setting up highly productive work groups
Developing effective engineering operations
Launching successful new marketing operations
Maximizing efficiency of production processes
Boosting revenues
Increasing value for shareholders

**EMPLOYMENT
PROFILE**

Meeram Systems   **Ft. Lauderdale, FL**
Senior Engineer / VP Operations (1991–present)
As of this writing, the nation's leading provider of sophisticated drug test equipment to private industry
- Reduced product costs by 32%
- Added $400,000 in cash flow through
- Negotiated financing that made possible key new product launch, which delivered $4.5 million in revenue in first year
- Worked with national sales staff to identify important new market areas representing $11.5 million in revenues
- Assisted in preliminary and final product design
- Supervised between 40 and 61 employees
- Named company's "Most Valuable Player" at annual banquet, 1995

**EARLY EMPLOYMENT
SUMMARY**

Crestview Information Products   **Miami, FL**
Process Engineer (1988–1991)

Sideco   **Atlanta, GA**
Engineer (1985–1988)

EDUCATION

Flausser College, Des Moines, IA (B.S., Manufacturing Processes) 1985

VP/FINANCE

VINCENT SMITH / 809 Symphony Avenue, Phoenix, AZ / 555-555-5555

Career Objective: Controller for XYZ Corporation

Qualifications: Eighteen years of experience as a key, top-level contributor for Greensboro Communications, Englewood Entertainment, a successful start-up operation, and DeVere Business Services. Familiar with all aspects of accounting and finance, with notable strengths in management, human resources, and business development. I specialize in the design and delivery of financial and human resource solutions.

PROFESSIONAL EXPERIENCE

1984–Present	VP/Finance, Greensboro Communications (Phoenix, AZ)
1981–1983	Controller/Director of Human Resources, Englewood Entertainment (Los Angeles, CA)
1979–1980	Associate, DeVere Business Services (Los Angeles, CA)

Key Accomplishments
* Responsible for managing all finances of Greensboro Communications, a company that grew from $2.5 million to $80 million in revenue in 36 months:

    Supervised staff that ranged in size from 7 to 23.

    Assisted in the development of two new business areas that resulted in $4.3 million dollars in annual revenue.

* Served simultaneously as Controller and Director of Human Resources for Englewood Entertainment:

    Wore multiple hats for this successful start-up operation; systems I developed praised as "one of the big reasons we were able to succeed in the marketplace despite intense competition." (Letter from president of firm upon my departure from Greensboro.)

    Retention rate among front-line employees 26% above published industry averages.

* Spent two years with DeVere Business Services, a top-10 CPA firm:

    Recruited upon graduation.

    Billings exceeded annual goals in each year.

EDUCATION

Bachelor's degree, Business Administration, Hartwell College (1977)

M.B.A., Vosburgh Institute (1979)

VP/FINANCE AND ADMINISTRATION

JOHN H. SMITH

316 Walnut Drive ■ Media, PA 19063
610-444-2374 ■ E-mail: jhsmith@greatnet.com

Exceptionally broad-based financial executive with an extensive background in financial management, with an emphasis on cost controls, budgeting, profit planning, competitive price analysis, forecasting and financial analysis.

Initiated control programs and new purchasing procedures resulting in a 21% reduction in inventory levels.

Installed a budgetary and reporting system to provide effective control of product line profits and manufacturing costs.

Managed a unique asset recovery effort from a liquidated Mexican subsidiary, recovering more than $14 million.

Successful at managing operations, negotiating loans and credit lines, and leading joint venture, merger and acquisition efforts.

Managed the transition from a single division $35 million company to a three-division $135 million company.

Negotiated the purchase of a $48 million subsidiary from a Fortune 100 company for 14% less than book value.

Prepared business plan for a seven-company operation that led to an extremely favorable sale of an unprofitable division.

Master of Business Administration • University of Minnesota   ✦   Bachelor of Science • Brown University
Certified Public Accountant, Minnesota

PROFESSIONAL EXPERIENCE

WONDER BUSINESS CORPORATION., Philadelphia, PA   **1991-Present**
VICE PRESIDENT FINANCE & ADMINISTRATION
Primary objectives were to manage the reorganization of the company, and to bring seven independent operating units under one formal reporting and operating structure. Direct all financial, accounting and administrative activities.

- *Elected Treasurer/Secretary of operating companies in 1993 and to the Board of Directors in 1994. Serve as the Chief Operating Officer in the absence of the President.*

- *Negotiated loans and credit lines of $38 million that allowed the company to grow sevenfold over a 6 year period.*

- *Negotiated building leases in excess of $1.4 million for use as corporate offices.*

- *Managed the installation of a new computer system -- including system definition and hardware conversion.*

- *Implemented new centralized accounting, order entry, invoicing, inventory control and sales analysis systems for seven operating divisions.*

BLENDEX ELECTRONICS GROUP, INC., Minneapolis, MN   **1986-1991**
CONTROLLER
Complete financial responsibility for a $78 million business with seven product lines. Responsible for all U.S. government contracts (Army, Navy, and Air Force) and SEC filings (3, 4, 10K, 8K, and 10Q).

- *Chaired a management task team that took a Fortune 50 division from a $16 million annual operating loss to a $8.4 million profit within four years.*

- *Effected a substantial increase in the effectiveness of the credit function through the installation of an automated billing and client record system with on-line management tracking.*

- *Improved cash flow by establishing credit and collection procedures that reduced the average account receivable from 58 days to 31 days.*

SOLAR INDUSTRIES, Minneapolis, MN   **1981-1986**
ACCOUNTING/OPERATIONS MANAGER
Responsible for day-to-day accounting operations, as well as the inventory control function. Supervised $5 million in monthly purchases, monthly physical counts and reconciliations for four warehouse locations. Prepared all statements and tax returns.

- *Redesigned the entire billing and statistical reporting system. Established office and warehouse accounting policies and a financial reporting and budgeting system to track profitability by salesperson.*

VP/FINANCE AND CONTROL

CAROL ANNE WESLEY
216 West Juniper Avenue
Clarksburg, OH 23622
709-559-3725 (Bus.) ◆ 709-865-2298 (Res.)

Accomplished, versatile financial executive with significant operations and general management experience. Demonstrated record of success in international/domestic financial management functions, with solid strengths in control, financial reporting, forecasting, budgets, mergers/acquisitions/divestitures, and treasury-related activities.

Expertise with external and internal auditors, counsel, financial analysts, stockholders, government compliance.

Mature management of human resources and seasoned business judgment.

Experienced in formulation, documentation, execution and control of strategic plans.

Excellent working knowledge of the planning and execution of medium and large scale MIS installations.

Record of success in directing complex operations with demanding time pressures, and the ability to motivate others to superior performance. Equal strengths in positioning operations for growth and building smooth running, cost-effective functions in periods of significant growth and down-sizing.

CAREER HIGHLIGHTS

MAXWELL MANUFACTURING CORP.
1989-Present   Vice President, Finance, Planning & Control
1985-1889   Controller
Direct all financial, accounting, and administrative activities of this $280 million subsidiary of General Engines. Heavily involved in the management of day-to-day operations and serve as the Chief Operating Officer in the absence of the President.

- *Played key role in highly successful effort to turn around divisional responsibility, resulting in a profit swing of $28 million over a two year period.*

- *Evaluated, recommended and purchased a $30 million preferred stock portfolio with leverage, yielding an after tax return of more than 20% per year. Realized capital gains of nearly $2.7 million in two years.*

- *Headed financial team on Philippines joint venture project requiring extensive involvement with U.S. EXIM bank, foreign governmental agencies and stateside commercial banking community.*

- *Introduced and implemented an innovative cash conservation program to intensify attention on working capital investment and administrative spending. Program was adopted as basis for monthly operating reviews at division and sector levels.*

- *Negotiated the sale of an office building which provided $1.8 in excess funds and retired a debt carrying a 16.5% interest rate.*

From 1981 to 1985, served as Assistant Controller for Webster Financial Services. Responsible for traditional controllership functions of this $60 million subsidiary of General Engines. Earlier experience includes a brief assignment as Budget and Tax Manager at Winston Financial Services and two years accounting work with Mitchell, Mitchell & Peak.

EDUCATION

M.B.A. - Accounting - Washington State University   •   **B.S.** - Accounting - Stanford University

Certified Public Accountant

VP/MARKETING

STEVEN S. WEINBERG
2225 Angel Lane
New York, NY 12345
555/555-5555

Senior Executive experienced in marketing/general management, strategic planning, business/product development, operations, and national multimedia advertising in start-up, nonprofit, and Fortune 200 arenas.
- *Took new division from $4 million to $75 million and from 1 to 8 products in 3 years.*
- *Led $50 million national ad campaign increasing brand awareness from 5% to 40%.*
- *Key in signing Bill Cosby to 3-year spokesperson contract and supervised production of 6 TV spots.*

Innovator with keen business sense who consistently orchestrated dynamic growth in market share and revenue through new product development and marketing of diverse products in wide variety of industries.
- *$65 million in sales by developing 2 new products (patents held) appearing on cover of* Business Week.
- *Achieved #1 in market share and increased sales from $23 million to $30 million by establishing nationwide, 24-hour distribution.*

Creative problem solver combining expertise in market research, broad-based technical knowledge, and excellent team-building and communication abilities to optimize results.
- *Reversed market share decline and increased unit sales from 420,000 to 500,000 in 1 year.*
- *175% increase in sales and 45% distributor expansion in 1 year for unique product.*
- *Developed and executed strategy which increased corporate volunteers from 40,000 to 78,000.*

Willing to relocate. Married. In excellent health.
M.B.A., University of California at Berkeley, 1975
Ph.D., Microbiology, University of California at Berkeley, 1969
B.S., Worcester Polytechnic Institute, 1964

EXPERIENCE

THE YOUTH GROUP, INC., New York, NY 1989–1997 Vice President, Marketing
Directed all marketing activities nationwide for this nonprofit education organization. Formalized market plan process for 167 U.S. franchises, increased corporate volunteers 195%, and negotiated $650K in contributions.

STEINBERG & ASSOCIATES, New York, NY 1986–1989 Principal
Marketing consultant to start-up and Fortune 500 firms. Successfully repositioned branded products for Litton and 3M. Increased sales from $1.4 million to $2.5 million in one year for new brand of golf cart. Developed/conducted seminars and workshops for groups up to 100, including Target Stores.

INFO CORPORATION, New York, NY 1983–1985 President, CEO
Recruited to turn around troubled high-tech start-up. Determined there was no market for sole product and reengineered for industrial applications. Technology sold off to a competitor.

TEXMARK, INC., Dallas, TX 1977–1983 Manager of Marketing and Communications, 1980–1983
Division Marketing Manager, 1977–1980
Developed/executed annual and long-range strategic marketing plans. Managed $50 million national marketing program increasing brand awareness eight-fold. At division level, increased sales from $4 million to $75 million.

PRIOR EXPERIENCE

Product Marketing Manager for medical equipment manufacturer, **FARSEK TECHNOLOGIES.**
Senior Research Microbiologist and troubleshooter for multiple plants at **BIGCORP, INC.**

VP MARKETING/ENGINEERING FOCUS

NATHAN SMITH

198 Truman Way
Troy, MI 48084
555/555-7168 (days)
555/555-7161 (evenings)

OBJECTIVE

To launch profitable new business operations for MarkCo Associates.

SUMMARY OF QUALIFICATIONS

Seventeen years of hands-on exposure to market development issues for highly respected engineering and manufacturing organizations. Skills that can be put to work for MarkCo immediately include:

* Product research and development
* Manufacturing process analysis
* Marketing design and launch
* Administration
* Capital funding
* Management of field operations
* International negotiations and licensing
* Plant management

PROFESSIONAL EXPERIENCE

Research Engineering (Troy, MI) 1994–present
VP/Marketing and Operations

* Helped launch most explosive market growth in company history
* New industrial marketing plan led to 45% revenue increases per year
* Boosted total revenues from $2 million to $19 million
* Served as main contact with financial institutions during critical funding meetings
* Assisted in development of new products yielding $1.9 million in annual revenue
* Negotiated favorable overseas equipment leasing agreements
* Established high standards for international plant output

Quality Fabricated Products (Oakland, CA) 1988–1994
Director of Marketing

VeeJay Products (San Francisco, CA), 1979–1988
Design Engineer (later appointed Field Representative)

EDUCATION

B.S., Mathematics, Burros University, Santa Cruz, CA

COMMUNITY SERVICE

Boy Scout den leader of 6 years' standing
With wife of eleven years, regular volunteer at WLPM, Troy (public radio affiliate)

VP/OPERATIONS

MELVIN WRIGHT
871 Smedley Court
Cambridge MA 02138
555/555-9181

19 years of experience in administration and manufacturing process management. Experienced in start-up, $600 million, and $3.1 billion working environments. Energetic, technically accomplished team player, with superior skill base in:

- Product design
- Testing
- Budgeting
- Training

- Product assembly
- Operations support
- Forecasting
- Technical writing

SIGNIFICANT WORK HISTORY AND ACCOMPLISHMENTS

3/86–present: Attosha Engineering (Cambridge, MA)
Successively: Process Engineer; Senior Process Engineering Specialist; VP/Operations

- Developed new product ideas in concert with Marketing Department resulting in annual sales of $14.5 million
- Designed and executed an 850-person manufacturing plan
- Personally responsible for $51 million operating budget
- Conducted staff training on testing and analysis procedures
- Developed 240-page resource and troubleshooting guide under tight deadline; this document was later described by CEO as "our production Bible"
- Developed working prototype for new MagnaCore analysis system in 14 days, paving way for early product release that secured significant market share

Canston Associates (South San Francisco, CA) Process Engineer (1984–1986)

Clements Technologies (Buffalo, NY) Engineering Associate (1978–1984)

EDUCATION

Vera Cruz University, class of 1977, concentration in Process Engineering

VP/OPERATIONS

JOHN H. SMITH

316 Walnut Drive • Media, PA 19063 • 610-756-2300 (W) • 610-444-2374 (H) • E-mail: jhsmith@greatnet.com

Executive with nearly 20 years experience in logistics and distribution management. Exceptional strengths in work and manpower planning, quality control, warehouse design and automation, receiving, shipping, and general management.

Developed and implemented a performance improvement program that boosted productivity by 18%.
Consolidated 3 geographically distant warehouse operations into a single 770,000 sq. ft. automated hub saving 43% in overhead.
Upgraded distribution output from a substandard rate to one of the highest in the entire country.

Acknowledged as one of the leading experts in the country at streamlining ordering and inventory tracking systems.

Featured in <u>Business Review</u> magazine for the development of a computerized international order control and shipping system.
Reduced inventory discrepancies more than 37% by developing a sophisticated receiving and internal tracking system.
Increased storage capacity 85% by installing a multi-tier system and standardizing inventory control procedures.

Master of Business Administration • Management Information Systems • New York University
Bachelor of Business Administration • Marketing Major • Bowling Green State University

---
PROFESSIONAL EXPERIENCE

LADY GLORIA APPAREL, Philadelphia, PA   **1993-PRESENT**
VICE PRESIDENT OPERATIONS
Manage all operations, warehousing and support services for the manufacture and distribution of products throughout the U.S. of this $600 million women's apparel manufacturer.

- Designed and installed a unique order entry and shipping control software package which was linked with 14 foreign suppliers throughout Latin America, the Caribbean, and the Pacific Basin.
- Revamped Customer Service and consistently met 24-hour turnaround for more than 90% of shipments.
- Introduced new packing materials and techniques which reduced shipping costs 17% and damaged goods 87%.
- Increased productivity 17% by establishing production standards linked to an innovative employee incentive program.

HERMAN'S GARMENTS, Pennsauken, NJ   **1988-1993**
OPERATIONS MANAGER
Responsible for customer service, receiving, quality control, warehousing, picking, shipping and returns. Administered $4.6 million budget. Directed 9 supervisors, and 127 administrative, customer service and warehouse persons.

- Reduced injury claims by 55% by working with insurance carrier and introducing an on-going safety awareness program.
- Upgraded warehouse output from nearly 20% below budgeted output to 103% with 9 months.

ATLANTIC PAPER PRODUCTS COMPANY, Atlanta, GA   **1985-1988**
WAREHOUSE MANAGER
Managed a 250,000 sq. ft. warehouse including receiving, checking, picking, packing, and shipping. Scheduled drivers, negotiated rates with truck lines and carriers.

- Increased productivity 11% by developing an operations manual and creating a cross training program.
- Awarded President's Club status for raising warehouse output from lowest in company ranking to number one.

EXCEL HOME PRODUCTS, INC., Atlanta, GA   **1981-1985**
WAREHOUSE MANAGER
Responsible for receiving, checking, storage, packing and shipping. Supervised 35 warehouse personnel and 5 support staff.
- Hired as Shipping Supervisor and promoted to Assistant Warehouse Manager and then Manager in 31 months.

VP/PURCHASING AND PRODUCT MANAGEMENT

JOHN H. SMITH
316 Walnut Drive ◆ Media, PA 19063
610-444-2374 ◆ E-mail: jhsmith@greatnet.com

Senior-level professional with an outstanding record of achievement in managing purchasing departments and operations, developing purchasing strategies, reducing costs, and directing inventory control and recovery efforts.

Background in large and small organizations. Skilled in the preparation of operating plans, budgets, and pricing analyses.

Master of Business Administration • Colorado State ◆ Bachelor of Science • North Carolina State
Former guest speaker Harvard University and Boston College

——————————————— PROFESSIONAL EXPERIENCE ———————————————

PACE MEDICAL MANAGEMENT   1994-Present
Vice President, Purchasing and Product Management
Led team which purchased in excess of $850 million in pharmaceutical and medical equipment for multiple hospitals and medical facilities.

- Prepared a strategic purchasing plan, leading to a more effective and stream-lined budget. Effort reduced purchasing costs by more than $500K in the first year.

- Saved more than $400K in purchasing expense in the first year by establishing new requirements for the vendor bidding process.

- Discovered and introduced more than 50 products which proved to be more cost-effective and superior in quality to previous products. Savings exceeded $140,000 per year.

- Consolidate two separate purchasing groups into one reducing labor costs by 18%. Assisted in the design of a new automated warehousing and shipping facility.

PAQUELL MEDICAL SERVICES   1989-1994
PURCHASING DIRECTOR
Responsible for a $6.4 million annual purchasing budget for hospitals, medical facilities, and medical supply houses throughout the U.S.

- Revamped the Computerized Inventory System which resulted in the recovery of more than $300K in fixed hospital equipment.

- Proposed and introduced a comprehensive software program which eliminated manual order processing, inventory control, shipping, and invoicing processes. Reduced man-hours by nearly 50% and errors by more than 70%.

- Instituted procedures and controls which guaranteed the availability of diverse materials and equipment to meet critical shipping schedules. Introduced product evaluation reports, permitting the use of less expensive substitute items.

GLOBAL PAPERS, INC.   1986-1989
PURCHASING MANAGER
Responsible for all purchasing activities of a $58 million paper products supplier.

- Implemented systematized procedures for purchasing which achieved economies of more than 3 times any previous efforts. Net result was a savings of more than $120K per year and a more satisfied customer base.

- Created a paper brokerage service which reduced purchasing costs by 14%. Expanded the brokerage business into a profit center selling paper to commercial printers, resulting in sales of $1.3 million within 18 months.

195

WHOLESALE SALES SPECIALIST

JOHN SMITH
225 Capitol Way, New York, NY 10000
555/555-5555
e-mail: johnsmith@vero.net

SENIOR EXECUTIVE
Sales & Marketing Management
High-caliber, results-driven leader with demonstrated ability to expand distribution, enhance branded image, increase market share and penetration, build solid account relationships, and position companies favorably in fiercely competitive markets. Combine real-world expertise in sales/marketing, information technology, business management, and strategic planning with keen sales savvy to:
▼ Establish win-win account relationships in a consultative selling framework
▼ Devise and implement comprehensive partnership programs yielding marked increases in account penetration and loyalty
▼ Develop and motivate staff in an environment of teamwork and creativity
▼ Create and introduce information technology innovations to increase sales, improve accuracy, and decrease order turn time
▼ Analyze operations and institute measures to maximize efficiency and minimize costs

PROFESSIONAL HISTORY

JULIAWAY CASUAL WEAR   1994–1996
$300 million international manufacturer, distributor, and retailer of branded apparel.

<u>Vice President—Wholesale Division, Los Angeles, CA</u>
Recruited to lead Wholesale Division with National Accounts, Customer Service, and National Sales management team directly reporting. Charged with expansion into department store arena, with concurrent responsibility for strategic planning, P&L, sales planning and operations, distribution, and inventory management. Conducted analysis of current distribution revealing very low account penetration in terms of categories and initiated measures to expand that penetration and revamp image.
▼ Invented and instituted two-barrel, consultative approach offering rebates for expanded SKUs and increased co-op advertising incentives:
  • Signed up 60% of account base within first six months.
  • Delivered volume increases for majority of program participants versus decreases for non-partners—in very tough retail economy.
  • Enabled control of product representation in marketplace through account base.
▼ Implemented cost reduction measures to cut administrative, travel, entertainment, and advertising expenditures, resulting in 21% decrease within cost center responsibility.
▼ Repaired tarnished image and poor account relationships: Reinstated Juliaway as #1 apparel vendor within firm's existing department store base, transforming adversarial relationship to one of mutual profitability and rapport.
▼ Developed five-year strategic business plan to effect turnaround through increased market share, broader distribution, upgraded quality, and focus on reinstating image as industry leader.
▼ Spearheaded sales force automation initiative implementing laptops for in-field sales direct order entry, e-mail, spreadsheet analysis, and contact management.

BW INC.   **1975–1994**
$175 million subsidiary of $5 billion manufacturer and distributor of cosmetic products.

Senior National Accounts Manager, Oakland, CA (1992–1994)

In conjunction with restructuring, selected as key individual to work directly with major buying offices nationwide, serving as corporate coordinator for all product lines with eight major department store chains. Held full accountability for promotions, planning, and bottom line profitability.

▼ Led sales force automation task force, personally training team in use of spreadsheet analysis to monitor and run their business:
  • Decreased product order turn time by 41%.
  • Dramatically increased accuracy and provided instantaneous information access.
  • Eliminated 27% of manpower needs for order processing.

Regional Sales Manager, San Francisco CA (1984–1991)

With sales responsibility for 16-state region accounting for over half of division volume, directed sales staff and managed all aspects of sales training, forecasting, tracking, key account negotiations, merchandising, sales office administration, and budgetary planning/control.

▼ Trained sales force in "consultative selling" approach, successfully positioning them as expert consultants providing valuable advice on conducting business profitably.
▼ Earned increased responsibilities from initial management of seven senior sales representatives/$7.5MM sales volume to ultimate sales force of 12/$26MM volume.

Regional Sales Representative, Omaha, Nebraska (1976–1983)

Promoted to Senior Sales Representative and assigned to Nebraska and South Dakota territory.

▼ Increased sales from $275,000 to $2 million. Corporate-wide analysis performed in 1983 revealed this territory to have highest sales/population ratio in division.
▼ Propelled BW to $1 million vendor status in chain where firm previously had no presence.

Sales Associate, Tulsa, Oklahoma (1975–1976)

Assigned as apprentice to senior representative to learn intricacies of cosmetics industry.

▼ Grew specialty store account base volume by 61%.
▼ Completed two-year training program in only eleven months.

EDUCATION

B.S. Marketing, Florida State University, Jacksonville, FL, May, 1975

A

Blank Resume Worksheet

Use this worksheet in conjunction with a sample resume from Chapter 13 that's appropriate to your situation.

This form is an outline, just to help you assemble your key material. It is expanded for easy entry, and has some suggestions or examples. In practice, you should generally fit information onto one spacious page. It shouldn't look cramped! Remember, you want the resume to pique your reader's interest—and leave you something to talk about at the interview. You might choose to set up several tailor-made resumes, each aimed at a different prospect.

Leave out:

- Long phrases.
- Anything confusing or emotional.
- Crowding.
- Dot-matrix.
- Second pages.
- Staples.
- Short or troubled jobs.
- Reasons for leaving.
- Past pay.
- Pay sought.
- Exaggerations.
- Personal weaknesses.
- Family conflicts or trouble.

Date_____

Your name _____

Address (street, box) _____

City, state, zip _____

Phone, fax, e-mail _____

(Your job goals here, briefly and in short, general sentences. Be careful. Talk of *their* interests.)

Goal is to provide _____

Postitions / Jobs Held (First, most recent. Two or three lines each. Double space.)

Example:

January 1990
to June 1995   Treasurer, Abbott Labs., $900 mill sales. Set up new cost and mgmt account system, and
                  wrote annual reports. Firm doubled in five years.

Dates
Title
Main action duty
Accomplished

To

To

To

Education

School/College	Years	Course	Degree	Awards
_____	_____	_____	_____	_____
_____	_____	_____	_____	_____

Key Outside Activities (Even short-term. Civic or church, offices, honors. Special skills, like languages, volunteering, licenses [pilot, medical], actor, author, artist, engineer, musician, teacher, speaker, leader. Important: Here is where you might list several and far exceed other candidates.)

_____

_____

_____

_____

Personal (Height, weight, health, hobbies. Spouse's job and education. Kids' ages.)

_____

_____

_____

_____

*All material here can be supported with documents, references, and other exhibits.

B

100 Largest Employers of $100,000 People

The firms are listed roughly in order of size. Check your library's regularly updated resources (such as the *Million Dollar Directory*) for the latest contact information on particular departments or individuals. Don't forget: You may be able to put yourself at an advantage by mailing to more than one spot within the organization!

General Motors
  3044 W. Grand
  Detroit, MI 48202

Ford Motor
  Box 1899
  Dearborn, MI 48121

Exxon
  225 Carpender
  Irving, TX 75062

Wal-Mart Stores
  Box 116
  Bentonville, AR 72716

IBM
  Old Orchard Rd.
  Armonk, NY 10504

General Electric
  3135 Easton Pke.
  Fairfield, CT 06431

Mobil Oil
  3225 Gallows Rd.
  Fairfax, VA 22037

Chrysler
  12000 Chrysler Dr.
  Highland Pk, MI 48288

Phillip Morris
120 Park Ave.
New York, NY 10017-5592

Prudential
213 Washington
Newark, NJ 07102

State Farm Group
1 State Farm Plaza
Bloomington, IL 61710

Du Pont
1007n Market
Wilmington, DL 19898

Texaco
2000 Westchester
White Plains, NY 10650

Johnson & Johnson
1 J&J Plaza
New Brunswick, NJ 08901

Sears Roebuck
Sears Tower
Chicago, IL 60684

K Mart
3100 Big Beaver Rd.
Troy, MI 48084

Procter & Gamble
1 P&G Plaza
Cincinnati, OH 45201

Chevron
225 Bush St.
San Francisco, CA 94104

Citicorp
399 Park Ave.
New York, NY 10043

Hewlett-Packard
3000 Hanover
Palo Alto, CA 94304

Pepsico
700 Anderson Hill
Purchase, NY 10577

Met Life
One Madison Ave.
New York, NY 10010

Amoco
200 E. Randolph
Chicago, IL 60601

Motorola
1303 E. Algonquin
Schaumburg, IL 60196

ConAgra
1 ConAgra Dr.
Omaha, NE 68102

Kroger
1014 Vine St.
Cincinnati, OH 45202

Dayton Hudson
777 Nichollet Mall
Minneapolis, MN 55402

Loew's
667 E. Algonquin
Schaumburg, IL 60196

Lockheed
4500 Park Granada
Calabasas, CA 91399

United Tech
UT Building
Hartford, CT 06101

Allstate
2775 Sanders
Northbrook, IL 60062

Fed National Mortgage
1759 Business Center
Reston, VA 22090

Merrill Lynch
100 Church St.
New York, NY 10007

JC Penney
1481 N. Dallas Pkwy.
Dallas, TX 75265

United Parcel
Greenwich Office Park
Greenwich, CT 06831

Dow Chemical
20430 Dow Center
Midland, MI 48674

Bank America
Box 37002
San Francisco, CA 94137

GTE
1 Stamford Forum
Stamford, CT 06904

International Paper
2 Manhattanville
Purchase, NY 10577

Boeing
Seattle, WA 98108

Xerox
800 Long Ridge
Stamford, CT 06904

Cigna
1601 Chestnut
Philadelphia, PA 19192

Coca Cola
Drawer 1778
Atlanta, GA 30301

Bell South Atlantic
1155 Peach Tree NE
Atlanta, GA 30367

Sara Lee
70 W. Madison
Chicago, IL 60602

Columbia/HA
201 W. Main
Louisville, KY 42021

Fleming
6301 Waterford
Oklahoma City, OK 73126

AMR
Box 6196
Dallas Airport, TX 75261

Atlantic Richfield
515 S. Flower
Los Angeles, CA 90071

Merck
Box 100
Whitehouse, NJ 08889

Travelers Group
1 Towers Square
Hartford, CT 06183

Supervalue
Box 990
Eden Prairie, MN 55440

Safeway
201 4th St.
Oakland, CA 94660

Nations Bank Corp.
101 Tryon St.
Charlotte, NC 28246

Intel
2200 Mission Col.
Santa Clara, CA 95052

New York Life
51 Madison Ave.
New York, NY 10010

3M
3M Center
St. Paul, MN 55144

Caterpillar
100 N.E. Adams
Peoria, IL 61629

RJR Nabisco Holding
1301 Avenue of the Americas
New York, NY 10019

American Express
World Finance Center
Tower C
New York, NY 10285

Home Depot
2727 Paces Ferry
Atlanta, GA 30339

Eastman Kodak
343 State St.
Rochester, NY 14650

MCI Communications
1133 19th St. NEW
Washington, DC 20036

Federal Dept. Stores
7th West 7th
Cincinnati, OH 45202

UAL
Box 66919
Chicago, IL 60666

Chem Bank
277 Park Ave.
New York, NY 10172

Compaq Computer
Box 692000
Houston, TX 77269

Allied Signal
101 Columbia Rd.
Morristown, NJ 07962

McDonnell Douglas
Box 516
St. Louis, MO 36166

Georgia-Pacific
133 Peach Tree NE
Atlanta, GA 30303

J.P. Morgan
23 Wall St.
New York, NY 10260-0023

Digital Equipment
146 Main St.
Maynard, MA 01754

Bristol-Myers
345 Park Ave.
New York, NY 10154-0037

Spring
8140 Ward Pkwy.
Kansas City, KA 64114

Phillips Petroleum
1237 Adams Bldg.
Bartlesville, OK 74004

Lehman Brothers Hold.
3 World Finance Center
New York, NY 10285

Bell Atlantic
1600 Market St.
Philadelphia, PA 19103

American Info. Tech.
30 S Wacker Dr.
Chicago, IL 60606

Bell Atlantic
335 Madison Ave.
New York, NY 10017

American Home Products
685 3rd Ave.
New York, NY 10017-4085

Texas Instruments
Box 655474
Dallas, TX 75265

Rockwell International
Box 4250
Seal Beach, CA 90740

Aetna Life
151 Farmington Ave.
Hartford, CT 06156

Archer Daniels
466 Faries
Decatur, IL 62526

SBC Communications
175 E. Houston
San Antonio, TX 78205

IBP
Box 515
Dakota City, NE 68731

Alcoa
Box 1491
Burlington, VT 05402

Albertson's
Box 20
Boise, ID 83726

Anheuser-Busch
1 Bush Pl.
St. Louis, MO 63118

Delta Airlines
Hartsfield Airport
Atlanta, GA 30320

May Department Stores
611 Olive
St. Louis, MO 63101

ITT Sheraton
60 State St.
Boston, MA 02109

Sysco
1390 Eclare
Houston, TX 77077

Walt Disney
500 S. Buena Vista
Burbank, CA 91521

Armstrong
Box 3001
Lancaster, PA 17604

Honda
Honda Parkway
Marysville, OH 43040

Nissan
Smyrna, TN 37167

Avis Rental
900 Old Country Rd.
Garden City, NY 11530

C

50 Special Recruiters for Jobs Paying $100,000 and Up

These professionals specialize in high-level employment "matchmaking." Remember, they're working for the employer, not for you.

1. **Allerton Henegham**
   70 West Madison
   Chicago, IL 60602

2. **Martin Bauman**
   375 Park Ave.
   New York, NY 10017

3. **Bishop Partners**
   708 Third Ave.
   New York, NY 10017

4. **Boyden**
   356 Elwood Ave.
   Hawthorne, NY 10532-1239

5. **Caldwell & Assoc.**
   1201 Wilshire Blvd.
   New York, NY 10033

6. **Callan**
   1550 Spring Rd.
   Oakbrook, IL 60521

7. **Cejka & Co.**
   222 S. Central Ave.
   St. Louis, MO 63104

8. **Clarey Andrews**
   1200 Shermer
   Northbrook, IL 60062

9. **Coleman Lew**
   326 W. 10th
   Charlotte, NC 28208

10. **Convex**
    18th Fl., 919 3rd Ave.
    New York, NY 10022

11. **Thorndike Deland**
    13 Fl. 275 Madison Ave.
    New York, NY 10016

12. **Diekmann & Assoc.**
    180 N. Stetson
    Chicago, IL 60601

13. **Diversified Search**
    2000 Market St.
    Philadelphia, PA 19103

14. **Early Cochran**
    55 E. Monroe
    Chicago, IL 60603-5805

15. **Fenwick Partner**
    57 Bedford
    Lexington, MA 02173

16. **Francis & Assoc.**
    Vista Drive W.
    Des Moines, IA 50266

17. **Jay Gaines**
    450 Park Ave.
    New York, NY 10022

18. **Gould & McCoy**
    300 Park Ave.
    New York, NY 10033

19. **Hayden Group**
    One P.O. Sq.
    Boston, MA 02109

20. **Heidrick & Stuggles**
    125 S. Wacker
    Chicago, IL 60606-4590

21. **Heidrick Partners**
    2020 N. Wacker
    Chicago, IL 60606

22. **Hetzel Group**
    Wm Village, 1601 Colonial
    Inverness, IL 60067

23. **Hockett Assoc.**
    350 2nd Ave.
    Los Altos, CA 94023

24. **Wm. Houze**
    48249 Vista De Nopal
    La Quinta, CA 92253

25. **Houze Shourds**
    1 World Trade
    Long Beach, CA 90831-1840

26. **Isaacson Miller**
    334 Boyston
    Boston, MA 02116-3805

27. **Pendleton James**
    200 Park Ave.
    New York, NY 10166

28. **A.T. Kearney**
    222 W. Adams
    Chicago, IL 60606

29. **Kenny Kindler**
    34th Fl., 1 Daghammer
    New York, NY 10017

30. **Korn/Ferry**
    237 Park Ave.
    New York, NY 10017

31. **Lamalie Ampro**
    489 Fifth Ave.
    New York, NY 10017-6105

32. **Herbert Mines**
    27 Fl., 399 Park Ave.
    New York, NY 10022

33. **Mirz/Morice**
    One Dok St., 3rd Fl.
    Stamford, CT 06902

34. **Nadzam Lusk**
    3211 Scott Blvd.
    Santa Clara, CA 95054

35. **Norman Broadbent**
    200 Park Ave.
    New York, NY 10160

36. **Preng & Assoc.**
    2925 Briar Park
    Houston, TX 77042

37. **Paul Ray**
    301 Commerce
    Fort Worth, TX 76102

38. **Russell Reynolds**
    A200 Park Ave.
    New York, NY 10166-0002

39. **Norm Roberts**
    1800 Cent. Park E.
    Los Angeles, CA 90067-1507

40. **Seitchik Corwin "C"**
    1830 Jackson
    San Francisco, CA 94109

41. **Smith & Sawyer**
    33F 230 Park Ave.
    New York, NY 10169

42. **Spencer Stuart**
    55 E. 52 St.
    New York, NY 10055-0102

43. **Stern & Watson**
    70 University Ave.
    Toronto, Ontario, Canada M5J 2M4

44. **Tan Ton**
    710-1050 W. Pender
    Vancouver, BC, Canada V6E 357

45. **Travis & Company**
    325 Boston Post Rd.
    Sudbury, MA 01776

46. **Ward Howell International**
    99 Park Ave.
    New York, NY 10016-1699

47. **Daniel Wier**
    333 S. Grand Ave.
    Los Angeles, CA 90071

48. **Wilkinson & Ives**
    1 Bush St.
    San Francisco, CA 94104

49. **Witt/Kieffer**
    2015 Spring Rd.
    Oak Brook, IL 60521

50. **Egon Zehnder**
    14 Fl., 55 E. 59th St.
    New York, NY 10022

D

How to Ace the $100,000 Executive Tests

Psychological tests are getting popular at $100,000 levels, because hiring the wrong person at this level can be costly. These tests are expensive. So if your prospective employer is willing to ask you to take a test, the odds are that you're on the short list.

Here are some thoughts on passing psych tests.

A *major secret,* when taking these tests, is to play the role of the "perfect candidate." Keep a highly positive attitude. Don't fight these tests, as some people do, destroying their chances.

There are three basic tests:

1. *IQ Tests:* Usually these are timed. Check the rules. The score is usually the number correct. So do all the easy ones first, then go back. Don't get hung up on any one question.

2. *Aptitude Tests:* These tests are usually about words, mechanics, and simple numbers. Again, to score well, go through these carefully but quickly. Skip the tough ones, then go back.

3. *Personality Tests:* These are so key that employers often check these the most carefully. The tests sometimes try to provoke hostile answers. Don't get fooled. Your deliberate, *positive mind-set* automatically helps you avoid errors. These are seldom timed; so don't hurry. Move carefully. Don't nit-pick. Assume that the questions are fair and honest, even if they seem odd.

There are three types of personality tests:

1. *Sentence completion tests* are tricky. These measure attitude and personality. Play the role: Ask yourself, "How would the *ideal* candidate answer?"

Suggestions:

They might ask you to complete, "My darkest secret is _____." ("Sometimes I work too darn hard.")

"The worst thing I ever did was _____." ("Get convinced I must excel, so that I feel badly when I don't.")

For each question, stop and think about how *you* would advise a perfect, upbeat applicant to answer this question.

2. *Psychological ink bot tests (Rorschach)* measure attitude and personality. You will see meaningless blots and be asked, "What do you see?" *Solution:* Be sure to see something pleasant, businesslike, and constructive, nothing violent or sexual.

3. *Picture tests* also measure attitude and personality. You will see photos of people, perhaps doing things, and be asked what the pictures mean to you. Keep playing the role of the ideal professional candidate. Think positive.

   Example: If you see a picture of a man with his feet in midair with his hands on a vertical rope, you'd best say, "Here is a man climbing a rope to success." Don't say, "This man is sliding down to total failure."

CASE STUDY

Lucy K. followed these guidelines and was hired. Later she said she had scored higher than anyone ever had. This system works, but is rarely known by your competitors. Use that to put you ahead of the others—and to get that $100,000 job.

Index

About the Author

Craig Scott Rice is a former business instructor at Northwestern University, major staffing director in both governmental and multi-billion dollar corporate environments, corporate president, consultant, and the author of ten published management and staffing books. The resume and personal marketing steps he outlines in his book are drawn from a variety of authorities, and have resulted in many job offers at the $100,000 level (and considerably higher). Mr. Rice has counseled and interviewed thousands of executives, read thousands of resumes, and hired and helped hundreds of people—including himself—to jobs paying over $100,000.